BMW Twins

BMW TWINS
The Complete Story

Mick Walker

The Crowood Press

First published in 1998 by
The Crowood Press Ltd
Ramsbury, Marlborough
Wiltshire SN8 2HR

British Library Cataloguing-in-Publication Data
A catalogue record for this book is available from the British
Library.

ISBN 1 86126 153 5

This book is dedicated to my Dutch friend Gennie Wolvers,
who is fortunate enough to own not only an R1100RS but also
travels some 45,000 kilometres on two wheels each year.

Frontispiece: 1979 BMW R100S

Typeface used: New Century Schoolbook

Typeset and designed by Focus Publishing, Sevenoaks, Kent

Printed and bound by Redwood Books

Contents

Acknowledgements

The motorcycle I aspired to own in my youth was an R69S BMW, but I never did. Instead, I rode and raced mainly Italian and British bikes, but my interest and affection for the German machines never quite went away. When I became a tester for and, subsequently, editor of *Motorcycle Enthusiast* magazine, I was at last able to sample these unique machines. My experience included a memorable day at Donington Park in the summer of 1987, when I got to ride every single machine in the range in the course of a few hours. Since then, besides compiling several books on the marque, I have also been an owner, so my interest and affection have turned to appreciation and respect.

Of all the BMWs, it has to be the long-running flat-twins that really best sum up the special character of these quality machines. This book sets out to look not just at the well known, but also at the not so well known, as well as some entirely new aspects of the Boxer story.

During the course of writing this book, I not only made many new friends, but also uncovered some old ones with whom, through time, I had lost contact. I was particularly pleased to re-discover Peter Mapes, whom I knew in Aden in the early 1960s when I was a teenager in the RAF (he owned the only Earles-forked BMW in the protectorate), and Joan and John Milligan, who not only ran the British Formula Racing Club during the late 1960s and early 1970s, but were also BMW enthusiasts of long standing.

A special vote of thanks is also needed for my local BMW dealer, Balderston Motorcycles of Peterborough, and their ever-friendly staff of Arthur Sneeden, Robin Homewood and Tony (TJ) Skrobot, who provided such friendly help with my many requests.

Many people provided photographs, information or memories, including Chris Hooper and Ron Slater (formerly of Hughendon M40 BMW dealers), the late Fred Secker, Andrew Kemp, Phil Schiling, the late Walter Zeller, and several members of the BMW Owners' Club. Emma Goode and Chris Willows of BMW GB provided both practical and moral help which was much appreciated.

Most of all, I enjoyed researching and writing BMW Twins. It's a fascinating story, spanning three-quarters of the twentieth century.

Mick Walker
Wisbech, Cambridgeshire

Milestones in BMW Motorcycle History from 1923–1998

1923   The R 32, BMW's very first motorcycle designed and built by Chief EngineerMax Friz, makes its debut at the Paris Motor Show and the German motor Show in Berlin. It already has all the characteristic features of BMW's two-cylinder machines: a boxer (flat-twin) power unit fitted in crosswise arrangement, the transmission connected directly to the engine, and shaft drive, all within a double-loop tubular frame.

75 Jahre BMW Motorrad
75 Years of BMW Motorcycles

BMW's R32 and R1200C

1924   Chief Test Engineer Rudolf Schleicher develops a sports engine out of the R 32 power unit, fitting the engine into the R 37 raced by Franz Bieber and bringing home the first German Road Championship for BMW.

1928   BMW's first motorcycle displacing 750cc, the R 62, enters the market. This is to remain the maximum engine size within the BMW range until 1973.

1928   Ernst Henne wins the Targa Florio in Italy on a BMW racing machine.

1929   Ernst Henne sets up the world motorcycle speed record on Ingolstädter Landstrasse near Munich: 216km/h or 134mph.

1935   BMW launches the R 12, the first-ever production motorcycle with a hydraulically dampened telescopic front wheel fork.

1936   A crankshaft-drive compressor is fitted into BMW racing machines for the first time; the R 5 sports machine features a thoroughly modified boxer engine with two camshafts.

1937   Ernst Henne sets up a new world speed record for motorcycles: 279.5 km/h or 173.3mph.

1938   BMW delivers its 100,000th motorcycle.

1939   BMW scores a one-two victory in the Isle of Man Senior TT. Schorsch Meier brings home the title on his compressor machine, becoming the first foreigner on a foreign motorcycle to win the race, followed by his British team-mate Jock West.

1941   BMW builds the R 75 military sidecar motorcycle.

1947   Schorsch Meier wins the German Road Championship for Motorcycles, repeating his victory in 1948, 1949, 1950 and 1953.

1948   BMW introduces the 250cc single-cylinder R 24, thus returning into the motorcycle market.

1950   The R 51/2, BMW's first post-war boxer, enters the market. 1952 The BMW R 68 becomes the first German production motorcycle to achieve a top speed of 160km/h or 100mph.

1954   Wilhelm Noll and Fritz Cron bring home the first World Sidecar Champion-ship for BMW, to be followed by 19 further World championships for BMW sidecar motorcycles up to 1974.

1955   The R 26, R 50 and R 69 all come with BMW's new full swinging-arm suspension.

1960   BMW's fastest boxer so far makes its entry into the market: the R 69 S.

1969   The /5 Series models make their appearance.

1973   BMW introduces the R 90/6 and R 90 S, the largest BMW motorcycles so far, displacing 900cc.

1976   BMW launches the 1000cc R 100 RS, the first series production machine in the world with full fairing.

1978   The sports fairing of the R 100 RS is converted into the tourer fairing of the R 100 RT. At the same time the 450cc R 45 and 650 cc R 65 round off the model range at the bottom end.

1980   BMW introduces the R 80 G/S enduro featuring single swinging arm suspension on the rear wheel, the BMW Monolever.

1981   French rider Hubert Auriol wins the Paris–Dakar Rally on a modified R 80 G/S.

1982   The 800cc R 80 ST and R 80 RT enter the market.

1983   The new K 100 Series makes its debut at the Paris Motor Show.

1985   BMW launches the three-cylinder K75 Series. BMW sets up a new production record, with a total output, of 37,104 motorcycles. Gaston Rahier repeats his victory in the Paris–Dakar Rally.

1986   Based on the R 80, the R 100 RS and R 100 RT once again enter the range at the request of many customers.

1987	BMW launches the largest enduro in the world market, the R 100 GS featuring a double-joint rear wheel swinging arm, the BMW Paralever.

1988	BMW becomes the first manufacturer in the world to offer motorcycle ABS featured on the K 100 models.

1991	BMW offers the first fully controlled motorcycle catalyst.
	The classically styled R 100 R makes its debut as BMW's new road model and becomes a best seller right away.
	The millionth BMW motorcycle since the start of production in 1923 comes off the production line at the Berlin plant.

1992	Jutta Kleinschcmidt wins the ladies' category on a standard BMW R 100 GS in the 12,700km Paris–Cape Town Rally.
	BMW launches the K 1100 RS and R 80 R at the Cologne Bicycle and Motorcycle Show.

1993	Celebrating the 70th anniversary of the company, BMW introduces an all-new generation of boxer machines, the first model making its appearance being the R 1100 RS.

1994	The R 1100 GS enduro and R 1100 R/R 850 R roadster models enter the market.
	The BMW Enduro Park is opened in the south German town of Hechlingen.

1995	A new BMW tourer enters the market – the R 1100 RT.
	All of BMW's four-valve models are fitted with a fully controlled catalytic converter as standard both in Germany and a number of other countries.
	The 100,000th BMW motorcycle featuring ABS comes off the production line.
	BMW sells more than 50,000 motorcycles in one year for the first time.

1996	The old boxer models with two-valve power units and the K 75 Series are phased out of production. At the same time the K 1200 RS makes its debut as the most powerful BMW motorcycle so far.
	The F 650 is joined by a sister model, the F 650 ST.

1997	BMW launches its first-ever cruiser, the R 1200 C.
At the Frankfurt Motor Show BMW presents the C 1, a two-wheeled city mobile for the next millennium.
	On 22 February Ernst Henne celebrates his 93rd, on 9 November Schorsch Meier his 87th birthday.

1998	A BMW team once again enters the Paris–Dakar Rally – now the 20th event – on New Year's Day 1998, 13 years after BMW's last victory in Paris–Dakar.

1 In the Beginning

THE COMPANY'S ROOTS

BMW – Bayerische Motoren Werke GmbH – can trace its origins back to the late nineteenth century. In 1896, well-known German industrialist Heinrich Ehrhart opened a factory at Eisenach, with a view to manufacturing military equipment; in the event, this was not to be, and Ehrhart soon switched his attention and resources to the production of bicycles and electric vehicles. The first of these debuted in 1898, and were chiefly notable for their transmission. Rather than employing a conventional chain or belt, Ehrhart's vehicles had toothed gear wheels and shafts with universal joints.

These early vehicles were constructed by hand, by a team of engineers. As a result, they were not cost-effective, and Ehrhart was forced to abandon production in favour of manufacturing Decauville cars under licence from France. This enterprise began in 1900, with both 'Eisenach' and 'Wartburg' being used as names for the German-built models. ('Wartburg', taken from the name of the local castle in Eisenach, was used again, after the Second World War, and by a completely different company, for a series of East German three-cylinder two-stroke cars that owed much to DKW; but that is another story.) Two of the Decauville cars built under licence in Germany were entered for the 1902 Paris-Vienna race, one featuring a five-speed gearbox! Both finished successfully, but this excellent debut in motor sport was not followed up. Ehrhart soon tired of the motor-car industry and the following year he quit the company he had founded. The original factory was taken over by a newly created organization comprising some of Heinrich Ehrhart's former associates, while Ehrhart's son continued to manufacture cars at one of the firm's other works. Ehrhart Junior still built according to the Decauville designs, using the name 'Ehrhart-Decauville' for his models. The new management team at the Eisenach factory decided to put into production a completely new range of cars. They chose the name 'Dixi'; the vehicles marketed under this new brand were clearly aimed at a clientele that would today be referred to as 'upmarket'.

Over the next few years, the remaining pieces in the BMW jigsaw were created. Aviation, rather than motoring, was to provide the key. In 1911, Gustav Otto (son of Nikolaus Otto, creator of the four-stroke Otto cycle engine), opened an aircraft factory on Lerchenauerstrasse at the eastern end of Munich's Oberwiesenfeld Airport. Two years later, Karl Rapp founded an aero-engine plant bearing his name –Rapp Motorenwerke GmbH. At the beginning of the First World War, the Eisenach, Otto and Rapp marques were not connected in any way, but each was to play a vital role in the development of BMW.

The first step in the emergence of BMW came on 7 March 1916, when Otto and Rapp, two of Munich's smallest aircraft factories, joined forces to create Bayerische Flugzeugwerke AG (BFW). The new company's two directors were Karl Rapp and Dipl. Ing. Max Friz. Their intention was to channel their combined energies and resources into the design and production of aircraft engines, and the start of this joint venture coincided with the rapid expansion of the fledgling German air force. Soon, many of Germany's front-line fighter squadrons, including the legendary Von Richthofen (the Red Baron) used aircraft powered by BFW products. In addition, BFW built a number of aircraft prototypes, including the Ch reconnaissance series, the monoplane, and the NI triplane night bomber; none of these projects reached production.

BFW's fame soon spread outside Germany, to the Austro-Hungarian empire, where a naval engineer on detachment with the Austro-Daimler aircraft engine concern, Franz Josef Popp, came to hear of their engineering prowess. Popp decided he must take his own special skills to Munich, and to BFW AG. On 29 July 1917, Bayerische Motoren Werke GmbH was formed. Popp was BMW's first managing director – a post he held until 1942. In the summer of 1918, the Munich-based company went public, and became BMW AG.

At that time, the company was at its war-time peak, employing over 3,500 people. (One director was Fritz Neumeyer, who later became one of BMW's biggest rivals in the motorcycle sphere, as boss of the Zündapp marque.) Aero-engine production was at its zenith. Fokker's new DVII was the arguably the world's finest fighter aircraft – although not especially rapid, its strong point was its great manoeuvrability at high altitudes. The power-plant was either a 160/180hp Mercedes or the 185hp BMW. The latter, neatly cowled and equipped with

Chief designer Max Friz, together with Martin Stolle, deve-loped BMW's first flat-twin motorcycle engine, coded M2B15, and intended to be sold to other manufacturers. Entering production in 1921, the 486cc unit developed 6.5bhp at 2,800rpm

11

One user of the M2B15 engine was the Nürnberg concern Victoria. Here, its designer Martin Stolle is seen on one of the machines after moving from BMW to Victoria in 1922.

a frontal radiator, offered superior performance and was much sought after by Germany's air aces.

But the war was nearly over and, just as BMW's rise had been meteoric, so its fall from grace following Germany's defeat was equally spectacular. Even as the victors and vanquished were gathering for the signing of the Armistice of Compiègne, chief designer Max Friz was completing the final preparations of a brand-new six-cylinder, inline, water-cooled BMW engine. Rated at an amazing 300hp, the power-unit was installed in a BFW biplane at the Munich production complex and underwent a series of top secret tests. Piloted by Franz Diemer, it achieved a new world height record of 9,760m (32,022 feet) on 17 June 1919.

Following these tests, virtually all BMW's materials and documentation appertaining to aviation were confiscated by the Allied Control Commission.

BMW was forced to turn its attention elsewhere, in order to remain in existence. Materials previously earmarked for aero-engine manufacture were diverted into an array of new uses, including agricultural equipment. Slowly, the company hauled itself back from the brink of disaster, both commercial and financial. Supplying metal castings to other enterprises led to a vital contract to produce components for railway braking systems. They also manufactured a new Friz-designed 8-litre (8,000cc) engine, for use in heavy trucks and boats.

THE FIRST MOTORCYCLES

The Flink

The real motorcycle breakthrough occurred in early 1920, when development work began on a 148cc two-stroke engine

The Helios, with a longitudinally installed M2B12 flat-twin engine and chain drive, was built and sold by BMW in 1922. However, sales were poor and the model was soon withdrawn

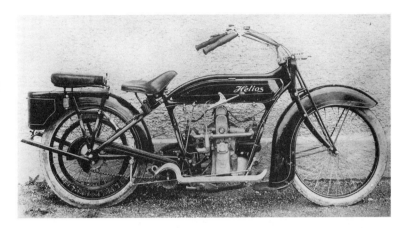

The first BMW car, the Dixi, was built in 1928; essentially, it was a licence-built British Austin 7

designed by Curt Hanfland. This unit was used as the basis of a lightweight motorcycle with direct belt drive, built by Kurier and sold under the name 'Flink'. It was built up to 1922, despite its lack of commercial success, and was the vehicle that led BMW on to two wheels.

Shortly after the appearance of the Flink, in 1921, the old Gustav Otto works were sold. They were used for the manufacture of Flottweg motorcycles and clip-on engine assemblies until 1937, when BMW bought the facilities back, as its own production expanded.

M2B15

Meanwhile, 1921 also saw the debut of an engine that was to represent the beginning of a real range of BMW motorcycles. Designed by Martin Stolle and designated the M2B15, it was a 493cc (68 x 68mm) flat-twin side-valve motorcycle, clearly based on the British Douglas design, which had been used in some quantity during the war by both the British and French armies. The M2B15 engine was supplied to several motorcycle marques, including Bison, Corona, Heller, Heninger, Scheid, SMW and Victoria.

1923 R32

Engine:	Side-valve flat-twin
Displacement:	494cc
Bore and stroke:	68 x 68mm
Maximum power:	8.5bhp at 3,300rpm
Carburation:	Single 22-mm BMW-made two-lever type
Ignition:	Bosch magneto
Lubrication:	Wet sump
Gearbox:	Three-speed, hand-operated
Clutch:	Single-plate, dry
Frame:	Twin-tube
Front suspension:	Leading-link, leaf-spring
Rear suspension:	None
Brakes:	Original model, no front brake (until end of 1924); drum thereafter; v-block on dummy belt at rear wheel
Tyres:	26 x 3 beaded-edge
Weight:	265lb (120kg) dry
Maximum speed:	57mph (91kph)

In 1923, Max Friz designed the first motorcycle to bear BMW's name, the R32. A gifted engineer, whose first love was aviation, he only worked on the motorcycle project because BMW was excluded from aircraft-associated work at that time

Friz's masterpiece, the R32, was the sensation of the 1923 Paris show. It had a tubular frame, a flat-twin engine installed at right-angles to the direction of travel, and cardan-shaft drive

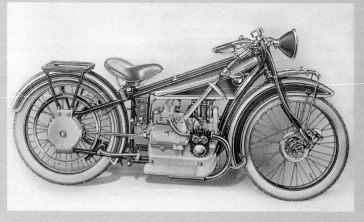

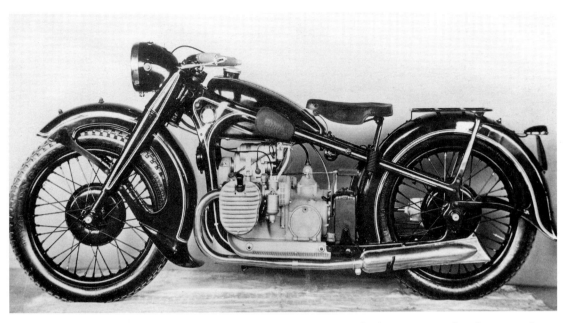

First produced in 1935, the 745cc (78 x 78cc) side-valve R12 was the first mass-produced motorcycle to feature telescopic front forks with hydraulic damping as standard.

The M2B15 was also used by BMW themselves, in 1922, to power the Helios; in this motorcycle, the engine (like the Douglas) was mounted fore-and-aft, driving the rear wheel by chain. The Helios was not a BMW design, although the complete machine was built at the company's Munich complex. Nor was it a particularly good motorcycle, partly, perhaps, because the personnel at BMW was more interested in aviation and, in fact, intensely disliked motorcycles. However, Friz's engineering talent allowed him to see the machine's shortcomings, and as a realist he knew that, for the present at least, there was no possibility of returning to aircraft manufacture. He set to work to create a new machine that would be worthy of carrying the blue and white BMW emblem, based on an aircraft's rotating propeller and in the style of Bavaria's chequered flag.

The R32

When the result of Friz's efforts was unveiled at the Paris Show in 1923, it created a sensation. Carrying the coding R32, the newcomer used what was virtually a direct descendant of the 493cc engine (even retaining the square bore of stroke dimensions). What was entirely new was that the engine was now mounted transversely in unit with a three-speed gearbox with shaft final drive. The frame was much more sturdy than that of the Helios and of a full double triangle design, while the front fork was sprung by a quarter-elliptic leaf spring. It was the beginning of a concept which was modern enough to endure decades and, indeed, is still what BMW motorcycles are about today. The R32 weighed in at 264lb (120kg).

Friz's idea behind relocating the cylinder's position was simple – to achieve

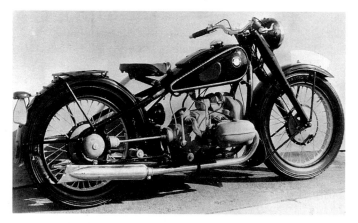

In 1936, BMW presented the R5 sportster with re-designed ohv engine, new tubular frame, improved electrics and toolbox located in the tank top. This is the 1937 model

In 1938, BMW updated its model range, the R5 sportster being replaced by the new R51, shown here, together with the side valve R6 tourer being axed in favour of the R61. Both newcomers benefited from rear suspension, a first for BMW.

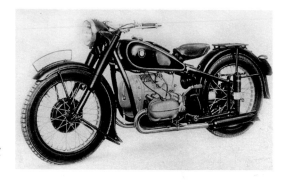

better cooling, why not swing the engine through 90 degrees so that the two cylinders stuck out on each side, to gather in the cool air! To eliminate chains, the separate gearbox was ditched in favour of one which was in unit with the engine – bolted to the rear, as in a car. Also following car design, the drive was to be via a large, single-plate clutch, by cardan shaft to the rear wheel.

There was nothing revolutionary about these changes. All had been tried and proven in previous designs, notably by the English ABC company, who marketed a horizontal transverse 398cc twin in 1919, and by the Belgian FN marque, who pioneered shaft drive on motorcycles in

1906. What set Friz's R32 apart from the rest was the fact that this was the first time everything had been brought together in a single package.

Although the R32 was not as powerful as some of its contemporaries, the BMW design was superior in several vital areas and offered potential buyers an ultra-modern concept in a world still dominated by unreliable engines, flimsy frames and temperamental transmissions. Only in braking did Friz and his team not take full advantage of best engineering practices; instead, they opted to use the already out-dated v-block on dummy belt rim at the rear and, initially, no brake at all at the front (although a small drum brake appeared for the R32 Series 2, which debuted in 1924).

In all, a total of 3,090 R32s were manufactured between the launch in 1923 and its demise in 1926 – a pretty good number for the early 1920s, and certainly for what was a luxury model.

The R37

Max Friz returned to aircraft design in 1924 and, with Martin Stolle joining Victoria, it was left to Rudolf Schleicher to take over the reins as chief designer at BMW. Besides being an excellent engineer, Schleicher was also a competition rider of some

The top-of-the-range side-valve R71 was built from 1938 through to 1941, for both civilian and military use.

note, so he brought an added touch of enthusiasm and expertise to the job, which a non-motorcyclist such as Friz had been unable to inject.

Schleicher's first project was the second pure BMW motorcycle, the R37. This retained the square 68 x 68mm bore and stroke but the performance-restricting side valves were abandoned in favour of the more efficient overhead valve layout. Combined with other minor engine improvements, this change doubled the power output from 8.5 to 16bhp (at 4,000), giving the 295-lb (135-kg) machine a maximum speed of around 70mph (110kph). The prototype was used by factory rider Franz Bieber to win the German road-racing championship, and in 1925 the R37 went on sale alongside the R32.

If the R37 had a fault, it was its cost. Only 152 machines were constructed over a two-year period, including ten special competition models, which were sold to selected riders for use in racing and trial events.

Probably the greatest moment for the R37 came in 1926, when J.P. Roth and designer Schleicher came to England to compete in that year's ISDT (International Six Days Trial). Based around the Derbyshire town of Buxton, the trial saw both German riders (as part of their national team) put up impressive performances; both returned to Munich with gold medals. This was the first time a German rider had struck gold in an ISDT held in the British Isles. The following extract from a letter written by Professor A.M. Low, technical chief of the organizing body, the ACU (Auto Cycle Union), shows how impressed the hosts were:

The most interesting machine of the whole meeting was undoubtedly the German BMW. A horizontally opposed two-cylinder

In 1949, shortly after BMW resumed its post-war motorcycle production, the 1000th R24 single-cylinder machine rolled off the assembly line.

engine which is mounted transversely in the frame – with completely enclosed valve gear, block construction and shaft drive. Even after the hardest days there wasn't a bit of oil to be seen anywhere, the machine was beautifully quiet and seemed to have an enormous power reserve. It is miles ahead of any British machine as far as design is concerned.

On home soil, Schleicher's masterpiece had won almost 100 road races in 1925, and had achieved victory in the 500cc class of the German Grand Prix.

R39, R42 and R47

The same year saw BMW expand their range, bringing out the R39 single. Although this sported a vertical cylinder, it retained the 68 x 68mm bore and stroke dimensions and other features, such as

shaft final drive. Other details included 6.5bhp at 4,000rpm, 58mph (100kph) and a dry weight of 242lb (110kg). A total of 1,000 machines were built, until production ceased in 1927. Again, BMW benefited from track exposure, with Josef Stelzer taking the 250cc German racing title aboard a specially tuned R39 in 1925.

The R42 came next, in 1926, replacing the R32. Improvements on the original included detachable light alloy cylinder heads, which replaced the R32's one-piece cast-iron cylinder and head assembly, and although it was still a side-valve set-up, the power was increased by 50 per cent, to 12bhp at 3,400rpm. To make room for a drum front brake, the speedometer drive unit was relocated from the wheel to the gearbox. During a two-year production run 6,502 R42s were built.

By 1927, BMW had manufactured its 25,000th motorcycle. In the same year, the ohv R39 was replaced by the R47, with the power output bumped up 2bhp, from 16 to

18bhp. From a sales point of view, the later machine was much more successful, selling no less than 1,720 machines over an eighteen-month period.

Larger-Capacity Twins

The next major event in the evolution of the BMW motorcycle came in 1928, with the introduction of two larger-capacity twins,

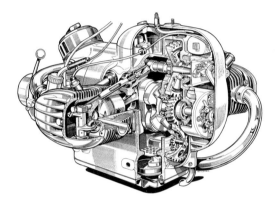

the R62 and R63. The former was a touring side-valve machine of 745cc (78 x 78mm), producing 18bhp at 3400 rpm, weighing in at 340lb (155kg), with a top speed of 73mph (115kph). The R63 was a more sporting overhead valve with a specifi-cation which included 735cc (83 x 68mm), 24bhp at 4,000rpm, a dry weight of 335lb (152kg), and could top 80mph (130kph).

The 735cc engine was also to be used as the basis for a series of world-renowned record-breaking sessions, with a small, shy local rider, Ernst Henne, in the saddle. Henne had first joined BMW back in 1926, and in 1928 won the legendary Targa Florio race in Sicily for them. He first became interested in breaking records while on honeymoon in 1929 in Paris. There, he found the French press full of stories about a battle between two Englishmen, Bert Le

Cutaway view of the R51/3 engine, showing valve gear, piston, crankshaft, camshaft, sump and electrical equipment

First of the post-war BMW flat-twins, the 494cc (68 x 68mm) R51/2. Between 1951 and 1953, some 5,000 examples were manufactured

Vack and Oliver Baldwin, to set the new motorcycle world record for outright speed on a stretch of route nationale at Arpajon, just outside the French capital. Le Vack eventually took the honours, setting the flying kilometre at 129.5mph (around 207kph) and 128.34mph (around 205kph) for the longer mile distance. Both men rode 998cc JAP-engined Brough Superior machines.

Henne went back to Germany, convinced that these records could be broken using one of the new 735cc short-stroke engines. At BMW's Munich plant work soon began on a likely machine. The factory already had some experience of supercharging, and Henne also used his expertise in the outline he presented to the factory engineers who were to work on the project. A Zoller supercharger was to be grafted on to the engine assembly above the gearbox and, with other tuning measures, this pushed the power output up to an incredible 55bhp. (This was gradually lifted, until, by the late 1930s, over 70bhp was available.) The machine was ready by the beginning of September 1929. The German team had also worked hard on other details – they were the first to make use of serious wind-cheating accessories, including a streamlined helmet,

close-fitting leathers and, eventually, an all-enclosing alloy streamlined shell for the motorcycle.

Henne repaid BMW for their faith in the project, not only setting a new record on the Munich-Ingoldstat autobahn with a two-way average of 134.68mph (around 215.5kph), but also going on to dominate the 1930s with a succession of ever-faster records.

The 1920s and 1930s: BMW's Return to the Car Industry

In the middle of 1928, BMW took over the Dixi automobile plant in Eisenach. During the First World War, the Eisenach facilities had built military trucks, but the Armistice left Dixi in dire trouble. They were taken over by the railway manufacturers Gothaer Wagenfabrik, and given the name Dixi Werke, Eisenach, AG. With an injection of cash, the company returned to car production in 1920, and, for much of the 1920s, its business centred around one model, the 1596 6/24 saloon. In 1927, after several years' steady growth, Dixi had new owners once again, when Gothaer Wagenfabrik

First manufactured in 1952, the R68 was the sports model in BMW's immediate post-war range. Most had low-level exhausts but some, as seen here, sported a siamesed hi-level system. Inspiration for the exhaust came from the company's involvement in the ISDT.

BMW's stand at the 1953 Frankfurt Show displayed the company's confidence in the future – this was not to last very long.

An R68 was used by a team of three riders – Jack Forrest, Don Flynn and Les Roberts – to win Australia's first-ever 24-hour race for production motorcycles, held in October 1954.

was taken over by the Shapiro organization. The following year, a licence was acquired to build the British Austin Seven; however, before production reached any significant quantities, Shapiro took the decision to sell off both plant and product range.

BMW stepped in, considering this the right time to make an entry into the car market, and acquired the Eisenach factory for 2.2 million Reichmarks (RM). Thus, the three roots of the BMW family tree finally merged to present a common corporate front.

The first BMW car was born out of the Austin. It was sold first as a Dixi, but from 1929 as a BMW. It was not until 1933 that

Iron Annie

The Junkers Ju 52/3m is rivalled only by the Douglas DC3 as the most famous transport aircraft of all time. It was conceived in 1930 as the last of a long line of corrugated metal-skinned aircraft, which began with the construction of the Junkers J4 of 1917. Used by a large number of the world's airlines and air forces, the Ju 52 remained in service for nearly forty years. Its best-known exploits were as a transport aircraft with the Luftwaffe (German Air Force), in whose service it was known as either 'Annie Eisen' ('Iron Annie') or 'Tante Ju' ('Auntie Junkers').

Together with the Douglas DC3, the BMW-powered Junkers Ju 52 is probably the world's most famous transport aircraft

The original Ju 52 was powered by a single 800hp engine of Junkers' own manufacture. However, of the many thousands of the 3m version (three-engined), virtually all used 525hp nine-cylinder BMW radial engines. Development of the Ju 52 design was led by Dipl. Ing. Ernst Zindel, and the first three-engined model flew in April 1932.

As well as its military role, the Ju 52/3m saw service with the airlines of Argentina, Australia, Belgium, Bolivia, Brazil, China, Columbia, Czechoslovakia, Denmark, Ecuador, Estonia, Finland, France, Great Britain, Greece, Hungary, Italy, Lebanon, Mozambique, Norway, Peru, Poland, Portugal, Rumania, South Africa, Spain, Sweden and Uruguay.

In 1934, a military version of the Ju 52 was produced for use by the still-secret Luftwaffe. Designated Ju 52 mg 3e, the aircraft was designed as a heavy bomber with a crew of four and armed with two machine guns. Although this aircraft was used by the German Condor Legion in the Spanish Civil War (1936–9), little use was made of it in a bombing role by the Luftwaffe. Instead, it was used as the main workhorse for transporting German forces and military equipment throughout the Second World War. It was also notable in the paratrooper role, and many aircraft were also fitted with floats.

The end of the conflict was certainly not the end of the Ju 52, which was manufactured under licence after the war in both France and Spain. Production of all versions exceeded 5,000; it was generally accepted as being one of the most reliable aircraft of all time, thanks in no small part to its BMW engines.

the first all-BMW car design, the 303, appeared on the scene.

The Wall Street Crash

The aviation side of the BMW business was also growing, especially since the acquisition of a licence to build American Pratt & Whitney radial engines. In common with other firms that were growing rapidly at this time (such as rivals NSU), this meant that BMW was very vulnerable in the storm that was about to engulf the industrialized world – the Wall Street crash, in October 1929. BMW, like NSU, had just completed a major investment programme, and the economic collapse, which bankrupted 17,000 German companies in 1931 alone, hit the firm terribly hard. Only a policy of diversification, and skilled financial management, meant that BMW was able to avoid the ultimate disaster of bankruptcy.

The Motorcycles

Less than a year before the Wall Street crash, BMW had displayed its new R11 and R16 models at Olympia, London, in November 1928, but teething problems delayed production until late in 1929. These machines look quite different from the R62 and R63 models they replaced. Gone was the duplex tubular loop frame used since the R32, and in its place was a pressed-steel frame. This soon became known as 'the star', for reasons that are now lost in the mists of time. (One theory is that the term was derived from the word shark, the German wording for 'strong'.) These new machines were particularly ugly, and their only real claim to fame was as the first series production motorcycles to employ pressed-steel frames anywhere in the world.

Unlike their chassis, their engines were largely unchanged and still featured three-speed gearboxes with hand change. The Series II models of each adopted twistgrip throttles late in 1930. Although the R11 and R16 were steady sellers – about 7,500 of the side-valve R11, and 1,106 of the more sporting twin carb ohv R16 were built in the five-year period before production was axed in 1934 – BMW aero engines, selling well in the Soviet Union and Japan in 1930, provided a useful lifeline to a struggling company.

More help to the business came with the R2, a 198cc (63 x 64mm) ohv single-cylinder

Sidecars

Once the motorcycle had become firmly established, the next question was how it could carry more people. The earliest example of the 'sidecar' arrived just after the turn of the century, in 1901–2, and by 1903 a couple of firms were already offering them for sale; most sidecar bodies at this time were made of wicker-work, mainly to keep down weight.

Martin Harmon of Ubach-Palenbury, near Aachen, with his 1961 R60/2 and BMW's version of the Steib TR500 chair, around 1964.

The Great War of 1914–18 was instrumental in putting the sidecar on the map. In the wake of the conflict, there was an urgent need to provide motorized transport for the family. Many specialized sidecar manufacturers began production, and several early motorcycle makers also entered the field, including BSA, Matchless, Royal Enfield, Sunbeam, Douglas, Phelon & Moore (later known as Panther), Dunelt, Raleigh, Ariel, New Imperial, Chater-Lea and Triumph. Of the many continental European manufacturers, the two most important names were German: BMW and Steib. BMW built its own sidecars for many years, while Steib made 'chairs', represented by dealers Bryants of Biggleswade, Bedfordshire, until 1938, and thereafter by Frazer Nash of Middlesex.

In 1936, there were half a million motorcycles on British roads, one-quarter of which hauled sidecars. By 1939, there were three sidecar combinations to every ten solos, and the third wheel had proved it was here to stay. The story was similar on the continent.

The sidecar's heyday came in the immediate post-war period, in the late 1940s and throughout the 1950s. With the end of the Second World War, established sidecar manufacturers returned with renewed energy. There was not only a demand for the traditional single-seater, but also for family saloons in the shape of either child and adult combinations, or double adult. These were mainly constructed using a wood frame and plywood panelling, with the outer made of aluminium or other metal sheet. With the increased demand, many new firms sprang up to join the established names, including Swallow, Watsonian, Blacknell, SA, Garrard and Panther, but BMW and Steib continued to produce the 'Rolls Royce' of sidecars at the top end of the market.

The mid-1950s brought the new plastic glass fibre. One of the first sidecars to enter production using this material was the Watsonian Bambino, a single-seater for lightweights and scooters.

With the advent of the 1960s, sidecar sales began to fall into the slump from which they never fully recovered. There were two main reasons for the decline: increasingly sporting motorcycles, many of which had frames unsuitable for a third wheel, and the creation of the Mini, which brought affordable four-wheel motoring to even the most economically minded family.

Sidecars survive today, but only among committed enthusiasts and as a tiny segment of the overall bike scene.

commuter bike. Sales of this machine were boosted not only by its low purchase price, but also by it being in a category in which the owner did not have to pass a driving test, or pay any road fund tax. Featuring a three-speed gearbox and a pressed-steel chassis, this utility machine sold well, with the Munich factory turning out no less than 15,207 between 1931 and 1936.

The motorcycle that really turned BMW's fortunes around during the dark days of the early 1930s was the 398cc (78 x 84mm) ohv R4 single, which ran parallel course to the R2 in production (1932–36). A total of 15,300 were sold, many of them to the German Army.

By 1933, the year Adolf Hitler came to power, BMW was rapidly climbing out of the hole caused by the Great Depression. By the end of that year, it boasted record production and a total workforce of 4,720, and it had produced its first six-cylinder BMW car. Its turnover rose from 19 million RM in 1932 to 82 million in 1934; its figures for 1935 were even more impressive, with a turnover of 128 million RM and 11,113 employees.

The year 1935 saw the introduction of the 754cc (78 x 78mm) R12 flat-twin, which was destined to become the company's most successful model of the inter-war years. The R12 featured telescopic front forks, but its one outstanding feature was the incorporation of hydraulic damping on a production model. Other features of the R12 included a four-speed gearbox (with hand change), 19-in wheels and a dry weight of 356lb (162kg). As before, BMW offered a version of the R12 with the more powerful ohv engine, coded R17. This produced 33bhp at 4,500rpm (against the R12's 18bhp at 3,400rpm), and

Zündapp's 'Green Elephant'

It will come as a surprise to many that the world-renowned Elephant Rally was named after a motorcycle – the Zündapp KS 601 'Green Elephant' flat-twin, the final version of the Zündapp twin-cylinder range, which for many years mirrored BMW's every move.

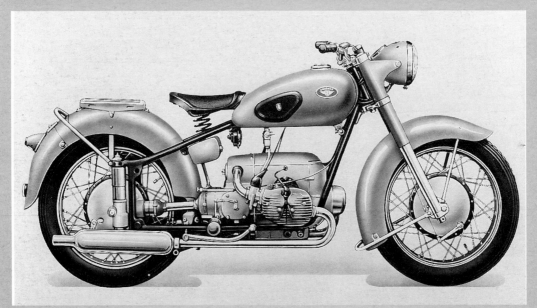

Zündapp's KS601 'Green Elephant' gave its name to Germany's famous Elephant Rally.

The first Zündapp motorcycle – a licence-built British Levis single-cylinder two-stroke – appeared in the autumn of 1921. By October 1922, 1,000 of these machines had been manufactured by a workforce totalling 600. Two years later, production had increased ten-fold. The success continued until the Wall Street Crash in October 1929, and the Great Depression that followed. At the peak of the economic crisis, over 55 million Germans were unemployed.

By 1933, Zündapp and the German economy was making a recovery. The company produced the first of its four-stroke flat-twins (in capacities of 398 and 498cc), and a flat four of 598cc. The models were the work of designer Richard Küchen.

The 200,000th Zündapp motorcycle was produced in 1938, and the first KS600 came the following year. This machine was a development of the previous KS500, and had an output of 28bhp at 4,700rpm. It featured aluminium pistons, removable cylinder heads in light alloy, triple-bearing crankshaft and forced lubrication. Other features included a four-speed gearbox in unit with the engine, shaft final drive and a pressed-steel frame with blade-type front forks. With a full tank of fuel, the KS600 weighed 210kg (462lb), and it could achieve 98mph (157kph).

In the Second World War, the KS750 was a special model developed by Zündapp for military purposes. It had an integral sidecar, its wheel driven via a lockable differential. The engine was

The brainchild of the leading German motorcycle journalist and writer Ernst Leverkus, the Elephant Rally, staged at the Nürburgring, became the most famous winter rally in Europe. This picture dates back to the mid 1960s

still an air-cooled flat-twin four-stroke, but it was unusual in having two sets of four forward and a reverse gear. Together with the similar BMW R75 outfit, the KS750 was the definitive German military motorcycle of the conflict.

After the war, the main excitement in Zündapp circles was the launch, in 1951, of a new 'sports' version of the flat-twin, the KS601. Besides a top speed of 75mph (120kph) with a sidecar, the 'Green Elephant' was also successful in long-distance sporting trials, such as the ISDT, during the early 1950s. The gearbox was devoid of gears, which were replaced by a series of sprockets and chains!

Even though the KS601 was a superb machine in many respects, Zündapp's attempts to outsell BMW were badly affected when BMW launched the new Earles-fork series in 1955. Manufacture of flat-twin Zündapps halted in 1959, when the last Green Elephant left the Nürnberg factory's gates late that year. A total of some 5,500 machines had been built.

could achieve 88mph (140kph). Between 1935 and 1938, 36,000 R12s were built and sold, while just 450 of the more exclusive R17 were manufactured. The R17 was the most powerful production roadster built by BMW, until the introduction of its R68 model in 1952.

In 1935, AFN Ltd of Falcon Works, London Road, Isleworth, Middlesex (now a Porsche dealership) become the first British importer of BMW. It was an inaus-

picious time – in 1936, the first signs of another world conflict began to appear on the horizon. At about this time, BMW set up a military equipment division at its Eisenach works to manufacture lightweight field guns. Meanwhile, motorcycle developments continued apace, most notably with two new production models – the R3 single and R5 twin.

The R3 was manufactured only in 1936, with around 750 being built. The 305cc

Isetta

During the early 1950s, BMW's motorcycle and luxury car sales were not meeting targets, so the company was forced to attempt to broaden its appeal. It built a scooter in 1954 using a four-stroke ohv engine, but this never left the prototype stage. Much more successful was the Isetta 'bubble car', which did reach production, and went on to sell in relatively large numbers.

Brochure proclaiming the virtues of the Isetta

The New 3-Wheeled **Isetta**

Outrageously cheap to run — comfortable — safe!

EASY PARKING
Since its length is no more than average car width, it can be placed nose-on to the kerb, and is therefore the easiest car in the world to park.

PLENTY OF ROOM FOR LUGGAGE
A very large shelf behind the seat gives plenty of room for luggage or shopping, and in addition a luggage grid can be fitted as an optional extra.

PERFORMANCE AND RUNNING ECONOMY
The Isetta will cruise "for ever" at 50 m.p.h. In a recent test, it was found to have a consumption of 93 miles per gallon at a steady speed of 30 m.p.h. Moreover, it is exceptionally economical and simple to run in other ways. An air-cooled engine: one sparking-plug only: a sump capacity of only 3 pints: only 6 greasing points — they speak for themselves. With four forward synchromesh speeds (and one reverse gear) the Isetta has remarkably quick acceleration. It is fitted with Dunlop tubeless tyres, with a life of 24,000 to 28,000 miles on the front and 35,000 to 40,000 on the back.

MAINTENANCE AND SPARES
In designing the Isetta, particular attention has been given to keeping costs of maintenance down to rock-bottom. The long-life tubeless tyres and the fully-tested, exceptional cheap-to-service engine are symptomatic of this principle. Good spares service is assured, wherever you go, by the Isetta world-wide Service Organisation with its work-trained engineers. Larger tyre section all round to give same suspension efficiency as a four-wheeled model. £5 only, road tax. Otherwise equipped with all the appointments of the four-wheeled model.

The Isetta was not a BMW original, but a tried and tested design from the Italian Iso concern, from whom BMW obtained a licence in late 1954. When the car first entered production in Germany on 5 March 1955, it was a four-wheeler, although the rear wheels were so close as to make it technically a three-wheeler in some countries. It was soon re-designed as a true three-wheeler, to take advantage of tax and insurance concessions available in several other markets, including Britain. It was a unique machine, and the typical BMW Series 3 owner of today would find it hard to believe that the Isetta carried that

Issetas were built with either 250 or 300cc single-cylinder engines, or in stretched form with one from the 594cc R60 flat twin.

world-famous and unmistakable white and blue symbol on its front door.

Power was provided by a fan-cooled variant of the single-cylinder R25 engine (later R26 and 27 assemblies), in both the original 245cc [(68 x 68mm)] and later 295cc (72 x 73mm) form from December 1955 onwards. Weighing in at 792lb (360kg) for the 250/300 versions, this unique machine had a maximum speed of 53mph (85kph).

Production figures for the period are impressive – between 1955 and 1962, when manufacture was finally halted, 74,312 of the '250' Isettas, and 87,416 of the '300' were built, as well as 34,813 of the stretched '600' version powered by the 594cc R60 flat-twin. Without this 'micro-car' BMW would have been in dire straits. Almost 200,000 of BMW's baby 'bubble car' were constructed – an economical form of transport for the austere 1950s, and an economic necessity for the company.

The design brief called for two occupants to be able to sit comfortably inside, in order to transport themselves and a minimum amount of luggage in a fair degree of comfort and for a minimum outlay in terms of both purchase cost and running costs (including fuel).

The problem of getting into this minimalist vehicle was solved ingeniously: open the front, get in standing upright, sit down, feel at home. The front door, essentially the entire front of the car, hinged at the left and opened to a wide angle. Even the upper part of the steering column moved out, complete with the steering wheel and instrument panel, to make access to the vehicle easy.

The Isetta was most definitely a concept belonging to its time. The strict safety standards that apply today call for vehicles of a specific minimum length. Despite its popularity and cute styling, the Isetta simply cannot conform.

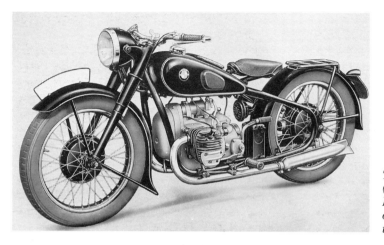

The R6 employed a 596cc (70 x 78cc) side-valve engine in R5 running gear. Production only took place in 1937, and a total of 1,850 were built.

(68 x 84mm) engine was basically a sleeved-down R4 engine, with the stroke unaltered. Power output was 11bhp at 4,200rpm. The real interest, however, was centred around the R5. This was powered by a re-engineered 493cc engine; the 68 x 68mm bore and stroke dimensions, and pushrod valve operation features were retained, but little else was. In order to achieve higher engine revolutions and, therefore, a higher performance, the design team spent much time ensuring that the individual engine components were lighter and stronger than before. There were now two camshafts, one on each side of the crankcase, rather than the original single shaft with its centred location.

The light alloy cylinder heads housed the more expensive hairpin valve springs, in place of the conventional coil variety. They were hidden away behind the massive rocker box covers that were a feature of this particular model. Another notable change in specification was, finally, the adoption of a four-speed gearbox, with positive-stop foot operation. To make room for this, the extensive aluminium footboards, used on virtually every BMW twin since the R32, were replaced by normal footrests. This

model also had the latest version of BMW's hydraulically operated front fork, and a neat tubular duplex frame in place of the ugly 'star' pressed-steel frame. The only feature still missing was any form of rear suspension; this had yet to reach even the racing BMW twins.

AFN sold the R5 in Britain for £115, about £15 more than an overhead cam International Norton of similar performance.

In the following year, 1937, BMW launched the R6, a side-valve 594cc (70 x 78mm) version of the R5 (1,850 were built), and a pair of new single-cylinder models – the 340cc (72 x 84mm) R35 and the 190cc (60 x 68mm) R20. The top seller was the R35, with 15,400 units built (all in 1937), most of them going to the German military; the R35 replaced the 398cc R4, which had been built in the preceding five years.

In 1937, BMW again took over the Flottweg factory, the same establishment it had sold in 1921. This was a period of intense activity on record-breaking and competition fronts, and it was only a short time before the racing technology was carried through into the BMW roadster line.

The Berlin show of February 1938, a much trumpeted occasion, was opened by

Adolf Hitler. In the previous year, over a million and a half motorcycles had been registered in Germany, with the leading manufacturers, BMW included, working on a prodigious scale. However, with Hitler's suggestion at the show that the 'people's car', which emerged as the Volkswagen Beatle, 'would be in production by 1939–40', planners within the German motorcycle industry began to foresee a decline in the demand for models of 500cc and above, and especially those intended for sidecar work. Despite these predictions, BMW engineers continued to work hard at transferring the technology developed in motorcycle sport to the machines on the street. The most notable outcome of this policy – on display at the Berlin Show – was the standardization of spring frames for all BMW's 1938 twin-cylinder models.

Included in the 1938 range was the entirely new R66. Based on the previous year's R5 five hundred, it featured a 597cc (70 x 78mm) engine, which was not based on the smaller unit, although it did retain the hairpin valve springs. Power was an impressive 30bhp at 5,300rpm, which was enough to break 90mph (145kph) in solo form, or 70mph (110kph) with a third wheel attached.

The sports R5 was replaced by the rear-sprung R51, while the R6 followed the same format and became the R61. The largest BMW twin that year was the R71, powered by a revised version of the long-serving 745cc side-valve motor with Graetzin carburettors. In this instrument, the jet block and float chamber were cast in a single unit. This motorcycle was, in fact, destined to be the last of the pre-war twin-cylinder models to be built by the Munich works and was phased out in 1941.

One interesting feature of all four 1938 flat-twins was that their air cleaner was situated inside the gearbox housing.

Completing the 1938 Berlin show line-up was the R23, a 247cc (68 x 68mm) with four-speed foot-change gearbox. It was also BMW's first true 'two-fifty' since the demise of the R39 in 1926. Producing 10bhp at 5,400rpm, the power unit was mounted in a neat tubular frame; the lightweight telescopic front forks lacked the sophistication of the hydraulic damping fitted to the twins.

In this year, 1938, the 100,000th BMW motorcycle rolled off the production lines.

Rider's-eye view of R68 controls, typical for BMW twins of the period. Note the tank-top toolbox, handlebar-mounted choke control and large headlamp-encased speedometer.

THE SECOND WORLD WAR

In 1939, on the eve of war, the BMW empire was still putting on weight, and now had a workforce of 26,919. In Britain, AFN was offering a full range of BMW production models for the 1939 season: the 250 ohv R23 at £59, the 350 ohv R35 for £85, the 500 ohv R51 at £123, 600 ohv R66 for £135, the 600sv R61 for £118, and the 740sv R71 for £123.

From the beginning of September 1939, the storm clouds of conflict gathered over the whole of Europe as the Second World War began.

The corporate strategy of BMW was now firmly set on military production. The aero-engine division was the leading player, but the production of motorcycles also continued to be an important part of the company's activities. The Wehrmacht (the German army) needed large numbers of machines, to use for troop transport and as fighting vehicles. These machines were provided by three main suppliers – Zündapp, NSU and BMW. There were single-cylinder BMW military bikes but, without doubt, the definitive German motorcycles of the war were the BMW R75 flat-twin, and the similar Zündapp KS750. Many of these machines were used for sidecar duties in all kinds of conditions, from the North African desert to the Russian steppes.

Many of Germany's leading aircraft, such as the Focke Wulf 190 fighter and Junkers Ju88 bomber, benefited from BMW piston engines. BMW was also at the forefront of jet-engine technology, and their units were used to power prototypes of both the Messerschmitt Me262 fighter and the Arado Ar234 bomber.

The war brought management changes at BMW. Franz Josef Popp, the first managing director, retired and was succeeded by Kurt Donarth. Just before the end of the conflict, on 11 April 1945, Hitler order Donarth immediately to destroy all production facilities. Heavy bombing had already taken its toll of the BMW facilities and, by 1945, about one-third of the Munich facilities had been destroyed. Donarth chose to ignore Hitler's order; he did the same when the order was repeated, in October, by the American garrison in Munich, who decreed that the plant should be dismantled and destroyed. Anything of value was to be shipped back to the United States. When the American forces took over Munich, they removed many of the remaining machine tools. In the East, Eisenach was occupied by Soviet forces and found itself in the Soviet sector of post-war Germany.

AFTER THE WAR

Post-War Restrictions

Because Munich had been the centre of BMW's wartime aero-engine production, Eisenach had been used as BMW's car and motorcycle divisions. Commandeered by the Red Army and, later, in the hands of the civilian Communist government, the plant was used to construct Soviet versions of BMW motorcycles and cars. At first, the new owners used the existing stock of spare parts, and later they manufactured their own components, before transferring motorcycle production back to the Soviet Union. Car production, originally of BMWs, then of EMWs (Eisenach Motoren Werke), continued at Eisenach, using pre-war BMW designs. From 1956, the East German plant produced three-cylinder two-stroke cars under the Wartburg name.

Meanwhile, in its stripped and shattered Munich plant, BMW was again fighting for its existence. Under the Allied Control Commission, immediately following the war, German companies were prohibited from making motorcycles. By September 1945, BMW was undertaking limited production of anything it could sell – cooking utensils, wood-planing equipment, and bicycle parts. Later, in early 1946, the plant (in common with that of NSU) was used to service American military vehicles, and then for the production of baking machines and household equipment. As Germany's need to become mobile again began to grow, the Allied Control Commission relaxed its regulations relating to the manufacture of vehicles and spare parts. Initially, BMW was allowed to build a batch of 100 pre-war R23 247cc ohv singles from existing components and 21,999 bicycles; this manufacture began in December 1948.

Post-War Motorcycles

The launch of the first real post-war BMW motorcycle came in 1949, with the debut of the R24. This was basically an updated R23, with an additional 2bhp, making 12bhp in all. It employed a rigid frame, spindly undamped telescopic forks, 3 x 19-in tyres on black painted rims, a small-capacity fuel tank (made smaller because of the toolbox built into its top), and single-sided, single-leading shoe drum brakes front and rear. It could not be called sophisticated, but in a country starved of personal transport it was a big sales success, with a total of 12,010 units sold in 1949. For 1950 it was replaced by the R25, which enjoyed the luxury of plunger rear suspension, but had virtually no other notable changes.

The other model introduced in 1950 was the R51/2, an updated version of the popular pre-war R51. This 494cc (68 x 68mm) ohv flat-twin provoked the following comment in the 23 March 1950 issue of *The*

Motor Cycle in the Geneva Show report: 'The reintroduced 500cc BMW transverse twin is a very trim, workmanlike-looking mount.' Workmanlike it certainly was, with its substantial mudguards, including the renowned 'elephant's ear' front assembly which was deeply valanced, and its comprehensive suspension, both at the front (hydraulically damped teles), and at the rear (plunger units). Notable improvements on the pre-war twin included new cylinder heads, the incorporation of a cam-type transmission shock absorber in the gearbox, and the fitting of a new (and much improved) four-speed gearbox.

At the beginning of 1951, the R51/2 was replaced by the R51/3. Although the power output was unchanged, at 24bhp, the engine was considerably revised and set a style which, in general appearance at least, was still visible as late as 1969, on the R69S. The crankcase – a 'tunnel' casting – had an outstandingly clean appearance. Behind a rounded timing cover at the front was the gear drive to the camshaft and magneto ignition. The rocker boxes on top of the cylinders on each side were of a new shape and carried cooling fins, while the Bing carburettors were fully waterproofed and ducted into the top of the gearbox, above which was bolted a housing for the external air filter. The gearbox itself bolted to the rear of the crankcase, carrying on its smooth lines, and for the first time it contained a switch which activated a light in the headlamp when neutral was selected.

There were also notable changes to the cycle parts, including, for the first time on a production BMW motorcycle, full-width brake hubs. Other updates included a larger-capacity fuel tank, alloy wheel rims, front fork rubber gaiters, and a new exhaust system, with silencers, and without the tail fins used on the earlier twins.

News of the R51/3 was released at the

Brussels Show in January 1951, where rumours also circulated that BMW was about to reintroduce a six hundred ohv twin. This prediction was proved to be correct a month later, when the R67 made its debut at the Amsterdam Show. Powered by a 594cc (72 x 73mm) horizontal opposed twin-cylinder engine, which followed the general layout of the R51/3, the new motorcycle produced its maximum power of 26bhp at 5,500rpm. Strangely, it used the cycle parts of the earlier R51/2, including the fishtail silencers, austere black-painted wheel rims, and less powerful single-sided brakes.

The R67's appearance was largely due to the market demand for a sidecar tug – many family men were looking for a motorcycle of suitable quality to haul a third wheel. It was significant as BMW's first post-war machine of over 500cc, although only 1,470 examples were built, all in 1951.

The R67 was replaced by the improved R67/2 at the end of 1951, and the R25 was given the /2 treatment at the same time. The third model in the range, the R51/3, remained unchanged for the season.

The three motorcycles were displayed at the first post-war German International Motorcycle Show which opened in Frankfurt on Sunday 28 October. Although there were over 300 stands, the sensation of the exhibition was another BMW – the new R68. This was the first genuine 100mph (160kph) production roadster from the German factory. Capable of 105mph (168kph), it was the flagship model that all enthusiasts of the marque had been waiting for. It was powered by a tuned version of the ohv 594cc twin, with a specification that included a high-level exhaust system (siamesed into a single silencer on the off side), special cams, timing gears and cylinder heads, a compression ration of 8:1, racing-type magneto, bigger-bore carbs (up from 22 to

26mm) and a twin leading shoe front brake. The power output had been increased to 35bhp at 7,000rpm. In a three-year production span a total of 1,452 R68s were built, ensuring the model's exclusivity.

The four models were imported into Britain, selling in 1952 at the following prices: R25/2, £215; R51/3, £339; R67/2, £343; the R68 was available only to special order, its price unpublished.

Steady Improvements

The only new production BMW in 1953 was the R25/3 single, which now offered 13bhp (at the same 5,800rpm), hydraulically damped front forks, an air filter housed within the fuel tank (with a long induction pipe to the carburettor), and the toolbox moved from the top of the tank to the side. Perhaps the most obvious change was the introduction of full-width alloy brake drums of a similar design to those found on the R51/3 model. When the new 250 went into production, the R25/2 was dis-continued; 38,651 had been made in the preceding two and a half years, making it the most popular model BMW had marketed up to that time.

For 1954, the three twin-cylinder models were equipped with the new type of air filtration system pioneered on the R25/3, together with a modified exhaust, so that both the intake and exhaust silencing were improved. The telescopic front forks on all three bikes featured improved hydraulic dampers, offering not only a softer ride but also improved roadholding.

While the rest of the German motorcycle industry seemed desperate to unveil new designs at a frenetic pace in a bid to stay competitive, BMW relied on steady improvements and refinements to the vertical singles and horizontally opposed twins. The company appeared, at least to the outside world, to remain true to this formula, which had proved so successful in the past; however, behind the scenes things were rather different. In reality, like the rest of the German two-wheel industry almost a decade after the end of the war, the BMW management was deeply concerned about what they saw as an uncertain future.

BMW's 100,000th post-war motorcycle had been built towards the end of 1953 and sales were at record levels. However, it was felt that the company was too exposed to the whims of the enthusiast market at a time when other manufacturers were becoming involved with scooters and micro cars. Even on the automobile front, BMW was potentially in a weak position, concentrating on the luxury end of the market with its large-capacity V8 saloons.

In order to broaden its appeal, in 1954 BMW instructed its engineering staff to come up with a scooter, in an attempt to rival the success of the Italian Lambretta and Vespa marques. In common with other European motorcycle manufacturers that attempted to break into the small-wheel sector, BMW plumped for a four-stroke ohv engine. Its scooter was destined never to reach production. It was too complex, and too expensive to compete.

Even though BMW did not hit the jackpot with the scooter, it did so with the micro, or bubble car. This time the company took an easier route, taking out a licence from the Italian company Iso, and developing the BMW Isetta. It could be said that the Isetta, together with a line of updated motorcycles, and a couple of automobiles (one of which used the famous flat-twin motorcycle engine), saved the company.

The year 1955 was a vital one in BMW's history, although this was not evident at the time. In fact, the company only managed to scrape into the 1960s by the skin of its corporate teeth.

With a 594cc (72 x 73mm) ohv engine, the 1954 R67/2 was equally acceptable in either solo or sidecar roles. It is shown here with a BMW Stetenwagen Special sidecar.

2 Racing and Record Breaking

BMW has had a proud record in all forms of motorcycle sport almost from the company's beginning. Grand Prix and TT victories, on both two and three wheels, and speed records have all played their role in creating a legend.

SOLO RACING

The R37

The first racing BMW was the 494cc (68 x 68mm) R37, the work of Rudolf Schleicher, who personally rode one of the models in the 1926 ISDT (see Chapter 3). In 1924, with Fritz Bieber at the controls, the R37 was victorious in the German national road-racing championships. From that moment, competition was to play a vital role in BMW's future. BMW constructed ten special versions of the R37, using them to test chassis and engine modifications, including the alloy cylinder heads that were such an innovation for the era. The model's last major success came in the 1926 German GP, when it was ridden by Paul Koppen.

The Kompressor

Although the company did enter long-distance road events such as the famous Targa Florio, BMW's main effort during the late 1920s and early 1930s was in record breaking and off-road sport. Lessons from

Diploma awarded to Ernst Henne and BMW for their world speed record exploits.

its record-breaking exploits were channelled into a return to tarmac racing via the Kompressor, a five-hundred twin cylinder model, which bore a close resemblance to Ernst Henne's 'world's fastest' machine. Both bikes were equipped with a Zoller supercharger built on to the front of the crankcase assembly, and coupled to the rearward-facing inlets via long pipes passing over the cylinders. The dohc 492cc (66 x 72mm) engine generated over 80bhp at 8,000rpm, giving an impressive maximum road speed of around 140mph (225kph).

The first examples of the Kompressor racer made their début in 1935. They employed telescopic front forks when the other factory racing teams could only manage blade or girder types. It was not until

Fritz Bieber, winner of the 500cc class of the 1924 German road-racing championships.

the end of the following year that BMW first made use of plunger rear suspension, but its use, combined with the teles, did not automatically provide the Munich works with a sufficiently competitive edge; they could not even equal the other machines, notably the normally aspirated British singles.

It was not until 1937 that BMW engineers had finally got their machine to a stage where a serious challenge could be launched. That year, the veteran Karl Gall became German national champion, while Jack West finished sixth in the Isle of Man Senior TT. The same riders went on to win the Ulster GP later that year, giving BMW considerable overseas publicity; it was the first time a German machine had won the event. Despite great hopes for 1938, not only was Gall injured during practice for the TT, but also Georg Meier (destined to become European Champion that year) was forced to retire. Jock West was left to try his best, but the Englishman could finish no higher than fifth.

Meier made history the following year, becoming the first foreign rider to win a Senior TT – the premier racing event in the world – on a foreign bike. Meier's team-mate Jock West came home second, but BMW's great 1–2 was tinged with tragedy following the practice crash and subsequent death of the third team member, Karl Gall.

AFTER THE WAR

A few short weeks later, the roar of the racing world was silenced by the outbreak of war. The European motorcycle industry transferred its industrial expertise to the military effort. During the immediate post-war period, BMW was one of the first manufacturers to campaign its machines in the defeated (and divided) Germany. Various examples of the pre-war flat-twins, including the works Kompressor models, were on song once again. Georg Meier, who had spent the war years in the Wehrmacht, was back in the saddle at the age of thirty-six. In 1947, Meier formed the Veritas team and selected a BMW for an attempt on the German national title. He was so successful that, in 1949, he was

The Deutsche Bundespost produced this special stamp in 1983 showing the BMW record breaker used by Ernst Henne in 1936.

Lessons from Ernst Henne's record breaker were used for a return to tarmac racing via the Kompressor, a five-hundred supercharged flat-twin. It first appeared in 1935.

voted the new West Germany's sportsman of the year in a national poll.

In 1950, a battle royal raged between the supercharged BMW and NSU twins for Germany's road-racing championship, with NSU coming out on top. When Germany was re-admitted to the FIM in 1951, all the German bike builders had to abandon supercharging. This move favoured the Munich factory more than their rivals NSU, and BMW romped home in the national title race that year. In April 1951, a re-engineered Boxer made its début at the Eilenriede Rennen races near Hanover. Unlike the newly created NSU four, the BMW twin not only lasted the distance, but took the victor's laurels. There was a new rider too – 23-year-old Walter Zeller, who won from old hand Meier.

GRAND PRIX

Although BMW was at the top of the tree in its own country, it was not yet ready to re-join the Grand Prix circuit. Against foreign opposition, notably the Italian fours and British singles, the Munich twins were not fully competitive. The revamped machine, named the Mustang, was hardly more than Meier's 1939 TT-winning machine, with the blower replaced by conventional air feed and two carburettors.

Meier rounding Quarter Bridge during his historic ride.

The 1939 Senior TT: Georg (Schorsch) Meier, the first foreign rider on a non-British machine to win the Isle of Man Tourist Trophy.

The 1939 Senior TT: Meier's winning machine.

After the war, Meier formed the Veritas Racing Team, using BMWs, of course! He was so successful that, by 1949, he was voted Sportsman of the Year in a national poll.

There was no real improvement in BMW's Grand Prix performance until 1953, when Zeller débuted what was to emerge as the Rennsport. The German Grand Prix that year was staged over the controversial Schotten circuit. This 10-mile (16-km), tree-lined course was considered too dangerous by the leading foreign teams, who withdrew from the race en masse, so the domestic factories had a clear run at honours. In the 500cc class, Zeller achieved a comfortable victory, riding a modified machine in which fuel was injected directly into the cylinders instead of the inlet venturis, as on earlier models. At the time, this was said to provide a considerable boost to the power output, and might have accounted for Zeller's 35-second lead over team-mate Hans Baltisburger, on a conventional carb model, after only two laps. Another factory-entered BMW, ridden by Hans Meier (younger brother of Georg), came home fourth.

The FIM later withdrew the points won at Schotten in both the 350 and 500cc class, due to the mass withdrawal of the leading teams.

Walter Zeller piloted another of the fuel-injected machines in the Senior TT that June. Unfortunately, lying ninth on the first lap, he fell early in the race, damaging the bike too badly to continue.

The Rennsport

There were three stages in the development of the BMW fuel-injection system. At first, the injector nozzle was fitted between the throttle slide and inlet port, spraying into the induction tract of an angle. Next came the layout employed for Zeller's 1953 Senior TT mount, in which the injector was situated in the induction bell mouth, upstream of the throttles and injecting axially. Finally, as first used at Schotten, the nozzle was transferred to the cylinder head, opposite the spark plug. Removal of the obstructions from the inlet system improved the cylinder charging appreciably, and resulted in an improved power output figure.

The definitive Rennsport appeared in 1954, and all subsequent factory and privately entered machines were developments of this basic format. At first, the Rennsport engine was of the long-stroke variety, with 66 x 72mm giving 492cc. In this form, maximum power was generated

Georg Meier on one of the new short-stroke 70 x 64mm dohc works racers at the beginning of the 1953 season. Much was new, not just the engine, but also the Earles forks, swinging arm rear suspension and duplex frame.

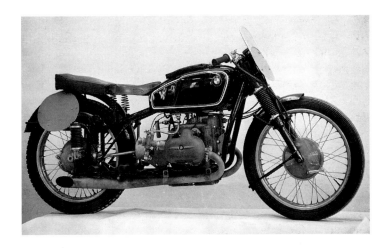

One of the official factory racers used in 1951. It was very much a normally aspirated version of the old pre-war model

at 8,000rpm. Later, however, with the need for more power, the bore and stroke measurements were altered to 68 x 68mm (493.9cc), resulting in the engine revolutions rising to 9,500rpm.

The crankshaft, with its 180-degree throws, was of built-up construction. Mainshafts were hollow and integral with the flywheels, which embodied balance weights. Each crankpin hole in the elliptical medial web of the shaft had a shallow counterbore on the side of the web, adjacent to the respective big-end. The radius of the counterbore was greater than that of the end of the web and of the big-end eye so that the shaft's overall length could be kept to the bore minimum.

Like the mainshafts, the hollow crankpins were of 35mm diameter, one end of each was pressed into the medial web and locked in position by a solid, forced-in expander plug. After the big-end bearings and connecting rods had been assembled on the pins, the cheeks were pressed on and further expander plugs driven in. The plugs at the outer ends of the pins differed from the inner type by having a small longitudinal hole for big-end lubrication.

There were three crankshaft main bearings. The one at the rear was of the self-aligning type, embodying a special variety of roller, while the one at the front featured a conventional bell-race. Another conventional bell-race was housed in the front cover as an outboard support for the firming pinion. The crankcase was a one-piece electron casting. There were two 35-mm main bearings which were fitted in separate housings. These housings were manufactured from different materials – cast iron at the front, steel at the rear.

Integral with the forward main bearing housing was the rear wall of the oil pump; the aluminium alloy pump body carrying the gears was fitted into a recess in the housing to which it was bolted. The pump itself was of the duplex-gear type, one part feeding the main big-end, while the other supplied the cam gear. Wet-sump lubrication was employed, with a sump (again in electron) of just over half a gallon (2.8 litre) in capacity being bolted to the base of the crankcase.

Oil for the cam gear flowed from the pump, through a series of oilways in the crankcase, to external pipes which lay between the cylinders. These pipes were flanked by a larger-diameter pipe through

1954 Production Racer RS54

Engine:	Bevel-driven, double overhead camshaft flat-twin
Displacement:	492cc
Bore and stroke:	66 x 72mm
Maximum power:	45bp at 8,000rpm
Carburation:	Twin Fischer-Amals 30-mm, with remote float chambers
Ignition:	Bosch magneto
Lubrication:	Wet sump
Gearbox:	Four-speed
Clutch:	Single-disc, dry
Frame:	Duplex
Front fork:	Earles-type
Rear suspension:	Swinging arm, twin shock
Brakes:	Front: 200-mm twin leading shoe, drum
	Rear: 200-mm single leading shoe, drum
Tyres:	Front 3.25 x 19. Rear 3.50 x 19
Weight:	291lb (132kg) dry
Maximum speed:	126mph (203kph)

Note: Factory racing model as used by Walter Zeller had oversquare 70 x 64mm bore and stroke dimensions.

which the oil returned to the sump. Lubricant (of the castor-based variety) circulated from each main bearing housing into a trap secured by screws to the adjacent face of each crankshaft cheek. The trap was essentially a disc which had its periphery turned inwards through 180 degrees to form an annular channel. Oil from the bearing housing was directed by centrifugal force into the channel; it reached the big-end through a small hole in the trap wall that aligned with the hole in the crankpin plug. Each of the crankpins had two radial holes, and, since they diverged outwards, the oil flow had the maximum centrifugal assistance. This type

of layout minimized internal oilways which otherwise could have weakened the whole crankshaft assembly. In addition, it simplified the building up of the shaft because no holes had to be aligned. The traps acted as very efficient centrifugal filters for collecting sludge, which is why only a gauze section oil filter system was needed.

Each big-end bearing comprised fourteen rollers measuring 10 x 7mm. Housed in a duralumin cage, these ran directly on the crankpin and the con-rod eye, both pin and eye featuring specially hardened surfaces. The connecting rods themselves were of particular interest, as they employed a very unusual flat section, rather than an

The factory exhaustively tested both fuel injection...

...and conventional carburettors.

I-section between the big- and small-ends. Each rod was quite short – about 180 per cent of the stroke. BMW's engineering team tried the more conventional I-section, but discovered that these were more prone to breakage, with fatigue cracks developing at the radius between the flange and the web.

The gear case at the front of the engine contained three pairs of spur gears. A steel gear on the crank drove an alloy half-speed gear immediately above it; the gears were lubricated by jet from the front main bearing housing. Also on the crankshaft was a steel gear that meshed with the alloy oil-pump driving gear. It was found necessary to embody a cush-drive in the steel gear to prevent the teeth of the alloy gear from breaking under the load produced by full throttle acceleration or deceleration of the crankshaft.

A steel gear on the half-speed shaft meshed with the alloy magneto gear which featured slotted holes for the timing adjustment. In front of the half-speed gear, and driven from it by a pair of pegs, was a ported sleeve which ran in the electron front cover and served as a timed engine breather. The breather sleeve contained the coupling for the fuel-injection pump drive. This coupling had holes that engaged with a trio of pegs projecting from the end of the half-speed shaft, and it was splined internally at its forward end to receive male splines in the pump-unit shaft.

At the rear end of the half-speed shaft, which was carried in a pair of ball bearings in a duralumin housing, was a bevel gear. This meshed with two more bevel gears embodying short, hollow shafts which transmitted the drive, via solid shafts, to the camshafts.

Engaging with the splines of the hollow shafts were male splines at the inboard end of the solid driveshafts. Each of these shafts had an integral bevel gear at its outer end and ran in a ball bearing pressed into the inboard half of a cast-iron housing. Split longitudinally in the vertical plane, the housing was held to the cylinder head by three pairs of studs; the two outer pairs also served to retain the electron cambox covers.

BMW technicians employed a most unconventional arrangement for the dohc system. In each cylinder head, the two camshafts lay close together within a split housing, and each operated its respective valve through a short, straight rocker. The design was a compromise between the usual sohc and the normal 'double knocker' layouts because, although the reciprocating weight with the rockers was higher than

1955 Racing Projects

During 1955, BMW engineers were involved in a highly secret development project involving three high-performance engines: a version of the Rennsport five hundred 'Boxer' engine with desmodromic valve gear; a twin camshaft, four-valve, four-cylinder car engine; and (the most interesting) the RS250.

Production version of BMW's dohc racer, the RS 54 Rennsport. displayed at the 1953 Frankfurt show with telescopic front forks...

Heading the development team was Alex von Falkenhausen, who was convinced that, whether for racing or production, a smaller BMW motorcycle engine could have nothing other than the Boxer configuration. At that time, international motorcycle development was focused on moving away from pushrod to overhead camshaft engines, so this route was taken with the RS250.

One of the main priorities of von Falkenhausen's team was to achieve the very minimum dimensions, especially with regard to overall width and weight. This engine was intended first for use in a racing environment, and later in a production high-performance road machine to compete with lightweight high-performance two-strokes, such as the Adler MB250 twin.

Extensive use was made of the magnesium-based alloy electron, with the crankcase, finned oil sump, front cover and unit-construction gearbox cast in the material.

The road unit was scheduled to use conventional coil ignition, but the racing motor had a specially designed thyristor ignition, developed expressly by Bosch for this engine.

Another unusual feature of the RS250 was the use of a horizontally split crankcase assembly –

after much heated discussion by the BMW board, which had voiced concern about giving up the traditional tunnel crankcase (ruling out the use of a centre bearing). There was a double-throw built-up crankshaft, with one-piece connecting rods and roller big-ends. The alloy cylinders employed chrome-alloy electro-plated bore totally unlike the conventional cast-in cylinder liners used by BMW at the time.

Bore and stroke measurements were oversquare, with dimensions of 56 x 50.6mm respectively.

Only one prototype engine was ever built, for a racing machine on which factory rider Walter Zeller could challenge the then world champions Werner Haas and NSU. It had only completed a few hours of testing when the whole project (together with the other two high-performance engines) was axed overnight, following a sharp decline in BMW sales and profitability.

with directly-operated valves, there was less power loss since two spur gears replaced the usual five. No doubt, this helped the Rennsport engine to run safely in excess of 9,500rpm.

Camshafts and rockers ran on needle rollers, while the rocker spindles were carried in the cam housings and had eccentric ends for valve clearance adjustment. Typical of the engineering skills shown in the design, the method of locking the rocker spindles was simple and ingenious. On one end of each spindle was a serrated washer, which was located on the spindle by flats. The serrations engaged similar serrations on a short arm, the other end of which was bolted to the housing. If the bolt was slackened and the serrations were disengaged, the spindle could be turned by one serration, or more, and then the serrations re-engaged. For valve timing, there was a vernier coupling between each camshaft and its driving gear.

Each cylinder head contained a part-spherical combustion chamber that provided

quite a wide valve included angle of 82 degrees. Inlet and exhaust valve seats were in different materials – manganese steel for the inlet, bronze for the exhaust. Both valve guides were also of bronze. Valve diameters were 40mm inlet, 36mm exhaust (the latter being sodium-cooled). Duplex coil valve springs and a stepped form of split collet were employed to keep cylinder head width to a minimum.

The downdraught angle of the inlet ports was 15 degrees, and their bore at the flange 32mm. On the 1954 factory Rennsport engine, as used by BMW team members that year, the third type of fuel-injection system was fitted. Like the fuel pump, magneto and spark plugs, the injector nozzles were of Bosch origin and had a minimum delivery pressure of 570psi.

Fuel was gravity-fed from the 5-gallon (25-litre) tank to a paper cartridge filter mounted on the off side of the crankcase, above the cylinder. From the filter, petrol passed to the pump, which was of the plunger type (similar to the type used on

Zeller held third spot for the first three laps of the 1957 Senior TT before being forced out with ignition trouble at Ramsey on lap four.

diesel engines). There was no direct rider control of pump delivery.

In the pump body was a diaphragm, which was subjected on one side to induction-pipe depression by means of a balance-pipe system connected to the two throttle boxes. Attached to the diaphragm was a rack-rod, which engaged with a gear on each of the two plungers. Movement of the diaphragm, activated by opening or closing the throttle, rotated the plungers; such rotation varied the internal porting end, and with it the amount of fuel delivered by the plungers. Surplus fuel was pumped back into the tank. An adjusting screw permitted basic setting of the mixture strength. Lubrication of the pump was taken care of by engine oil from a separate container. Apart from providing a useful gain in performance, BMW also claimed at the time that its fuel-injection system produced a 15 per cent improvement in fuel economy.

Another aspect of the Rennsport engine of considerable technical interest was the piston design. Almost fully-skirted, the 10.2:1 pistons had an oil scraper ring below the bosses of the gudgeon pin. Three compression rings were also fitted in the conventional position, the lowest of these featuring a tapered face and drainage holes to assist oil control. The piston crown was of nearly pent-roof shape and fitted closely into the head space at each side to promote squish. To accommodate the contour of the valve head, the valve cutaways under the inlet and exhaust valves were convex and concave respectively.

The cylinder barrels normally featured shrunk-in cast-iron liners, but BMW also experimented with chromium-plated bores – the finish being applied directly to the aluminium – with complete success.

A taper at the rear of the crankshaft accommodated a flywheel car-type clutch. The clutch body was in two halves, held together by a ring of eight bolts; the inner face of the rear half formed one of the driving surfaces. Sandwiched between that face and the pressure plate was a single, faced drive plate. This had a splined centre, which transmitted the drive to the gearbox mainshaft.

The rear section of the clutch body had internal peripheral teeth, which engaged with similar external teeth on the pressure plate. Actuating force for the pressure plate was supplied by six non-adjustable springs that were seated in the front half of the clutch body. Clutch withdrawal was by means of a thrust rod passing through the hollow gearbox mainshaft; a hemispherical pad, jointed to the end of the rod, sat on a cap in the centre of the pressure plate.

The forward half of the clutch body had a spigot that fitted into a bore in the back of the rear main bearing housing. There was an oil seal within this bore, and the spigot had a spiral groove to assist in preventing oil from entering the clutch housing. Clutch cooling was effected by a series of concentric ribs on the rear of the clutch body, and by air ducts in the housing.

Of conventional, all-indirect design, the gearbox had a top gear reduction of 1.3:1 and normally featured five ratios (although four were used for certain circuits). The complete engine and gearbox assembly was supported at three points in the frame: one each at front and rear of the lower portion of the crankcase, and the third at a steady point above cylinder level in the crankcase half of the gear case. The frame was of the cradle type with a tubular extension to carry the racing seat and to provide anchorages for the rear suspension legs. On the factory

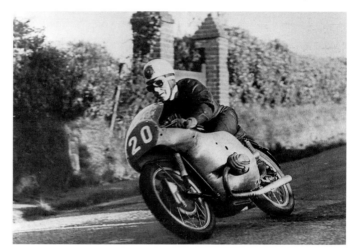

Six-times world champion Geoff Duke rode for BMW in 1958. He is seen here competing in that year's Senior TT.

Ernst Hiller surprised many with a spirited performance at the International Thruxton road races in August 1958. The BMW rider won his heat and then chased Derek Minter (Norton) home in the Senior Final.

Helmut Fath

Helmut Fath made history one Sunday in October 1968, when he became the first person to win a world title with a home-built machine.

Fath had a unique talent – he was a brilliant sidecar driver and a superb engineer. He first sprang to public attention in 1959 when, partnered by Alfred Wohlgemuth, he finished fifth in the World Sidecar Championship. The following year, still using a BMW Rennsport outfit, the duo dominated the title race. Out of the five rounds, they won in France, the Isle of Man, Belgium and West Germany.

In 1961, Fath looked set to repeat this performance and retain the title, beginning the series with a runaway victory in the first round at Montjuic Park, Barcelona, in April. Fath and Wohlgemuth lapped the entire field. But tragedy was to follow. The next weekend, during the annual Eifrennen at the Nürburgring, the partnership crashed in heavy mist and rain. Wohlgemuth lost his life, and Fath not only lost his friend but was also put on the sidelines for five long years. At the time, it was reported that he had lost a foot, but he had in fact badly broken his right leg, left ankle, and a bone in his hand.

Most men would have quit, but Fath retained his single-minded love of racing, even during his enforced absence from the circuits. With the aid of some friends, including Dr Peter Kuhn (formally a lecturer at Heidelburg University), he designed, built and ultimately tested his own across-the-frame four-cylinder dohc racing engine. Fath named it the URS, after the village of Ursenbach where he lived. The URS engine featured large valves, twin-spark ignition and fuel injection.

Fath made his debut on the URS outfit in May 1966 at the West German

Fath and Wohlegemuth, winners of four of the five rounds counting towards the world championship that year, on their way to victory in the 1960 Sidecar TT. A serious accident at the Nürburgring in 1961 left Wohlegemuth dead and Fath seriously injured. After many months in hospital, Fath returned to racing in 1966, with great success, although not on a BMW.

Helmut Fath and passenger Alfred Wohlgemuth after winning at an international meeting at Hockenheim in May 1960.

GP at Hockenheim some five years after the Nürburgring accident. His reappearance, and the new engine, created a sensation, even though he failed to finish the race. Testing and racing continued throughout 1966 and 1967, before the successful championship year of 1968, when he won, passengered by Wolfgang Kalouch.

Later, during the early 1970s, Fath designed and built a flat-four cylinder two-stroke engine, and tuned Phil Read's 1971 250cc championship-winning TD2 Yamaha twin. He also had a less than successful tie-up with the Münch organization. In 1979, he decided to call it a day in his bid to be both a world champion and one-man motorcycle constructor.

Helmut Fath died in 1995, but his legend lives on through his unique achievements.

bikes, three quite different frame layouts were built to ensure that each rider could tuck himself away to the maximum advantage.

Pivoted-fork rear suspension, first seen on the factory racers in 1952, was employed, with the driveshaft enclosed within the offside fork tube. Likewise, the Earles-type front fork first appeared for the 1953 season, replacing the telescopic fork which BMW had done so much to popularize. Front and rear suspension legs were similar in design and embodied two-way hydraulic damping; variations in rod conditions or rider weight could be met by fitting legs with the appropriate spring and damper characteristics.

Both brakes were cable operated, the front being of the 2LS pattern. BMW stated that the new fork improved front-wheel braking by eliminating 'dip' when the brake was applied.

The 1954 specification factory Rennsport engine produced significant power from around 6,500rpm, with a maximum output of 58bhp at 8,500rpm using injectors, and 52bhp with conventional carburettors.

Besides the works entries, a batch of twenty-five Rennsports were constructed during 1954 for sale to private customers. These engines, together with the factory units, were not only used in solo racing, but also went on to achieve unparalleled success in sidecar racing.

THE END OF THE 1950s

In solo racing, 1956 was to be BMW's best-ever year. Walter Zeller finished an impressive runner-up in the world series, to none other that the legendary pairing of John Surtees and MV Agusta, and in front of the entire Gilera squad. The only negative aspect of the season was the infamous riders' strike of the Dutch TT, which affected the scoring of several stars, including Geoff Duke.

By this time, Zeller was using a very special short-stroke engine, with new 70 x 64mm bore and stroke dimensions, giving well over 60bhp. There were several other differences compared to the Rennsport engine, notably the driveshaft, which ran alongside the fork leg, not inside it. Full streamlining was a feature of the machine, although this was not fitted when Zeller finished fourth in the 1956 Senior TT.

At the end of the 1957 season, there were two vital developments that affected BMW's solo racing plans – the FIM's ban on full streamlining and Walter Zeller's retirement from the sport.

For 1958, Geoff Duke and Dickie Dale both campaigned factory-supported models (Duke's was said to have been Zeller's best bike). Neither of these established stars could match the success gained by Zeller, although several German riders, among them Ernst Hiller, put up some good performances, and Dale continued to ride for BMW. In 1959, followed by the dashing Fumio Ito (better known for his Yamaha exploits) in 1960, the German flat-twin's effectiveness as a competitive solo racer at Grand Prix level was over. Instead, the factory decided to commit its small race budget into helping the sidecar class. Events were to prove that this was a wise choice.

Sidecar Racing

'Phenomenal' is the only suitable word to describe the overwhelming success of BMW's flat-twin engine in the sidecar world championship series during the period from 1954 to 1974. In total, the team won nineteen titles, a figure that was never to be beaten.

The effectiveness of BMW's dohc Rennsport-type engine in solo racing declined as the 1950s wore on, but in the sidecar category, for a number of reasons, the situation was just the reverse. In sidecar racing, neither the engine's width nor the shaft final drive are the disadvantage they are on a solo, while the BMW's silky smoothness and great engine torque were a positive advantage. Another plus was the fact that the flat-twin engine could be mounted ultra-low, allowing corners to be taken faster, while the cylinders were cooled more effectively. Also a great boon were the high standard of engineering quality and the reliability. The 180-degree crankshaft was extraordinarily robust, as were the engine's other major components. Until 1954, the world of sidecar racing had been dominated by British Nortons and British drivers, most notably Eric Oliver. During the early 1950s, the highest position any BMW-powered outfits had finished in the race towards the world title (instigated in 1949), had been third (Kraus and Huser in the 1953 Belgian GP, and Wilhelm Noll and Fritz Cron in the 1953 Swiss GP).

The Seasons, 1954–74

In 1954, Eric Oliver began his championship defence in his usual winning style, taking the Isle of Man, Ulster and Belgium in the first three rounds of the series. The next round was in Germany, at the Solitude circuit, near Stuttgart. A week earlier, both Oliver and his passenger, Leslie Nutt, had been injured when their Norton outfit had skidded off the track at a non-championship international meeting near Frankfurt. Oliver had a broken arm, and Nutt was nursing a shoulder injury. With the British pairing sidelined, the German GP proved a walkover for the two works BMW entries of Noll and Cron, and Schneider and Strauss. Although Oliver bravely raced in the next round, in Switzerland, Noll and Cron ran

BMW's Swiss star Florian Camathias (left) after winning the sidecar event at the Scarborough International, 19 September 1959. On the right of the picture is a youthful Mike Hailwood, who won the 350cc final on his 7R AJS.

out clear winners, as they did in Italy. This left the British and the Germans equal, with three wins apiece. The German's superior finishing positions in the other three rounds made the difference, and BMW had gained its first-ever world road-racing title.

In 1955, Willi Faust and Karl Remmert retained the world crown for BMW, with wins in three of the six rounds – in Spain, Germany and Holland. Fate then dealt the team a cruel card. The newly crowned champions suffered a serious practice accident at Hockenheim, and the partnership was broken by the death of Remmert. Fraust eventually recovered from his injuries, but he never raced again. The void left by this loss was filled by the 1954 championship pairing of Noll and Cron, who took the 1956 title, after victories in Belgium, Germany and Ulster; they also finished second in Holland.

After this second championship success, Noll announced his retirement. He switched to cars, but never achieved the same level of success.

Next in the line of BMW world sidecar title-holders came a former Luftwaffe pilot, Fritz Hillebrand, and his passenger, Manfred Grünwald. BMW was dominating the 1957 season, with victories in Germany, the Isle of Man and Holland, when tragedy struck the BMW team once again. Hillebrand was killed in an accident during an international race meeting in Bilbao in August.

Following a drastic fall-off in sales of its production models, BMW cut its sidecar support to only one crew for the 1958 season – Walter Schneider and Hans Strauss, who had finished runners up the previous year to Hillebrand and Grünwald. If the factory-supported team thought it was in for an easy time, they were soon brought down to earth. Swiss privateers Florian Camathias and Hilmar Cecco, on a home-tuned Rennsport outfit, gave them a tremendous fight at every one of the rounds. The Swiss pair, who ran out winners in the Dutch round at Assen, also raced solos – Camathias a Norton single, and Cecco a 125cc Ducati). The other serious contender that year was another new face, Helmut Fath, whose name would certainly be heard in the future.

Schneider and Strauss went on to record championship number two in 1959; once again, their biggest challenge came from Camathias and Cecco, whom they beat by the slender margin of only four points. In the five-round series, the Germans won three races, and the Swiss won two.

Schneider and Strauss then decided to hang up their leathers. Like Noll, Schneider tried his hand at racing on four wheels, but

Wilhelm Noll and passenger Fritz Cron won the sidecar world championship in 1954, laying the foundations for an unparalleled run of success in this branch of racing.

achieved no more success than his predecessor.

Following the retirement of the Germans, many observers expected Camathias and Cecco to pick up the championship. However, things did not go to plan; Cecco decided to switch partners, and left Camathias to join his rival, Edgar Strub. With his new passenger, Camathias had a poor year, his best placing coming in the last round, at the German GP; his final placing in the points table was fourth. In front of him were Fath as champion, Fritz Scheidegger, and Englishman Pip Harris.

With four wins out of the five Grand Prix making up the 1960 championship series, Helmut Fath and Alfred Wohlgemuth ran away with the title that year. Tragically, a serious accident at the Nürburgring in 1961 completely changed Fath's future, leaving Wohlgemuth dead. Fath's accident was not the only one; Camathias also had his share of grief. The diminutive Swiss star had been re-joined by his former passenger, Hilmar Cecco, but his campaign also had tragic consequences. At a non-championship meeting in Italy, Cecco sustained fatal injuries when the BMW outfit crashed. Camathias did not race for the remainder of 1961.

Following these tragedies, BMW's official entry of Max Deubel and Emil Hörner took the 1961 championship, pursued by privateers Scheidegger and Burckart who finished runners up.

If they had been fortunate in 1961, it was definitely skill and determination that brought Deubel and Hörner their second championship title in 1962. They gave their challengers, Camathias and Scheidegger, and their partners, little chance of glory. The three teams dominated the series, except in the Isle of Man, where all three retired, presenting victory to Chris Vincent and Eric Bliss, riding a specially prepared, pushrod, A7 BSA roadster-engined outfit.

In 1963 and 1964, Deubel and Hörner retained their championship laurels, their only real challenge coming from old rivals Camathias and Scheidegger. Their run of glory came to an end, when Scheidegger (partnered by Englishman John Robinson) won the title in 1965, and repeated the feat the following year. Meanwhile, Deubel and Hörner had retired, the former to run his hotel in Muhlenau, and the latter to return to his former occupation of car mechanic.

Although he was using BMW power,

Scheidegger, with fellow Swiss Camathias, had brought to an end the long supremacy enjoyed by the BMW works sidecar drivers. However, the hand of fate was to strike once again at the very top of the sidecar world. First, Camathias (at Brands Hatch, on 10 October 1965) and then Scheidegger (at Mallory Park, on 26 March 1967) were fatally injured in horrific crashes. In Scheidegger's case, brake failure caused his outfit to crash at Mallory's Hairpin.

Sidecar racing did not stop, and the next BMW champions were the pairing of Klaus Enders and Ralf Engelhardt, who won five of the eight rounds to lift the crown in 1967. Then, in 1968, Helmut Fath stunned the racing world by becoming the first and, so far, the only man to win a world championship using a machine constructed by himself (see pages 48–9).

Enders and Engelhardt, with renewed backing from BMW, won their second title in 1969. With a new passenger, Wolfgang Kalouch, Klaus Enders scored his third championship in 1970. At the end of the season, he decided to quit, at the age of thirty-three, and moved over to four wheels. This let in Horst Owésle and Peter Rutherford, who took the title for the Münch team (using a development of Fath's engine) in 1971.

For 1972, three-times champion Klaus Enders re-entered the fray. His four-wheel career (also with BMW) had not brought him the level of success he had expected, and he had decided to don his leathers and go sidecar racing once more. His results proved that his decision had been a sound one; partnered by his old friend Ralf Engelhardt, Enders became champion for the fourth time. This put him on an equal footing with three-

Former Luftwaffe fighter pilot Fritz Hillebrand (passengered by Manfred Grünwald) took the world sidecar title in 1957, with victories in Germany, the Isle of Man and Holland. Later that year, Hillebrand was fatally injured in a racing accident in Spain.

Max Deubel (with passenger Emil Horner) during the German GP at Solitude, July 1960. They finished 4th behind the BMW trio of winner Fath, Camathias and Scheidegger.

BMW Sidecar World Champions

1954	Wilhelm Noll/Fritz Cron
1955	Willi Fraust/Karl Remmert
1956	Wilhelm Noll/Fritz Cron
1957	Fritz Hillebrand/Manfred Grunwald
1958	Walter Schneider/Hans Strauss
1959	Walter Schneider/Hans Strauss
1960	Helmut Fath/Alfred Wohlgemuth
1961	Max Deubel/Emil Hörner
1962	Max Deubel/Emil Hörner
1963	Max Deubel/Emil Hörner
1964	Max Deubel/Emil Hörner
1965	Fritz Scheidegger/John Robinson
1966	Fritz Scheidegger/John Robinson
1967	Klaus Enders/Ralf Engelhardt
1969	Klaus Enders/Ralf Engelhardt
1970	Klaus Enders/Ralf Engelhardt
1972	Klaus Enders/Ralf Engelhardt
1973	Klaus Enders/Ralf Engelhardt
1974	Klaus Enders/Ralf Engelhardt

wheel legends Eric Oliver and Max Deubel. Renewed success spurred Enders on to even greater things and, in 1973, he not only became the first man in sidecar racing to win five world titles, but also won all of the seven rounds that he contested!

It was perhaps fitting, therefore, that Klaus Enders should be the man to win BMW's last sidecar world title, in 1974, thus creating a record that still stands. However, this final year did not present Enders and BMW with the relatively easy series of victories to which they had been accustomed. Instead, there were problems with the new Büscher-tuned motor, as well as the ever-increasing challenge from the two-stroke brigade, headed by König (using modified horizontally opposed, water-cooled, boat engines).

At the end of 1974, Enders decided to retire (this time for real), rather than race a two-stroke. He had scored a record total of twenty-seven GP victories, all on BMWs. Since that final championship year, not a single BMW-powered sidecar has won another Grand Prix.

The Chassis Design

During the twenty-one seasons in which BMW had been a serious contender for sidecar championship honours, the power output of the double overhead camshaft flat-twin engine remained virtually unaltered, except for the final couple of years. What did change, however, during this time was the chassis design, to which the engineers turned their attention in a bid to improve lap times.

From 1958, a major change had been introduced for the official factory BMW outfit (pioneered by Eric Oliver's Norton/Watsonian outfit, back in 1954). This was the kneeler; as the name suggests, the riding position was transferred from the conventional sitting to a kneeling position. The resultant lowering of gravity provided an immediate improvement in cornering. The fuel tank was also relocated. At first, it was split into two and lowered; later, it was joined in one unit again, housed in the sidecar.

Another important development was the replacement of the telescopic front forks with a type of suspension that was more akin to that of a car rather than a motorcycle. In many ways, the same could be said of changes introduced to the wheels, tyres and brakes.

Streamlining played a pivotal role in the development process from the old to the modern racing sidecar outfit. The 'chairs' had not been affected by the revised FIM regulation, which had banned full streamlining on solos after the end of the 1957 season. Also significant was the change from direct BMW factory involvement to entries through other companies, notably Büscher and Krauser.

In 1974, the curtain came down on what had been one of the longest-running success stories in motorcycle racing at the highest level. BMW could be justifiably proud, having achieved a record number of championship titles in a branch of the sport which was exciting, competitive and fraught with danger.

Record Breaking

In the field of speed records, BMW motorcycles have a proud and long history, which began not long after the first R32 was built, in 1923. However, the real heyday of the marque in this form of competition came in the late 1920s and during the 1930s.

During this period, one man, Ernst Henne, set about creating new records in a highly professional and most successful manner. Riding 750cc and, later, 500cc twin-cylinder

A superb action-packed photograph of sidecar racing at its best. This 1968 Dutch TT shot shows the BMW outfits of Georg Auerbacher (40), Pip Harris (12), Tony Wakefield (13), Johann Attenberger 96) and Klaus Enders (1). Odd man out is Helmut Fath (2), who was piloting his home-built four-cylinder URS.

On 5 October 1955, Wilhelm Noll set a new world sidecar speed record of 174.13mph (280.22kph) over the flying kilometre.

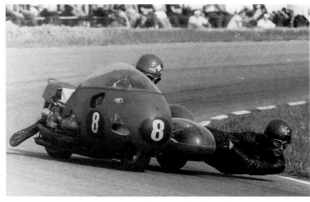

Fritz Scheidegger and John Robinson in action during the 1964 Dutch TT at Assen.

machines against the stopwatch, Henne assembled an impressive series of speed records at venues both inside and outside Germany. After success in the ultra-tough Targa Floria races in Sicily, on 9 September 1929, Henne began a remarkable series of world speed record-breaking achievements on Germany's first autobahn at Ingoldstat near Munich. Riding a supercharged 750cc BMW, he set a new world speed record over the flying kilometre of 134.25mph (216.050 kph).

Over the next eight years, Henne went on to smash his own record, and those set by others. The culmination of his achievements

came with a final outing, on 28 November 1937, when, riding a 500cc supercharger, he travelled at 173.68 mph (279.503 kph). This record stood for an amazing fourteen years before it was beaten in April 1951 by NSU-mounted Wilhelm Herz.

Much of the success achieved by the pairing of Henne and BMW was made possible by supercharging. This had first been tried in early 1929, when a production R63 had been fitted with a positive-displacement blower, mounted on the top of the gearbox and driven by the magneto shaft. Lessons gained from this trial were not only applied

BMW World Records

1929	9 September: Ernst Henne (750cc)
	Munich, flying kilometre 134.25mph (216.05kph)
1930	20 September: Ernst Henne (750cc)
1931	September various: Ernst Henne (750cc solo) and
	(750cc sidecar) Vienna, solo 148.08mph (238.3kph) and
	sidecar 118.58mph (190.83kph)
1932	3 November: Ernst Henne (750cc)
	Tat, Hungary, flying kilometre 151.87mph (244.399kph)
1934	10 October: Ernst Henne (750cc)
	Tat, Hungary, flying kilometre 152.9mph (246.059kph)
1935	27 September: Ernst Henne (750cc)
	Frankfurt, flying kilometre, 159.1mph (256.046kph)
1936	12 October: Ernst Henne (500cc)
	Frankfurt, flying kilometre 169.02mph (272.006kph)
1937	28 November: Ernst Henne (500cc)
	Frankfurt, flying kilometre 173.68mph (279.503kph)
1954	12 May: Georg and Hans Meier with Walter Zeller set a nine-hour record of
	103.55mph (166.64kph) at Montlhéry, France in 500cc category
	30 October: Wilhelm Noll (500cc sidecar)
	Montlhéry, France, 10km. 132.17mph (212.7kph)
1955	3 October: Wilhelm Noll, Fritz Hillebrand and Walter Schneider
	(500cc/sidecar) at Montlhéry, France set 24-hour record at an average of
	89.67 mph (144.3kph)
	5 October: Walter Zeller (500cc) at Montlhéry, France 10km 150.25mph
	(241.8kph)
	5 October: Wilhelm Noll took a 500cc/sidecar over 1km to average
	174.13mph (280.22kph)
1961	3 March: Ellis Boyce, George Catlin, John Holder and Sid Mizen rode a
	R69S entered by London-based dealers MLG at Montlhéry, France to set a new
	24-hour record of 109.36mph (176kph)

to record breaking, but also to BMW's Kompressor Grand Prix racer, which used much of the technology developed initially around Ernst Henne's record-breaking attempts.

After the war, BMW gained publicity from new records at various distances, both with solo and sidecar BMWs, and most notably in the endurance field. In May 1954, the trio of Georg and Hans Meier, and Walter Zeller travelled to Montlhéry near Paris. There they set a new nine-hour record of an average speed of 103.44mph (166.64kph). Montlhéry was the venue for another BMW record-breaking feat, in March 1961, when an MLG-entered R69S set new twelve and 24-hour records with a team of British riders.

3 Off-Road Motorcycle Sport

Although its off-road activity and achievements have been much less heralded, BMW has always taken a keen interest in this aspect of the motorcycle sporting scene. In fact, BMW's success during the 1980s in the Paris–Dakar Rally was nothing new for the German company.

THE INTERNATIONAL SIX DAYS TRIAL

Early Days

Long before the setting up of the Paris–Dakar Rally, the major off-road event

was the legendary International Six Days Trial (ISDT). The ISDT began in 1913, as an event for standard production machines, and rapidly established itself as the most important test for the world's manufacturers. The highest award was the Trophy, which was not only an issue of national pride, but also of enormous commercial benefit too. Teams were motivated to achieve unprecedented feats of heroism. The event also inspired engineering excellence – without it, the machinery would not last the full six days. There was also a Vase contest, introduced in 1924. Both the Trophy and the Vase drew riders prepared to pit themselves against the world's best in cross-country riding, through mountains,

BMW has made its mark on the off-road scene, almost from its inception. This photograph shows the German Trophy team at the 1937 ISDT in Wales: (left to right) Ludwig Kraus, Josef Stelzer and Georg Meier.

forests and sometimes even peat bogs.

BMW's first success in the event came in 1926, when the R37's designer Rudolf Schleicher (together with team-mate Roth) won gold medals. This was particularly significant for the German team because the trial was staged that year in Buxton, Derbyshire, at a time when Great Britain was the world centre of motorcycle construction.

The 1930s

In the 1930s, BMW's Six Days star really began to burn brightly. The 1933 event, staged in Wales, saw a straight fight between host nation Great Britain and Germany; the German three-man Trophy squad of Mauermeyer (sidecar), Stelzer, and Henne (holder of the world speed record) were all BMW-mounted. For the first time, Germany came out victorious, losing only one mark in the whole six days. The 'Editorial Opinion' in *The Motor Cycle* of 28 September 1933 commented as follows:

The result of the trophy contest provided another signal success for the multi-cylinder engine, and the horizontally opposed ohv twin in particular, since the winning trio were using 750cc BMW transverse flat-twins, which, as the majority of motorcyclists know, have unit construction, shaft drive, and pressed-steel frames. The manner in which the machines were prepared and the team organized furnishes, we suggest, a lesson for Britain.

The 1934 ISDT began at the end of August. Organized by the Deutsche Automobil Club, because of Germany's victory in the previous year, it attracted a record entry of 220 riders. Four teams, representing Italy, Czechoslovakia, Britain and Germany, were competing for the International Trophy, while six countries, with two teams apiece, were contesting the silver Vase. There were also no less than thirty-four manufacturer's teams. A total of 1,211 miles (1938km) had to be covered, concluding on the final day with a speed test.

BMWs taking part in the speed tests at the 1937 ISDT. Numbers 85 and 143 (members of the Vase team) are mounted on the German flat-twins as they negotiate Redgate Corner, Donington Park.

THE MOTOR CYCLE REPORT TAKES UP THE STORY:

The sixteenth International Six Days Trial, which concluded last week-end, will live long in the memory of the 200-odd competitors, of ten different nationalities, who competed in it. They will retain vivid recollections of early morning starts while the stars still glimmered over the Bavarian Alps; of long, gruelling runs on mountain roads and narrow lanes with surfaces that changed their character at almost every yard; of incessant rain and wintry cold, of the superb organization and unbounded hospitality of the German organizers.

Germany's victory, secured by the same riders on the same type of BMW, was a well-deserved one. It was won by a margin of a few seconds from the Italian team (Gilera-mounted) in the final speed test, both teams having retained a clean sheet throughout. One interesting feature was the pristine white overalls worn by all the BMW riders, who were issued with fresh, clean suits after each day. According to *The Motor Cycle*, 'Our [British] men looked untidy by contrast.'

After winning the 1934 ISDT, the Germans played host to a gathering of twenty-five riders from all over Europe to compete in the 17th event in the series. Centred on the town of Oberstdorf in the

German and British competitors sit side by side in the sun in Salzburg, Austria, in late 1939. A few days later, their two countries would be at war.

One of the factory prepared R68 ISDT bikes, 1952.

Bavarian Alps, the route took in not just the Alps, but also the Black Forest further to the north, with riders having to complete daily runs of 300 miles (480km) or more. The high mileages and the high average speeds required took a great toll on both riders and machines, with the sidecar entrants receiving more than their fair share of trouble. One major problem throughout the week was the blinding and choking dust, caused by the long absence of rain. The sun shone brightly every day, but the nights were cold – below freezing – and the thickening oil that resulted caused many early-morning starting problems.

A highlight of the second day was a 25-mile thrash up the newly completed

Like Georg Meier before him, Walter Zeller rode for BMW both on tarmac and dirt. They were real motorcyclists in an age that is now only a distant memory.

Munich autobahn, with the new super-charged BMWs leading the way.

On the last day – a 150-mile (240-km) run to Füssen for the final one-hour speed test – the Germans were in the lead, ahead of the Czechs, with zero marks lost compared with the Czechs' twenty-two. However, on the run-in, Stelzer smashed the cam box of his supercharged 500 BMW when he came off the machine at a corner; the resulting repairs cost him, and the team, twenty-five marks and reversed the positions at the top. During the speed test, the positions changed again, when Vitvar blew up the engine of his 350 Java and saddled the Czechs with a further forty marks, giving the Germans the Trophy for the third time.

In 1936, Deutsche Automobil Club again took on the responsibility of organizing the ISDT, which was based around the Black Forest town of Freudenstadt. Against tradition, it started on a Thursday, rather than a Monday. The first half of the event was held in the Black Forest, but on the Saturday evening riders reported to the Winter Olympic Stadium near Garmisch-Partenkirchen, which was to be the base for the second part. In view of the importance of the event, military training was curtailed for the duration, freeing the vast resources of the German army to help with the organizational and marshalling duties. German military teams even entered the event, top club honours going to Kraftfahr Lehr-und Versuchs-Abtig Wünsdprf on a trio of army BMWs. The German Trophy team comprised Henne and Stelzer, with Kraus in charge of the sidecar.

Up to the start of day five, Britain and Germany were level. The sun shone on the assembled riders as they gathered to tackle the Ammerbrucke hill climb, which, although only 1 mile (1.6km) long, was extremely dusty. During this section, disaster struck at the BMW squad when Henne's

One of the 57bhp GS80 enduro bikes which the factory built to take part on the 1979 German Enduro Championships. These were effectively pure-bred competition models and pre-dated the production R80 G/S streeet enduro.

The 1979 BMW works enduro squad: (left to right) Ekkehard Rapelius (chief engineer), Laszlo Peres, Fritz Witzel Jnr., Karl Gerlinger (business manager), Herbert Schek, Richard Schalber, Rolf Witthöft, Kurt Fischer, Dietmar Beinhauer (team manager).

engine seized, not once, but twice, and he lost two marks in the process.

Before leaving Garmisch on the final day, Henne fitted a new piston to his BMW in an attempt to stop any further seizures, but in

doing so he dropped a further fifteen marks, which put Britain even further in the lead. Thus, the three-year domination of the ISDT by Germany and BMW came to an end.

Having lost the Trophy on home ground

1979 GS80 Enduro

Engine:	Overhead-valve, flat-twin
Displacement;	870cc
Bore and stroke:	95 x 61.5mm
Maximum power:	57bhp
Carburation:	Twin 32-mm Bing CV carburettors
Ignition:	Electronic
Lubrication:	Wet sump
Gearbox:	Five-speed
Clutch:	Lightweight Fitchel & Sachs single-plate
Frame:	Duplex in 1-mm chrome-molybdenum tubing
Front forks:	Maico air-assisted enduro forks with 260mm travel
Rear suspension:	Monoshock with Bilstein gas damper unit giving 245mm of travel
Brakes:	Front: 150mm (5.9in) single leading shoe drum Rear: 200mm (7.87in) single leading shoe drum
Tyres:	Front 3.00 x 21. Rear 5.00 x 17
Weight:	308lb (140kg) with fuel and tools.

Note: One bike is preserved in the BMW Museum, Munich

in 1936, the Germans were determined to win it back when the 1937 ISDT returned to Britain. Having arrived in Southampton by sea the previous week, the German contingent (seventy-nine riders and sixty back-up crew), made their way to Llandrindod Wells, where practice and course reconnaissance began in earnest. The German team included many members of military personnel from all sectors of the German army, their units identifiable by the riding outfits they wore. The normal army units wore field-grey leathers, the Storm Troopers had light-brown one-piece suits, and the SS were in black leathers. The Trophy trio comprised Josef Stelzer and Georg Meier on 500 BMWs, with Ludwig Kraus piloting the 600 BMW outfit. Henne had been forced to stand down, owing to injuries sustained while racing cars.

Traditionally, the International Six Days Trial was held in September, but in 1937 the organizers brought it forward to July in the hope of beating the wet weather typical in Wales in early autumn. Again, the finish was tight, and the final day's speed test session was decisive. The result hinged on the solos, with the two 500 BMWs having to complete nineteen laps against the eighteen of the British 350s. Meier led for most of the test, but Rowley and Britain stayed with him to take the Trophy for Great Britain by the merest margin of just ten seconds, after six days of competition!

The Germans went home to rethink their strategy, and to practise for next time. Their national pride was at stake, and they simply had to win the Trophy in 1938, having been denied the Trophy by the smallest of margins in the previous two

BMW Comeback in the 20th Paris–Dakar Rally

Coinciding with the 75th Anniversary of BMW motorcycles, Edi Orioli, Oscar Gallardo, Jean Brucy and Andrea Meyer took part in the Paris–Dakar Rally, which ran from 1–18 January 1998, on factory-supported single-cylinder F650s.

The 1986 BMW team: (left to right) Eddy Han, Belgian Gaston Rahier and Frenchman Raymond Loizeaux.

After winning the Paris–Dakar four times on twin-cylinder Boxers (in 1981 and 1983, with Frenchman Hubert Auriol, and in 1984 and 1985, with Belgian Gaston Rahier), BMW's works team did take part in the 1986 event, but with sponsorship from Marlboro.

Some thirteen years later, the new BMW Team Schalber, under the management of former BMW works rider and world off-road champion Richard Schalber, from Hindelang in Germany, made a return to the toughest endurance event in the world. All four BMW entries began the rally on the morning of New Year's Day, at Versailles.

The prominent member of the four-rider team was Edi Orioli. Celebrating his 35th birthday on 5 December 1997, this legendary Italian rider had already won the Paris–Dakar no less than four times – in 1988, 1990, 1994 and 1996. The other three members were also highly experienced in Paris–Dakar: 32-year-old Spanish rider Oscara Gallardo finished second in 1997, 35-year-old Frenchman Jean Brucy was fifth in 1995, and 29-year-old Andrea Meyer from Germany won the Ladies Cup in 1996.

Prepared for the event by Richard Schalber GmbH, with technical support from BMW, the special F650 competition bikes developed an output of some 60bhp (48bhp on the standard production models) and weighed in at 370lb (168kg) dry.

In a test prior to BMW's decision to re-enter Paris–Dakar with a works team, Edi Orioli and Andrea Meyer entered the Dubai Desert Challenge, in early November 1997. Riding on behalf of Enduro Equipe Schalber, Edi Orioli came home fifth, while Andrea Meyer won the Ladies' Cup; both F650s performed brilliantly.

Gaston Rahier, riding a BMW, won the Paris–Dakar in 1983 and 1984.

years. They mounted an all-out effort, retaining Kraus, together with his 600 BMW in the sidecar section, and equipping the solo riders with a trio of blown two-stroke DKWs. This different strategy failed, and the Trophy stayed in Britain for another year. The Germans did not go home empty-handed, however, taking the Silver Vase, the Hühnlein Trophy and the Club Challenge Trophy. The last two awards were won by the SS team of Patina, Mund-heuke and Zimmerman, mounted on 494cc BMW flat-twins. Runner-up position in both these contests went to the NSKK (Mobile Storm Troopers) squad, mounted on similar motorcycles.

The infamous Salzburg ISDT during late August 1939, with Europe almost on the brink of war, led to most of the British riders leaving half-way through the week of the ISDT. War was declared on Sunday 3 September. Although the Germans (with two BMWs in the Trophy team) were declared the winners, after the war the sport's international governing body decreed the result void.

After the War

West Germany was re-admitted to motor-cycle sport in 1951, and BMW decided to contest the ISDT in 1952. In early September, the final selection of the West German teams for the ISDT was announced. In the Trophy, Maico and NSU were preferred over the larger BMW flat-twins, although three of the newly released BMW R68 sports models had been chosen for Georg Meier, Walter Zeller and Hans Roth, members of the Vase team. The factory also entered a manufacturer's team, with Ludwig Kraus and Max Klankermeier on R66/2 sidecar outfits, and Hans Meier riding one of the machines in solo trim.

The 27th ISDT was held in Austria between 18-23 September, where 260 riders battled it out over a strenuous 1,250-mile (2000km) course. But for an amazing piece of bad luck, when a valve broke on the nearside cylinder of Roth's machine, the Vase would have been won by the BMW-equipped team, instead of by the Czechs. Although it did not win, the performance of

In January 1983, Hubert Auriol on his BMW repeated his 1981 victory in the gruelling Paris–Dakar Rally. The 30-year-old Frenchman beat the entire Japanese works teams in the 6,200-mile (9,200-km) marathon.

the BMW team was superb, and this was reflected in gold medals for Hans and Georg Meier, and Zeller, and the sidecars of Klankermeier, Klaus, Thornblom and Vandernoll. Following a poor showing by the NSU entries in the 1952 ISDT, and the good record of BMW, Germany's team selectors opted for a mix of BMW and Maico machinery for the 1953 Trophy team.

Held in Czechoslovakia, the 28th ISDT got under way on 15 September 1953. The German Trophy squad consisted of a pair of 175cc Maicos, together with three 594cc BMWs, ridden by Roth, Georg Meier and Zeller. BMW had also entered its own manufacturer's team. Zeller's retirement with a broken universal joint on day three dropped the Germans back to fourth at the finish, with 460 marks lost. The other BMW retirement in the event was a private entry riding an R68 solo – the Swiss rider Florian Camathias, who was later to win fame for his sidecar-racing exploits. BMW gained a total of seven gold medals – five solo, two sidecars.

BMW took a break until 1958, when its twins were back at the ISDT. The competition was staged on the Germans' home ground once again, among the mountains of southern Bavaria, in late September. Gold medals were won by a trio of converted R50s, ridden by Hartner, Hans Meier and Roth; it was an impressive performance, even though none were members of the official factory team.

By 1960, the 'Gentle Giant' Sebastian Nachtmann, on his factory-supported R50, was the only BMW included in any of Germany's ISDT squads. In almost every case, the machines chosen were two-stroke powered lightweights, such as Maico, Hercules and DKW. However, Nachtmann proved his worth by completing the event as part of the highest-placed German team; West Germany B finished second in the International Silver Vase contest, with Nachtmann gaining a gold medal for his efforts.

Throughout the remainder of the 1960s Nachtmann continued to impress, with a string of medals and superb performances. With the demise of the British motorcycle industry, he was often one of very few riders to be mounted on a large-capacity four-stroke (usually a specially kitted-out R69S), among a much larger number of small-capacity two-strokes.

From 1964, BMW took more of an interest in endurance competitions, and used events such as the ISDT as a development ground for its forthcoming range of twins – the Stroke 5 series, which was launched in 1969. Many of the series' components were developed in the white heat of competition, including telescopic forks, and other chassis and engine modifications. For the rest of the 1960s, BMW retired again, and did not re-surface until 1978, when development of an upcoming new model – the R80 G/S – led to their re-entry into the ISDT Arena. The model was developed too late to compete in that year's event, but a series of prototypes was built, culminating in a specially prepared 57bhp works GS80 enduro mount. Ridden by Fritz Witzel Junior, this motorcycle won the over-750cc class of the 1979 ISDT.

In 1980, Rolf Witthöff won the over-500cc European Enduro Championship and went on to win a gold medal at the final ISDT, held in France.

In 1981, the BMW factory once again withdrew from the event (now named ISDE, the 'E' standing for enduro), claiming that the revised rules meant that the event had lost its publicity value. They were later to be proved correct in this assumption.

Paris–Dakar

Long-distance rallying has always been seen by the major car manufacturers not only as an excellent means of publicity, but also as an extremely useful all-round test of a design's reliability and performance under the most severe conditions. It is not surprising, then, that BMW should support a long-distance rally in the two-wheel world. Although other such events have been run, the Paris–Dakar Rally has proved to be the premier event in what is now an established branch of motorcycle competition.

The Paris–Dakar was first organized in 1979, its original route running some 6,200 miles (10,000km) from the French capital to Senegal on the West African coast. The race, for both bikes and cars, is staged annually over several days in January, and its real test comes with nearly 2,000 miles (3200km) of off-roading in the very harshest of conditions, much of it across barren desert. Not only does deep sand pose a problem, but there are also rocky tracks and hilly terrain, all of it in intense heat, with dust storms and sudden flash floods to catch out the unwary or inexperienced.

BMW first took part in the 1981 rally, in which a total of 101 bikes and 130 cars, including a Rolls Royce, competed. There were also factory teams from Honda and Yamaha. The French BMW team of Hubert Auriol (1st), Jean-Claude Fenouil (4th) and Bernard Neimer (7th) gave the German company both the motorcycle award and the team prize.

The twenty-day battle had been prepared by BMW with great precision. Their back-up squad included three Puch-Daimler four-wheel drive cross-country vehicles, with enough mechanics and tools to cope with any emergency. Nicknamed the 'Desert Foxes', this group included Dipl. Ing. Helmut Pohl, the head of BMW's race shop.

The bikes were one-offs, which, although based on the production R80 G/S street Enduro, were hand-built. Their specification included strengthened frames, specially tuned engines and long-range fuel tanks. The ultimate BMW works Paris–Dakar bikes employed a special 1040cc, 70bhp

Andrea Meyer (left), winner of the 1997 Dubai Desert Challenge Ladies Cup. Also in the picture is Edi Orioli, who took fifth overall. Both rode single-cylinder BMW F650s.

version of the flat-twin engine, which provided a maximum road speed of 115mph (185kph) and torque figures of 64ft/lb (87Nm). With a full 13-gallon (60-litre) tank of fuel, spares and tools, plus water bottles, the machines weighted 507lb (230kg). One particular (and vital) modification was a hi-level air filter built into the fuel tank.

Although considerably heavier than that of its rivals, BMW's robust flat-twin engine proved surprisingly adept at coping with the conditions encountered in such a harsh environment. The fact that the shaft drive rose under initial acceleration proved a boon for extracting the rider from deep-sand conditions.

Hubert Auriol, known to the rest of the BMW team as Der Afrikaner, finished the rally three hours in front of the next machine, a Yamaha XT500 single. The 28-year-old textile salesman had been born on the other side of African continent, in Ethiopia. Later based in Europe, he had been a trials champion in 1977, 1978 and 1979, and therefore in many ways was an obvious choice for BMW. Auriol's team-mate Jean-Claude Fenouil was a journalist and a veteran of the desert, having been the first motorcyclist to cross the Sahara

alone, in 1973. In 1978, he had created a record of 12 hours, 34 minutes for a trans-Saharan motorcycle ride of over 900 miles (1,450km) between Algiers and Tamanrasset. The third member of the team, Bernard Neimer earned his inclusion through his previous record in the Paris–Dakar – he had finished 2nd in 1979. When not competing, he was an officer in charge of a Paris-based motorcycle police unit.

During the 1981 rally, privateers Karl Frederick Capito and Karl Schek rode their own bikes with BMW support. Only twenty-five of the motorcycle starters made it to the Dakar finish line in 1981. BMW was able to boast of having a higher percentage of finishes than any other make that year.

The organizers bill the Paris–Dakar as 'The World's Toughest Race'. BMW dominated the event during the first half of the decade, going on from their success in 1981 to win in 1983, 1984 and 1985, a record four victories. A poor result in the 1986 event led to the factory announcing its retirement from the rally towards the end of that year, but the Paris–Dakar of the early 1980s had none the less represented a glorious chapter in BMW's history.

4 Earles-Fork Models

TWO NEW MACHINES

A new era for BMW began at the 38th International Brussels Salon, which opened to the public on Saturday 15 January 1955. Unlike several European exhibitions at the time, the Belgian fair was truly international, with entries from as far afield as the USA and the Soviet-bloc countries. The 'sensation' of the show, according to *The Motor Cycle*, was on the BMW stand. Two sensations, actually, in the shape of two brand-new machines – the five-hundred R50 and six-hundred R69 – featuring Earles-type front forks, and full swinging-arm rear suspension closely related to that pioneered on the factory's racing motorcycles campaigned by Walter Zeller.

New Features

The treatment of the rear section of the frame was very unusual, bearing a marked resemblance to the old plunger design, with main loops that extended down and rearwards almost as far as the wheel spindle. Instead of the rear frame carrying top and bottom mounts for the old-style plunger boxes, however, the rear shock absorbers were supported from the middle by the upper portions of the loops. A welded bracket extended rearwards to form the base of a top shroud for the spring damper assembly, which was secured in place from the top by a threaded alloy boss. The upper section of the shrouds also formed the rear mudguard mountings. This arrangement provided for

The first of the Earles-forked models appeared in early 1955, following the launch in January that year at the Brussels show. This is the top-of-the-range R69.

an extremely rigid frame and was of great importance in the design's aspirations to sidecar work. For the same reason, the front forks had dual mountings for the swinging bottom link and suspension units, allowing trail to be adjusted with relative ease. The rear suspension pre-load could be varied simply by turning a handle built into the base of the unit.

The rear swinging fork pivoted on taper roller bearings from a pair of adjustable stub spindles screwed into each side of the frame just behind the gearbox. Where previous BMWs had always employed an exposed final shaft drive, the driveshaft was now contained within the offside leg of the swinging arm assembly, which was bolted to the rear bevel drive casing.

Other differences from earlier models included a deeper fuel tank (but with its capacity unchanged, at 3.2-gallons/17 litres), which featured a large, lockable toolbox of which the lid formed the nearside knee-grip. There were smaller-diameter (18-in) alloy wheel rims, new silencers, new mudguards (although the rear still featured

Touring R60 engine. Whereas the sports model had rocker covers with only two fins, the R60 (and the R50) had the six-fin type.

All Earles-fork twins had expensive timing gears, not the cheaper chains found on post-1969 models.

the much-appreciated hinged section, allowing easy wheel removal). There was also a dual seat option, at an additional cost.

The Engines

As for the power units, these were largely unchanged, but output had been increased – 26bhp at 5,800rpm for the R50; 28bhp at 5,600rpm for the R60; the more sporting R69 offered 35bhp at 6,800rpm. The R50's 494cc (68 x 68mm) engine had a compression ratio of 6.8:1 (against 6.3:1 on the outgoing R51/3), 24-mm Bing carbs, and a slight increase in cam lift profile. On the larger 594cc (72 x 73mm) engine, the R69

ran an 8:1 compression ratio, with the cams and 26-mm carburettor size remaining the same as on the R68, the machine it effectively replaced.

Both engines benefited from a newly designed diaphragm clutch and a new three-shaft gearbox in an equally new housing, the rear of which carried the output flange which bolted the universal joint for the driveshaft, and also supported the rubber gaiter which protected the joint. Although the gearbox was basically a similar four-speed design with a cam lobe shock absorber on the input shaft, it was none the less successful in speeding up what had previously been a rather lethargic change. Ratios were: 1st, 5.33:1, 2nd, 3.02:1, 3rd, 2.04:1, and top, 1.54:1.

Distinctive features of the Earles-fork models: internal details of BMW's bevel-driven twistgrip throttle.

Alternative positions for solo or sidecar use.

The rear section of the frame is virtually unique.

Hinged rear mudguard, allowed easier wheel removal.

The only twin-cylinder model to continue from the previous series was the R67, which was now in its /3 series. Compared to the Series 2 model, of which a relatively large 4,234 examples were manufactured, a mere 700 R67/3s were built in 1955 and through the first part of 1956. Power output remained at 28bhp.

Reviews and Prices

Motor Cycling tested an example of the R69 in its issue of 19 April 1956. A maximum speed of 102mph (163kph) was recorded, with 61mph (98kph) being set for the standing quarter-mile dash. The tester made the important point that, even though the R69 was the 'sports' model in the BMW range, it was still a touring machine at heart, albeit a fast, luxurious one. As *Motor Cycling*'s man put it, the machine represented 'a vast improvement over its predecessors, which themselves held an enviable reputation'.

Back in July 1955, rival magazine *The Motor Cycle* had tested the R50. Recording a top speed of 94mph (150kph), they commented: 'Acceleration was zestful without being tigerish, but chiefly notable for its sweetness whether the engine speed was high or low.'

In October 1955, British importers AFN announced that the range-topping R69 would cost a hefty £489, compared to the home-built 646cc BSA A10 Golden Flash, which cost half as much, at a shade under £250. This difference in price was partly due to the fact that, at this time, there was a large import duty levied on non-British bikes sold in the UK and in other Commonwealth countries. The R50 was priced at £378, as was the R67/3.

The result was that, in the British Commonwealth at least, BMWs sold in very

This view of an Earles-fork model shows the staggered cylinder, with the near side more forward than the off side.

small numbers, to the wealthy few who could afford the asking price.

Problems in 1956

In 1956, the R67/3 gave way to the R60, which was basically an R50, but with the 28bhp engine from the R67/3. The R60 was also offered with the option of various sidecar ratios within its rear bevel box. BMW catered even further for sidecar fans, with a range of purpose-built outfits and accessories, including a specially badged Steib TR500 with flat sides (not the 'Zeppelin' style almost universally associated with Steib products), wide handlebars,

Rocker box removed to reveal rockers, pushrods, valves and coil springs. Tappet adjustment by simple lock-nut.

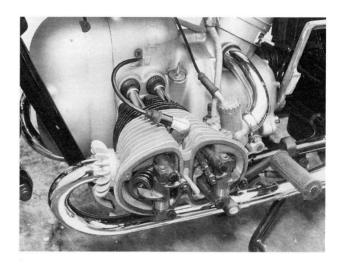

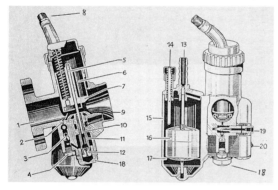

Working components of the Bing slide-type carb: 1, body; 2, central venturi; 3, idling jet; 4, retaining screw; 5, needle; 6 and 7, slide; 8, cable adjuster; 9, air intake port; 10, tapered needle valve; 11, needle jet; 12, main jet; 13, hose fitting; 14, tickler; 15, float chamber; 16, float; 17, damper ring; 18, base nut; 19, idling mixture adj. screw; 20, throttle valve limiting screw.

heavy-duty suspension springs, strengthened wheels, special speedometers to suit the particular gearing, sidecar wheel braking (using a hydraulically operated linkage in the motorcycle's rear brake rod), and a spare wheel (to be mounted on the sidecar). This spare was interchangeable with both of the wheels on the motorcycle.

Even though the factory had a much-improved line of machines, the year 1956 did not prove a success commercially. During September, in common with other German factories (including NSU, DKW and Horex), BMW began laying off workers; the first serious problems at the Munich works began, with the dismissal of 600 workers, owing to falling demand. The year's figures revealed the serious nature of the problem, with production plummeting from the 23,531 motorcycles being built in 1955, to only 15,500 in 1956.

Despite the depressed state of the market, BMW continued to display its products at the various international exhibitions that were staged in all the major capitals of Europe. For example, even though the vitally important domestic motorcycle show was a mere two weeks away, on 5 October 1956 the German company put on an impressive display at the 43rd French motorcycle show in Paris. At that time, France was enjoying a vibrant two-wheel industry, with almost

BMW launched its 1961 model range at the Frankfurt show in September 1960. Besides a new 250 single, there was also more power for the flat-twins, with sports versions of the R50 and R69 – the R50S (seen here) and R69S – while the R60/2 superceded the earlier R60.

five million machines on the roads, mostly mopeds, scooters and ultra-lightweights. The 3rd International Frankfurt Motorcycle Exhibition followed, billed as Europe's largest bike show. In 1956, however, there was a very different story hiding behind the glitz and glamour of this vast affair. Things had gone very wrong within the German domestic industry, and BMW was suffering along with the other factories.

Even as the Frankfurt extravaganza was taking place, new motorcycles were being built, and the three- and four-wheelers were also proving difficult to sell. Production was down by almost half, to 120 a day, and stocks were rising rapidly in the firm's warehouse. In fact, had it not been for BMW's local Munich bank providing additional working funds, the company could

well have ceased to exist there and then. But, continue it did, unlike many of its rival German bike builders.

The Problems Continue

No improvements were seen in 1957, which was to prove even more dire, at least for the motorcycle side of the business, with production dropping to 5,429. Isetta sales were, however, improving year on year, and this allowed BMW to reduce their over-stock on these vehicles. At least BMW was able to continue in business, unlike rivals Adler, DKW and Horex, which all ceased motorcycle production in that year.

During this period, virtually all the twin-cylinder motorcycles produced by BMW were being exported; the USA was by far the biggest market; sometimes taking up to 85 per cent of the company's production during the late 1950s. In Britain, too, BMW continued to attract an enthusiastic following. In October 1957, AFN listed four models that would be available for 1958. All were displayed a month later at London's Earls Court Show. *The Motor Cycle*'s special show edition said: 'Quietness, smoothness and excellence of design are the outstanding features of the BMW range.' Prices were: R50, £380, R60, £392, and R69, £495. The other model, the R26 (BMW's first single with swinging-arm rear suspension), came in at £258.

Financial problems meant that BMW presented no new models for 1958 or 1959, although motorcycle production, at 7,156 and 8,412 respectively, did show some improvement. Overall, however, the situation was not improving for the Munich company; as expected, the annual financial report, presented in December 1959, showed BMW heavily in the red.

A New Business Plan

Prior to the publishing of this report, it had been widely speculated that BMW would accept a takeover bid from Daimler Benz but, under the leadership of Dr Herbert Quandt, the shareholders rallied and came up with a viable business plan that was acceptable to the creditor banks. It was a close-run thing. The success of the new corporate plan relied on raising capital not only from the banks, but also from the realization of assets. One of the first moves was to dispose of the aero-engine business, to MAN Turbo GmbH.

The BMW stand at the Zurich Show, 2 February 1965.

Dr Herbert Quandt successfully rallied support amongst other shareholders to save BMW from takeover in 1959.

George Catlin being pushed off on the record-breaking MLG-entered R69S at Montlhéry, 3 March 1961. Together with Ellis Boyce, John Holder and Sid Mizen, he set a new 24-hour world record, averaging 109.36mph (176kph).

New Products

The plan called for a number of new products, including a new small saloon car – the 700 – powered by a larger-capacity 697cc (78 x 73mm) version of the flat-twin motorcycle engine. This proved to be an inspired move and, with improvements to the motorcycle line, helped set BMW on a course towards profit once again. The new two-wheelers were first shown to members of the press at the famous Nürburgring race circuit in August 1960, a month before their public debut at the Frankfurt Show, in time for the 1961 model year.

Although a new two-fifty single, the R27 (featuring a rubber-mounted engine), replaced the R26 (with a total of 30,236 being built between 1956 and 1960), it was the twins that really attracted attention. Most interesting were the R50S and R69S sportsters ('sports-tourers' would be a more apt name); about the R69, BMW was truthfully able to claim, 'The fastest German machine – of royal standard indeed – represents the top line of BMW motorcycle production: 42bhp – 110mph!'

The Motor Cycle went overboard on the superlatives when they tested the new top-of-the-range model in March 1961; their headline read: 'Luxury roadster, with superb high-speed performance, yet docile traffic manners; magnificent steering, roadholding and brakes.' The magazine's fastest one-way speed, of 108mph (173kph) in a very strong side-wind, seemed to show BMW's 110mph (175kph) claim to be accurate. The only downside, at least to British enthusiasts, was the £530 price tag; in comparison, a 649cc Triumph Bonneville was £288, a 597cc Norton 99 Dominator De Luxe, £294, and a 646cc BSA A10 Super Rocket, £273.

While the extra power of the R69S endowed it with a 110-mph (175-kph) potential, the smaller twin was still capable of cracking the magic ton, without sacrificing in any way the high degree of comfort and silence of its touring brothers. Both sportsters used the cycle of the earlier R50/60/69 models, with only the addition of a hydraulic steering damper and Hella-made indicator lamps fitted to the ends of the handlebars as obvious external differences. The engines could be distinguished from the other models externally by their rocker covers – the R50S/R69S had two

An official factory shot of a 1967 model R69S; in truth, the bike remained virtually unchanged during its nine-year production run. A total of 11,317 were built.

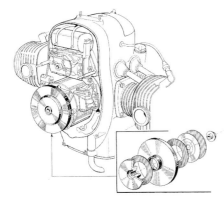

Crankshaft-mounted vibration damper as fitted to the 'S' models, R50S and R69S. Essentially a series of clamped-up discs, it helped provide these bikes with their famous silky-smooth power delivery.

horizontal ribs, while the touring models had six (although, obviously this is not a reliable guide almost four decades on).

The extra zip in these engines was due to modified internals including raising the compression ratios – 500, 9.2:1; 600, 9.5:1. Both engines also featured a timed rotary breather disc mounted at the front end of the camshaft and connecting it with passages into the crankcase. The other major difference was the fitment of close-ratio gear clusters; this was necessary because of the higher revving and less flexible nature of the 'S' power units.

MLG's Involvement

London BMW specialists MLG were partly responsible for the development of these machines; thanks to a racing programme they had begun back in 1958, when they entered an R69 in the Thruxton 500-mile race. This was an event for series production roadsters, and *The Motor Cycle*'s race report shows how impressive the BMW's debut was: 'So unobtrusive that its high placing surprised many onlookers, a BMW R69 was ridden into fourth place by John Lewis and Peter James. Quietly, smoothly and cleanly, the German flat-twin, one of the most ordinary (read standard!) looking models on the course, circled with admirable regularity, calling at the pits only for fuel and change of riders, never for oil or repairs.' Compared with the race-winning 649cc Triumph Tiger 110, ridden by Mike Hailwood and Dan Shorey, which completed 220 laps in 7 hours 35 minutes at an average speed of 66mph (106kph), the MLG BMW recorded 215 laps in 7 hours 35 minutes 49.6 seconds, at an

Earles-Type Front Fork

In the early days of motorcycling, suspension was largely non-existent. First came girder forks, followed in the mid-1930s by telescopics – thanks to BMW – with, of course, a similar story at the rear. First, they involved a rigid frame, then 'spring-in-the-box' as used by Moto Guzzi and others during the inter-war period, the plunger-type and, finally, swinging arm with twin shocks.

In the late 1940s and early 1950s, a Birmingham-based engineer named Ernie Earles started a new fashion in front suspension. Earles was also a prevalent 'specials' builder. Most notably, he was later responsible for a 498cc Ariel-Arrow-based four-cylinder engine, which powered a sidecar raced by Bill Boddice during the early 1960s. Although virtually ignored in his own country, Earles' fork design was widely adopted by the Germans – DKW, Hercules, Horex, Kreidler and BMW – and, for a short period, by the Italian MV Agusta racing team. The Earles-type fork was selected by BMW largely because of its suitability for sidecar work, and because of the fact that it did not dive under hard front-wheel braking. For solo use the design has two main problems: an aversion to fast rippled curves, and a tendency for the front end to become light when a passenger and laden panniers are carried.

Drawing showing various components; hydraulic steering damper denotes one of the 'S' models.

The Earles fork operates in the following way. The front wheel is suspended in two swinging arms, which pivot in a fork that bends back behind the wheel. The fork itself turns in the steering head in the usual way. These swinging arms pivot in adjustable taper roller bearings at the lower end of the fork. A pair of shock absorbers mounted in rubber bushes and cast-alloy carriers are connected to the swinging arms and to the fork. In each shock absorber, a non-linear suspension spring is seated at the base of the inner telescopic tube. A bi-directional damper is screwed into the lower part of each shock absorber, and its piston rod is fastened to the upper section. The suspension spring is prevented from bottoming out by rubber bushings at the top, and is limited at the bottom by the hydraulic action. An important point is that the units are re-buildable.

For sidecar operation, the front wheel swinging-arm pivot bearing is transferred from the rear position to the front position in each fork, which results in a smaller trail angle and, hence, easier steering. The top mounting is also adjusted to suit.

1961 R69S

Engine:	Overhead-valve flat-twin
Displacement:	594cc
Bore and stroke:	72 x 73mm
Maximum power:	42bhp at 7,000rpm
Carburation:	Twin 26-mm Bing
Ignition:	Bosch magneto
Lubrication:	Wet sump
Gearbox:	Four-speed, foot-operated
Clutch:	Single-plate, dry
Frame:	Twin tube
Suspension:	Front: Earles-type fork
	Rear: swinging arm, twin shock absorbers
Brakes:	Drums, twin leading shoe at front
Tyres:	3.50 x 18 on both wheels
Weight:	445lb (202kg) dry
Maximum speed:	110mph (177kph)

average speed of 64.38mph (103kph).

MLG returned in 1959 to win the event, with John Lewis partnered by Peter Darvill. Even more success came later that year, with victory in the arduous Barcelona 24-hour race, Darvill now partnered by Bruce Daniels. With some added support from the factory, via importers AFN, MLG continued in 1960, and again won both the Thruxton and Barcelona events. These performances did much to promote BMW's range of motorcycles and, at the same time, provided an ideal testing ground for trying out modifications being assessed for the R50S/R69S series.

Another milestone was passed in 1960, when an MLG team of four riders (Ellis Boyce, George Catlin, John Holder and Syd Mizen) piloted a specially prepared and streamlined R69S around the Montlhéry circuit near Paris. They broke the world 24-hour record, with an average of 109.24mph (174.78kph), covering a total of 2,622 miles (4195kph).

The R60/2 was another 'new' model for 1960. Except for minor changes to aid reliability, and an increase in the compression ratio, from 6.5:1 to 7.5:1, which upped power to 30bhp at slightly increased engine revolutions, the R60/2 was identical to the R60. Of the six-hundred series Earles-fork models, the R60/2 was to prove the most popular, with a total of 17,306 being sold between 1960 and 1969. Next popular was the R69S, with 11,317 sold over the same period. Of the smaller-engined five-hundreds, the R50 sold 13,510 between 1955 and 1960, the R50/2 sold 19,036 between 1960 and 1960. The R50S was only produced for three years (1960–62), and was a slow seller, with only 1,634 units being manufactured. As such it is now quite a rarity and commands special attention from collectors.

Turn of the Tide

Cars have been important in the development of BMW as an international company, but none has played a more vital role than the 1500 model, which was launched at the 1961 Frankfurt Show. The 1500 was to be the forerunner of a whole range of new BMW cars, leading to the 1600, 1800 and 1800ti models, and later to the '02 range', comprising the 1502, 1602, 1802 and 2002, which made their mark in the early to mid-1970s. These cars gave BMW the massive success it has enjoyed since the beginning of the 1980s, and the 3 Series models are still very much current, in updated forms, as the last days of the 20th century approach.

A total of 23,557 standard 1500 saloons were built and sold from the beginning of 1962 to the end of 1964. Compared with any of BMW's other post-war cars up to this time (excluding the Isetta 'bubble' car), this represented real mass production.

The car's four-cylinder engine, with a capacity of 1499cc (82 x 71mm), produced 80bhp at 5,700rpm. Its boxy four-door body shell masked a technical package that held the promise of considerable development potential. This was to serve BMW particularly well. The 1600, manufactured between 1966 and 1970, sold no less than 92,833 units, while the 2000 limousine was also a big sales success, with 51,324 built between 1966 and 1968.

The new four-cylinder cars were soon being used in competitive events, including the Monte Carlo Rally and the Tour of France, saloon-car racing and 24-hour endurance; there was even a BMW Formula 2 racing squad during the late 1960s.

The humble 1500 saloon of the early 1960s was the real forerunner of BMW's success on four wheels; certainly, without it, BMW would not be where it is today.

The 1960s

What really secured BMW's long-term survival was the various 1500, 1600, 1800 and 2-litre cars produced during the 1960s. An entirely new 1500 (actually 1499cc) car made its debut at the Frankfurt Show in 1961 and, from that moment, BMW car sales rocketed. On 1 January 1967, BMW took over control of the Glas car company, more as a means of gaining production space than anything else; for a while, BMW went on making and selling Glas cars.

The 1960s was largely a period of rapid advance for BMW on four wheels and stagnation on two. Even so, the company never lost its name for quality during this time. Attention continued to be lavished on the tiniest details: the tank badges on the early 1960s BMW motorcycles were still made of genuine glass enamel, while the rear brake rod linkage comprised no less than six major components (plus 18 fasteners and other pieces), designed to ensure that the pedal was unaffected by suspension movements.

From March 1965, British imports were handled by BMW Concessionaires of Victoria Road, Portslade, Brighton, Sussex. Four models were available – the R27 single at £384, the R50/2 at £449, the R60/2 at £451 and, finally, the range-topping R69S at £524.

Although it was fairly common knowledge that a new range of BMW twins was under development, it was to be almost another five years before these bikes went on general sale. In the mean time, the existing range soldiered on unchanged, except for the axing of the R27 single at the end of 1966.

For the USA market, importers Butler & Smith, of 160 West 83rd Street, New York, were able to list no less than six models for the 1968 season. The R50/2, R60/2 and R69S were all available, either with the Earles forks or, for the Stateside market only, telescopic front forks. The latter were referred to differently, as follows: R69US. Butler & Smith offered, for an additional charge, the following accessories or options: standard-width dual seat, extra-wide dual seat, electric turn signal, 6– (US) gallon sports tank, safety bars and a white, or black paint job.

Costing US $1188, the R50/2 with Earles-type forks cost only US $108 more than the equivalent R51/2 had cost eighteen years earlier, in 1951!

The telescopics and the higher and wider handlebars reflected the changing requirements of the American rider, who was becoming more and more interested in taking his machine off the freeways and interstates and on to dirt roads and rough byways. The teles coped better with this sort of going, and BMW duly responded to the needs of what was, after all, its biggest market outside Germany.

Just around the corner (see Chapter 6) was the new Stroke 5 series. But, even today, those machines that BMW built for a decade and a half from 1955 onwards are viewed with genuine enthusiasm by BMW-lovers by around the world.

5 Military and Police Service

Besides its reputation for providing top quality up-market motorcycles for the enthusiast, BMW has also always proved popular with governments around the globe, both in war and peace, for police, military and public authority work. In addition, in more recent times, BMWs have been used as courier machines, where the demand for fast, dependable delivery of items such as documents, drugs and other vital supplies has grown rapidly.

During the 1930s, the Wehrmacht (the German army), under the impetus of the Third Reich, began to build up its strength. The first BMW model to be used was the single-cylinder 398cc R4, which began production in 1932, although a few R52 and R62 twins had been supplied in 1928 and 1929.

The R12, R61 and R71

The first of the flat-twins to be used following Hitler's rise to power, in 1933, was the 1935 side-valve 745cc (78 x 78mm) R12. A single carburettor supplied both cylinders via inlet tracks and the exhaust ran back

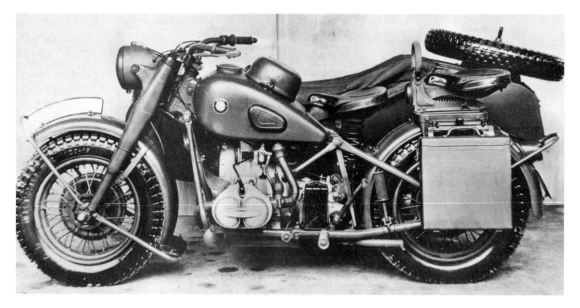

The R75 military motorcycle, built mainly for use with a sidecar, with drive to both the rear and sidecar wheel. There were no less than eight forward gears and two reverse.

1941 R75

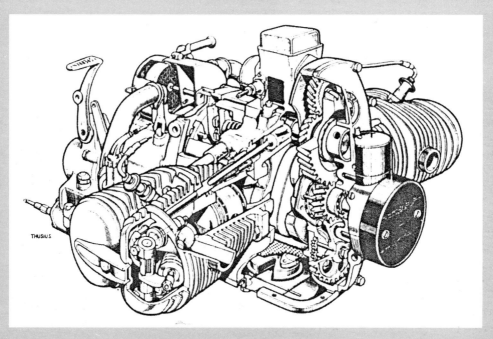

A sectioned view of the R75 engine with the air filter still located on the top of the gearbox. Service experience led this to be relocated in the fuel tank

Engine:	Overhead-valve flat-twin
Displacement:	745cc
Bore and stroke:	78 x 78mm
Maximum power:	26bhp at 4,000rpm
Carburation:	Twin 24-mm Graetzin carburettors
Ignition:	Noris magneto
Lubrication:	Wet sump
Gearbox:	Four-speed, foot-operated; hand change for reverse and high-ratio gears
Clutch:	Single-plate, dry
Frame:	Bolted-up tubes
Front forks:	Telescopic, hydraulically operated
Rear suspension:	None
Brakes:	Drum brakes front and rear, the latter hydraulically operated
Tyres:	5.00 x 16 front and rear
Weight:	620lb (281kg) with sidecar, dry
Maximum speed:	58mph (93kph)

low down on each side. Construction of the engine and gearbox assembly followed traditional BMW practice, with the magneto and dynamo mounted on top of the crankcase, with wet sump lubrication and an engine speed clutch. The gearbox contained four speeds and employed a car gate-type hand change mechanism, with the final driveshaft running on the off side. The R12's most notable feature was its front suspension, representing as it did a giant leap forward, with its hydraulically damped telescopic front fork assembly. This was a world first, at least on a series production model.

The frame followed the pressed-steel 'star'-type construction used in BMW's civilian models of the era (see Chapter 1), with a rigid rear end and the fuel tank set between the upper members. At first, the military authorities chose to retain the civilian footboards and extensive front mudguard. Later, after service experience, these were changed for conventional footrests and a less comprehensive mudguard. Panniers could be used with the frame provided and a pillion seat was mounted some way above the rider, to provide a better view for the passenger, who

might be surveying the terrain while the rider piloted the machine.

The majority of military R12s were employed with a sidecar, and lower gearing to suit. This third-wheel device was a stark affair, with very little in the way of creature comforts provided. The body was built to be functional, and not for style or comfort, and, without a screen or door, the passenger was probably even less comfortable than the rider on the bike itself. A spare wheel was carried, which was interchangeable both with the sidecar and the motorcycle.

Later, in 1938, the 597cc (70 x 70mm) R61 and the 745cc (78 x 78mm) R71 (also side-valves) were both adopted by the German armed forces to replace the ageing R12. They were supplied in both solo and sidecar versions for escort, despatch and general reconnaissance duties. However, with only 18bhp, none of the machines was really up to the task, and this was soon proven in the first campaigns of the war.

BMW and Zündapp were asked to co-operate on a project to provide a new generation of twin-cylinder models. To understand the reasoning behind this, it is necessary to examine the thinking of the Nazi authorities. The German motorcycle industry at this time was influenced by

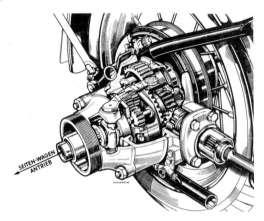

Close-up details of the motorcycle rear-wheel drive on the R75, very specialized and very expensive to manufacture.

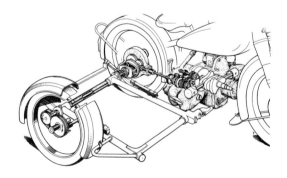

The drive train layout for the R75 and sidecar unit, including both rear wheel and sidecar wheel.

politics rather than commercial considerations. Long before the outbreak of war, the Nazi party had begun to streamline production on all industrial fronts. The motorcycle industry benefited from these moves, as its product was seen as a most effective use of materials, both in its construction and in its fuel economy when in operation. There was also close co-operation between civilian motor-sport bodies and the state, with the authorities encouraging club members to train on military equipment, ensuring that a ready source of personnel would be at hand.

The German motorcycle industry was rationalized late in 1938 by Colonel (later General) Oberst von Schell, who was given complete power to act. The Berlin show report in the 23 February 1939 issue of *The Motor Cycle* describes the situation well:

The fact is that the German motorcycle industry is in a state of flux. The same applies to the automobile and commercial vehicle industries. It has been decided that in the national interest there must be a drastic reduction in the number of models offered to the public. Obviously, the

The R67 combinations of the German ADAC highway patrols were nicknamed 'Angels of the Road'. The 594cc (72 x 73mm) flat-twins were built between 1951 and 1954.

production of a large number of different types means comparatively small quantities of each, this adding to the retail price. Reduce the variety of models and it is possible to go in for mass production – or at least 'flow' production – to keep down the number, and therefore cost, of the jigs and tools required for manufacture, to provide better servicing facilities (fewer parts and wider distribution of these parts), and to get down to prices that spell wider markets, particularly abroad. There can be savings in many directions! Of course the Berlin show was primarily a civilian affair – but the overtone was very much of a country preparing for war.

Colonel Oberst von Schell announced that he would be reducing the number of different types of motorcycle built from around 150 to just 25, cars from 55 to 23 and commercial vehicles from 110 to 24.

At around the same time as these decisions were being implemented, BMW and Zündapp were starting development of the models that would ultimately appear as the R75 and KS750. The Wehrmacht's requirements called for a special motorcycle and sidecar unit, which could be not only used for conventional communications and convoy work, but also, more importantly, as an attack vehicle for light motorized brigades; in addition, it needed to have the ability to tow a light gun. However, this final requirement proved impractical, and was abandoned after tests showed that the towbar weight lifted the front wheel off the ground.

The R75

The first prototypes of R75 were constructed in 1939 and 1940, influenced by the Belgian FN and French Gnome-Rhone. Both of these pioneered sidecar-wheel drive, a feature exploited by BMW and Zündapp. The original development of the R75 was undertaken by Dipl. Ing. Alex von Falkenhausen, who had joined the company in 1934. The differential gear drive to the two-wheel drive (on the rear motorcycle and sidecar wheels) was the work of Zündapp, both for BMW's R75 and their own KS750 outfits. The R75 was built in BMW's Eisenach factory. From the beginning of series production, in June 1941, and its end, in mid-1944, almost 18,000 were put into service.

The R75 engine was based on that of the side-valve R71, but with several changes and pushrod-operated valves. Thanks to an ultra-low compression ratio of 5.8:1, it could operate on low-grade fuel. A pair of 24mm Graetzin carburettors was connected to a single air cleaner. Early production models had this assembly mounted on top of the gearbox, but service problems on the Russian front, where deep mud often left the gearbox covered up, led to a larger filter box being mounted on top of the fuel tank. The exhaust was also modified in view of Russian service (from 1943), so that it could direct heat over the rider's feet and hands, and even into the sidecar.

The most interesting technical feature of the R75 combination was its transmission, with only the usual single-plate clutch remaining from previous models. The gearbox contained, in effect, no less than ten ratios – the normal four speeds forward were doubled up, giving a two-speed set for high or low overall gearing, and two reverse ratios were also provided. Control of all the gear ratios was via a foot-operated pedal on the near side, with two hand levers in and beside a gate bolted to the off side of the tank. The inner lever was protected by a button set in its top that selected the direction of travel, while the outer one looked after the choice of ratios.

An R80/7 police model, dating from around 1978. After their service life, these models were sold off for civilian use. Note features such as a single seat, radio tank-grid, small panniers and other smaller items. The fairing is based on the RT type.

The driveshaft to the rear wheel drove a differential. Power was taken from the differential to the bevel box at the rear wheel, as well as to the sidecar wheel via a transverse shaft. The differential not only split the power between the two driven wheels in a ratio to suit the load, and the outfit's centre of gravity, to prevent it running in circles, but the differential could also be locked to provide full power on both drive wheels.

The frame was a complete departure from conventional BMW design. A fabricated steel backbone held the steering headstock, which was welded on, and all other components of the duplex frame were suspended

from that central piece. Lengths of tubing were butted at the ends and bolted together. A steel pressing strengthened the rear section of the frame, between the end of the central section and the bottom tubes. The upper part of the engine was also attached to that point under the seat.

All three wheels featured extra heavy-gauge straight spokes, to withstand both load and cornering stresses. There was an interchangeable spare wheel normally carried on the sidecar rear panel. Tyre size was 4.50 x 16in, with a block-pattern tyre tread. All three wheels were braked. The rear sidecar brakes were coupled and operated hydraulically by a single pedal on the near

Alain Boutiller and Jean Bartier of the Paris Police Service at the National Motorcycle Museum, Birmingham, in July 1986, with their R80 police bikes.

side. They operated the piston of a master cylinder, which was attached to the underside of an extension of the gearbox casting. The front brake was cable-operated, with the wire entering the back plate and coupling to a balance linkage between the shoes. In this way, there was no external mechanism to foul obstructions and no cam internally (a design shared by Zündapp). Stopping was, in fact, rather a problem, owing to the unit's massive weight of no less than 925lb (420kg). Other technical features included a Noris magneto, and telescopic front forks with a rigid rear.

A few R75s were issued as solo machines, with the threaded connection for the sidecar drive blanked off with a large knurled cap nut. Producing 26bhp at 4,000rpm, the bike's maximum speed was 58mph (93kph).

Although a match for any other vehicle in the most trying conditions, the R75 and its Zündapp counterpart had two major problems. The first was cost, and the second

the need for an experienced crew. These two factors conspired to see these machines finally forced to give way to the cheaper mass-produced Volkswagen Kubelwagen four-wheel vehicle.

The Germans continued to produce lightweight two-stroke DKWs, and TWNs (German-made Triumphs) for the remainder of the war. Although BMW had supplied a number of its more standard twins (and singles) to the German military during the Second World War, the R75 and its Zündapp brother remain the epitome of the German wartime motorcycle, like the American HD or Indian V-twins, or the ranks of Britishsingle-cylinder machines on the Allied side.

Police Duty

The BMW concept also proved to be ideal for police duties. Well before the end of the 1920s, the German police had begun to use

BMWs for various types of work, including patrol escort and communications. By the 1930s, regular police traffic patrols had been introduced. As the autobahn system of motorways was constructed, linking major German cities, so speeds rose. This led to the need for high-speed police vehicles, including motorcycles. The sporting R51 flat-twin proved an efficient (and popular) choice, capable of apprehending most offenders.

With the coming of the war, and its restrictions on the civilian population – with virtually the whole of the male population on some form of military duty – crime and road-traffic offences became much less common.

As post-war Germany clawed its way back to normality, in the early 1950s, the government again began purchasing new equipment for its police. From 1955 onwards, the most popular motorcycle was the R50, equipped with polizei fairing, blue light and pillion-mounted radio equipment. Many German police motorcycles of the era were white. It was also during the 1950s that BMW began selling motorcycles to police forces overseas. This trend accelerated with the introduction of the Stroke 5 series in 1969, and by 1980 no less than 83 countries, from Abu Dhabi to Zambia, relied on BMWs for a host of duties ranging from patrol to escort work.

The prestige of the BMW name made, and indeed still makes, the German motorcycles eminently suitable for official escort duties. In a number of countries, a special squad of BMW motorcycles is employed for royal or presidential ceremonial functions.

In Britain, the conversion to BMWs for police work did not happen until the mid-1970s, when it came about as a result of a lack of spares for the existing Triumph and Norton machines already in service. The first force to employ BMWs was the Thames Valley Police, and, once the process had begun, with two R75/6s, the transition was rapid. In 1975, only four UK police forces had been equipped, with some fifty R80/7s on duty, but, by 1980, forty-eight of the fifty-five police authorities had purchased 2,000 machines between them.

This rapid development of the police market was very much the result of the efforts of British importers TKM, based in Chiswick, London. They saw the police business as a marketing priority to be pursued with a special vigour in-house, and not left to individual dealers, although this did lead to a certain amount of friction between the dealer network and BMW Concessionaires GB. To improve communications, BMW Concessionaires GB recruited Neale Shilton to head up the police-sales side; he had already established a reputation selling Triumph Saints and Norton Interpols to the police forces. His experience, combined with BMW's quality and direct selling approach (which meant a competitive price struc-ture), made BMW virtually irresistible, and led to the sales success which followed his appointment.

During the mid- to late 1980s, many police forces around the world switched to the new K-series of three- and four-cylinder machines. However, many continue to oper-ate a fleet of the Boxer (flat-twin) models, finding these ideally suited to a wide range of police and public service duties.

6 Stroke 5, 6 and 7

THE STROKE 5 SERIES

BMW's long-awaited 'new breed' did not appear until September 1969, when the /5 (or 'Stroke 5') series machines made their public debut at the Cologne show.

The Spandau Facility

After a long production run, of fifteen years, the last of the Earles-fork BMWs were constructed in the summer of 1969, the last motorcycles to be built at the Munich works. The development of their replacements had finally been completed at the same time; for

the construction of these, a completely new production facility had been built at Spandau in the western sector of Berlin, on the site of a former aircraft-engine factory. This site had originally been part of BMW's massive wartime operations and in the post-war era had been used for the production of an ever-increasing number of car and motorcycle components. After the end of this production, and before the beginning of the motorcycle manufacture, the Spandau plant had been enlarged and totally modernized. The original Munich factory was now to be used exclusively for car production, which had increased to such an extent that there was simply no room in which to house the

The new Stroke 5 series was launched in late 1969. Both engine and frame were substantially different from what had gone before. The model shown is an R75/5.

bike division. The administration and development offices remained in Munich, but everything connected with the manufacturing process was relocated to the Berlin site, including the assembly lines, the foundry, and the frame-building, machinery, plating and paint shops.

Harry Louis' Test Ride

Plans for the new bikes and for the production facilities had been conceived many years previously, and had even been reported in the British press as early as the spring of 1965. In their 22 April 1965 issue, *The Motor Cycle* had carried a story about BMW's plans for the production of a new series of flat-twins, which were then reported to be in the early prototype stage of their development cycle. *The Motor Cycle*'s highly respected editor Harry Louis had even been invited by BMW to test such a machine.

The essence of the new-look Boxer was its lighter weight. Over the preceding years, BMWs had put on fat rather than taken it off, as their specification had become more luxurious. At 445lb (200kg), the R69S was in danger of becoming ponderous, even if it could not be accused of lacking performance. BMW engineers decided, therefore, that its next generation of flat-twins had to be leaner and fitter, while retaining the marque's traditional quality.

The first indication of what was to come had been seen when the factory's specially prepared models were rolled out for the 1964 ISDT (International Six Days Trial), which was staged at Erfurt in the German Democratic Republic. These new trials machines sported telescopic front forks, a lightweight duplex frame and a specially tuned engine reputed to develop 54bhp.

Harry Louis rode one of these bikes, it

Front view of an R75/5 showing narrow, flat handlebars, square-section direction indicators, and mudguard support-cum-brace.

weighed in at 380lb (172kg), some 60lb (27kg) lighter than the current production models. Louis immediately noticed the weight difference, even when easing the machine off its stand. Galloping around Bavaria, it became, in Louis' words, 'a sheer joy to heel through fast corners, to switch from one angle of lean to the other in an 'S' bend, to take…round tight hairpins, to wiggle slowly along slippery farm tracks'. He went on to sum up the bike's appeal as follows: 'Like middle age spread, the weight climb of luxury bikes is usually in small stages with the cost in convenience and handling going almost unnoticed. Only when the weight is cut back is the deceit really

1970 R75/5

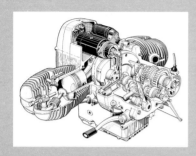

Cutaway view of the engine and gearbox of the Stroke 5 series. They were built in 500, 600 and 750 class sizes.

Engine:	Overhead-valve, flat-twin
Displacements:	745cc
Bore and stroke:	82 x 70.6mm
Maximum power:	50bhp at 6,200rpm
Carburation:	Twin 32-mm Bing CV type
Ignition:	Battery/coil
Lubrication:	Wet sump
Gearbox:	Four-speed, foot-operated
Clutch:	Single-plate, dry
Frame:	Twin tube
Suspension:	Front: telescopic fork
	Rear: swinging arm, twin shock absorbers
Brakes:	Drums, twin leading shoe at front
Tyres:	3.25 x 19 front; 4.00 x 18 rear
Weight:	419lb (190kg) dry
Maximum speed:	112mph (180kph)

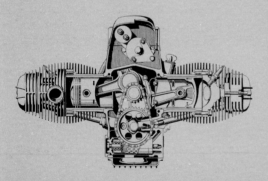

Fitted from 1970 to 1979, the duplex timing chain (shown here in a Stroke 5 engine) will often last in excess of 100,000 miles (160,000km); it is difficult to reassemble when the time comes for replacement. Post-1979 models have a less hardy simplex chain, but it can be replaced in a fraction of the time.

exposed. That's how it is with the Bee-Em.'

Lower weight was not the whole story. There had also been a complete face-lift, which had given the bike a much tidier front end, neater, narrower handlebars, blade mudguards, a shallower seat, a deep tank to fit the frame, and a re-designed exhaust system. Louis commented, 'Yes, my guess is that when the lean look roadster does appear it will be very much a plus on the BMW escutcheon. Trouble is, a long, long wait is certain. Like Rolls-Royces, the Munich men set their sights high and won't be hurried.'

Harry Louis' prediction proved to be spot on, and BMW's existing models continued for almost five more years.

The Stroke 5s

At the launch in Cologne in September 1969 there were three new bikes – the R50/5, the R60/5, and the first post-war BMW seven-fifty, the R75/5. The 'Stroke 5s', as they became known, appeared just at the right time. Spearheaded by the launch of the Japanese Honda CB750 four a year earlier, motorcycling was heading out of recession and into the era of the superbike series.

The Stroke 5 series totally replaced the old BMW models. While the engines were still the traditional flat-twins, largely retaining the layout pioneered by Max Friz back in 1923, there were some important changes. The most noteworthy of these were to the crankshaft and the position of the camshaft.

The earlier crank had been a pressed-up affair, but this was replaced by a simple but strong two-throw forging. To improve the balance of the flat-twin layout, BMW engineers devised small counterweights, which were bolted on to the crankshaft web and selected to suit the weight of the respective pistons. The alterations enabled the engines to have a larger cubic capacity than would otherwise have been possible.

The crankshaft was mounted in plain bearings at each end. The rear bearing was housed directly in the large light-alloy crankcase casting, while the forward bearing was held in a detachable support plate. The one-piece assembly meant that split shell big-end bearings were needed, which in turn required a new higher-pressure lubrication system. An Eaton-type oil pump (a new departure for BMW) was driven

STROKE 5 ENGINE COMPONENTS

(top left) Cylinder barrel – an alloy muff, with cast iron liner. Note pushrod tubes and sealing rubbers.

(top right) The one-piece crankshaft brought with it split con-rods and white metal big-end shells.

(bottom left) The one-piece crank brought with it split con-rods and white metal big-end shells.

(bottom right) One-piece crankshaft.

Telescopic Front Fork (Post-1969)

The telescopic front fork, introduced in late 1969 on the Stroke 5 series machines, was developed from the type used on the factory's ISDT machines campaigned during the 1960s. A feature of these was that the front-wheel spindle was carried ahead on lugs cast into the front of the sliders (this method being referred to as the leading axle type), rather than centrally, thus allowing a greater spring/damper length.

Technical operation is as follows. The fork stem of the BMW telescopic front fork turns into two tapered roller bearings located on the steering, which provides a superior operation to the cups/cones/balls set-up found in the preceding Earles-fork models. An upper steel fork yoke (triple clamp in the USA) and a lower forged-aluminium fork yoke hold the 36-mm diameter hard chromed steel fork tubes (stanchions). The aluminium fork legs (sliders) move up and down the tubes. Shock absorbers are fastened into the base of each fork leg. The shock absorbers thus slide inside the fork tubes. A nozzle is screwed into the base of each tube. These nozzles provide damping on extension, while calibrated holes in the shock absorber itself provide damping on compression. An important role is played in this process by the damper chamber, located between the hydraulic piston screwed into the shock-absorber tube and the damping nozzle. The valve attached on the bottom of the hydraulic piston closes the damper chamber on extension (in tension), so that oil must flow through the damper nozzle, and opens it under compression so that the oil can escape through the calibrated holes in the damper tube and return from the spring chamber into the damper chamber. Since the outside diameter of the damper tube is tapered conically at both ends, the damper nozzle provides for a hydraulic stop in the lowest and highest fork position. A valve at the lower end of the shock-absorber tube prevents the fork tubes from jamming, should the fork be moved beyond the hydraulic stop.

There is one replaceable 36 x 46 x 7.3mm oil seal in each fork leg. A progressively wound spring in the fork tube supports itself on top in a fixed spring retainer, and at the bottom against the hydraulic shock absorber.

The turning angle of the front fork is 46 degrees in both directions. This design of telescopic fork remained basically unaltered until the introduction of the K-series revised type, which made its twins debut on the new 'monoshock' R80 model on 1985.

from the end of the camshaft and supplied the lubrication via a cartridge filter. Whereas, on the earlier models the camshaft had been gear-driven and mounted above the crankshaft, it was now carried below the crank and driven by chain.

A distinctive feature of the old cylinder barrels had been the pair of pushrod tubes on the top, but these had now disappeared underneath, while the barrels themselves were now cast in light alloy instead of iron, with pressed-in cast-iron liners. The cylinder heads were light alloy as before, but of improved design and with the conventional BMW detachable one-piece rocker covers.

Besides the R75/5, there was also the 599cc (73.5 x 70.6mm) R60/5...

...and the 498cc (67 x 70.6mm) R50/5.

The Bing CV (Constant Vacuum) carb. First used on the R75/5, this was to become a standard fitment for BMW twins.

Each of the three engines used a stroke of 70.6mm, with cylinder bore sizes of 67, 73.5 and 82mm, giving 498, 599 and 746cc. The fact that the specification was otherwise nearly identical gave rise to a quip that only BMW could get away with charging more money for a bigger hole!

Carburettors on the smaller models were conventional Bing instruments, but on the 750 they were of the CV (Constant Vacuum) variety. The power outputs were 32bhp for the R50/5, 40bhp for the R60/5 (both at 6,400rpm), and 50bhp at 6,200 rpm for the R75/5. All three shared a common

The Maudes Trophy

In May 1973, two completely standard R75/5s won the coveted Maudes Trophy for BMW.
The trophy was originally the gift of Mr Pettyt from Maudes of Exeter and was first known as the Pettyt Trophy. Only awarded to motorcycle manufacturers for a really meritorious performance, it had been won nine times before the war. In the post-war era, the judges rewarded BSA in 1952, Honda in 1973, and BMW in 1973. Since 1973, it has only been awarded two more times.

BMW's submission deserved to join this select band of winners. A team of no less than 14 riders, made up mainly from the British motorcycling press, and also including racer Tony Jefferies (also a BMW dealer) and TT Chief Travelling Marshall Alan Killip, were to ride the two R75/5s for seven continuous days and nights over the 37.75-mile Isle of Man TT circuit.

The weather certainly did the team no favours, changing from blazing sunshine to lashing rain within a lap. During the dry periods, rear tyre wear was found to increase dramatically. Until half-way through the week, both machines ran like clockwork, but then disaster struck. The rider of the B machine swung wide at Brandish Corner and caught a projecting rock. He was pitched off, unhurt, but the bike was less fortunate, cartwheeling down the road. The front fork, wheel and headlamp all had to be replaced, and BMW UK's service boss, Alberto Crisuolo, and his team did a magnificent job, with the machine losing only six laps before it was back in action. Then the other machine hit trouble, when rider Mick Hemmings was in collision with a lorry at Quarter Bridge, and more spares were needed. Later problems were restricted to a slipping clutch, which eventually needed replacement, and the cylinder head of the other machine, which needed to be removed for maintenance.

The final session for both bikes came with Ken Heanes and Alex Smith crossing the finish line in Douglas at four minutes past noon, on Thursday 10 May. Machine B, the first to crash, had clocked 225 laps, 8,490 miles, of which 8,451 qualified for the week-long test. Bike A clocked 217 laps – 8,187 miles, with 8,150 in the test. Average speed was 48.68mph, with a total mileage of 16,658 miles.

The last time the Maudes Trophy had been won in the Isle of Man by a manufacturer had been when Dunelt clocked 350 laps, or 133,200 miles, at 34.8mph, in 1930.

BMW, and its team of riders and back-up crew, had to wait almost six months before the ACU (Auto Cycle Union) finally announced that their performance had been successful and the coveted Maudes Trophy was theirs.

three-shaft gearbox with the same internal ratios.

Another change was the replacement of the former 90-watt dynamo/magneto electrics with an 180-watt alternator and coil ignition, and, for the first time, 12-volt electrics. Electric starting was standard on the two larger machines and, although the headlight was similar to the old type, built in with speedo and ignition on the top, the fitment of a full set of four direction indicators with rectangular lenses was an innovation for BMW.

However, the most obvious change to the whole motorcycle was that the engine assembly was now mounted into a frame

In 1983 BMW celebrated its 60th year of motorcycle production, from the original R23 through to the then-current R100RS.

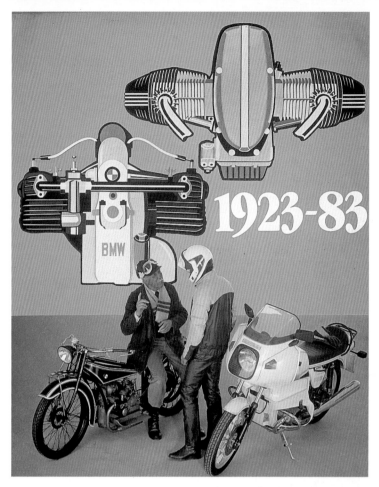

First introduced in 1955, the 594cc R60 with its Earles-type front forks was an excellent sidecar machine. The other machine is a British HRD Vincent.

Georg Meier's 1939 Senior TT-winning supercharged 500 flat twin racer. He was the first foreign rider on a foreign machine to win the event.

Introduced in 1960, the R69S was the top-of-the-range BMW model throughout that decade.

The West German rider Otto Kolle was a leading contender in the 1962 sidecar world championship series, which was dominated by BMW machines.

(Left) BMW enthusiast Peter Mapes with his son and R69S, Aden, April 1964.

(Left) *BMW twins in both standard two-valve and Krauser four-valve versions proved effective in Battle of the Twins (BOTT) racing throughout the 1980s.*

(Right) *KT Durham BMW R69S at Snetterton circuit in September 1964.*

The R65 was a popular middleweight which ran from 1978 through to the beginning of the 1990s with very few changes.

(Right) *Racer Paul Iddon with his Krauser BMW at Brands Hatch, April 1984.*

(Left) *To celebrate its 50th year of building motorcycles, BMW launched the R90S sports model in 1973. It was to prove its worth, both on the street and race circuit.*

Another very successful BMW twin was the R80G/S of 1980. This opened up a whole new market for larger road-going enduro models.

(Right) *The R80 and R100 were relaunched in updated form at the end of 1991. The last examples, tagged 'Classics' were built in 1995.*

(Left) *Superb R100RS with Hedingham sports chair, circa mid-1980s.*

Later version of R80G/S with factory options, including panniers.

(Right) Developed from the R65 which had first appeared at the end of the 1970s, the R65LS was styled by Hans Muth and made its debut in 1983.

The 1988 R100GS proved that the two-valve Boxer could still rule the roost, in this case the large capacity enduro class.

(Left) *Finally, in 1997, BMW stunned the motorcycle world with its first ever cruiser, the R1200C.*

(Right) *In 1996 the R1100RT made its bow, to provide enthusiasts with the latest technology in full touring trim.*

In 1993 BMW launched the first of its new breed of Boxer, with four valves per cylinder, the R1100RS. This example has optional full fairing.

which was not only considerably lighter than the old one, but also used a completely different layout. It was built up using oval section tubing, joined by an inert gas welding process, which produced very strong, and very well-finished joints.

The frame was in two sections: there was a separate main duplex cradle around the engine, and a rear sub-frame carrying the seat and the top mountings for the rear suspension., which bolted to the main frame loops in four places. The main section was based around a single, substantial top backbone welded to the base of the

Dahne taking part in an Isle of Man TT race with a racerized version of the R75/5 production model.

Metzeler tyre tester Helmut Dahne was probably the best-known European-based BMW racer of the 1970s, campaigning either standard production models or race-kitted versions of standard stroke series models.

Start of the 1971 Production TT in the Isle of Man. Number 24 is Tom Dickie, who came home 7th on his R75/5; Hans-Otto Butenuth (4th) and Tony Anderson (9th) were also R75/5-mounted.

headstock. A pair of tubes ran down diagonally and splayed out from the top of the headstock, curved round and back to form a double cradle under the engine, then up and around to meet the main backbone under the nose of the seat. There was a cross-brace just below the steering head, and a further tube ran back from this to the underside of the backbone.

The rear suspension pivot points and swinging arm arrangement were similar to those on the models replaced, and the rear shocks retained the useful load-adjusting handles. As on the 1965 prototype that Harry Louis had ridden, a telescopic front fork was fitted, developed from the ISDT mounts, and, as on the competition machine, rubber fork gaiters were specified. The front wheel spindle was carried forward on lugs cast into the front of the fork sliders, rather than centrally, as on the majority of machines, and so a greater spring/damper length was possible. One change regretted by existing BMW owners was that the interchangeable wheels had gone; where these had been of a standard 18in diameter, featuring identical (and very expensive) hubs and spokes, for the rear drive, the front tyre was now 3.25 x 19in, and the rear 4.00 x 18in.

Disc Brakes

The first production BMW twins to employ disc brakes as standard equipment were the R75/6 and R90/6 (single front disc), and the R90S (dual front discs), at the end of 1973, for the 1974 model year.

These models featured 260-mm diameter brake discs; it was the first time, BMW claimed, that perforated (drilled) discs had been used on a series production motorcycle. It was also claimed that this technique prevented fading when the discs were dry and the formation of water when they got wet.

The master cylinder, with a hydraulic stop switch, was located underneath the fuel tank. It was held to the top of the frame by a single jubilee clip – not exactly BMWs usual standard of engineering excellence. At the time, BMW stated that 'this means it can't be reached by unauthorized persons, nor can be damaged or even broken if the machine topples over'. A warning lamp (on the dash) informed the rider when the brake-fluid level was low.

The original calipers were of German manufacture (ATE). Initially, they were 38mm piston diameter, and later uprated to 40mm; both types were of the floating variety. For simple identification, the calipers are clearly stamped '38' or '40'. The ATE-made calipers are eccentrically mounted to adjust run-out on the disc – unlike any other calipers found in the two-wheel world.

From 1979 onwards, BMW switched over to Italian-made Brembo calipers (with the 'Brembo' name cast on to the piston boss). By the 1981 model year, every BMW had Brembo equipment. Besides offering improved braking performance, the Brembos have other advantages. The caliper are fixed and need no adjustment for pad wear. The brake-fluid reservoir (from the 1981 model year) was moved from its much-admired location beneath the fuel tank to a more conventional place, up on the handlebar. This allowed BMW engineers to dispense with the fluid warning light. It is widely thought that Brembo advised BMW that a fully hydraulic system would out-perform the previous Bowdon cable actuated system, and they were correct.

Whether fitted with ATEs or Brembos, most BMWs of the period, with their long travel forks, and the considerable length of standard rubber-type brake hoses, still need a strong squeeze of the brake lever. Regular bleeding helps, as does the use of DOT4 or 5 brake fluid. DOT3 universal fluid is not up to the task.

For many BMW enthusiasts and others, the new Stroke 5 models did not quite offer the air of quality or the charisma of their forerunners, even though they might have been more efficient motorcycles. There was more use of modern materials such as plastic, and simplification in order to speed up production. Some observers were also suspicious of the soundness of having a bolted-up rear sub-frame, and it was also noted that for the first time BMW openly did not recommend the Stroke 5s for sidecar use. In addition, almost sacrilegiously, the new range went as far as offering a wide choice of colour schemes! This was in stark contrast to the traditional black with white coachlining (which did, however, remain available).

For 1972, BMW fitted a smaller 3.85-gallon (17.5-litre) tank. Most buyers chose to pay extra for the larger 4æ-gallon (22-litre) tank, as fitted as standard to earlier Stroke 5 machines. The 1972 chrome-plated side panels also proved exceedingly unpopular.

Throughout 1970 and 1971, the new range remained unchanged. In August 1970, the British price of the top-of-the-range R75/5 had reached a figure of £998; the day of the £1,000 BMW motorcycle was not far off. The R60/5 was £826 and the R50/5 £762.

THE WORKS

BMW faced another problem around this time, experiencing great difficulty in finding labour to build its new range of motorcycles. The chief executive for the Spandau works was 40-year-old Horst Spintler, whose official title was managing director of the motorcycle sales division. Spintler had joined BMW early in 1964 after four years with the German branch of Agip, the Italian oil giant, and five years with the German industrial conglomerate, Krupp. Initially, the Spandau complex was essentially an assembly, rather than a manufacturing plant. After five years and several millions spent on tooling, the only parts of the motorcycle still manufactured

at BMW's Munich headquarters were crankshafts and gearboxes – and even some of these were made at Spandau.

By the late 1960s and early 1970s, the workforce had increased from the original 850 workers to some 1,500, over half of them non-German, and a high percentage of them Turkish Gästarbeiter. There was even one Irishman on the line, who had ridden all the way to Berlin on his own BMW in search of work! It may seem strange today, with high unemployment throughout Europe, but Horst Spintler's most pressing task was to recruit enough workers to keep the production line moving. The management openly advertised throughout Europe, and many British workers who had formally been employed by the once-great British bike industry went to work for BMW.

Changes to the Stroke 5

BMW introduced several alterations for the Stroke 5 range during late 1971, in time for the 1972 model year. Mechanically, these were mostly of a minor nature, although

The Stroke 6 series made its debut at the Paris show in October 1973. The range consisted of the R60/6, R75/6 (shown here), and the new, larger-capacity R90/6, plus a brand new sports model, the R90S.

within the engine the flywheel weight was reduced. This made for a slightly more revvy power delivery, particularly on the smaller unit. The size of the rear wheel rim was increased from WM2 to WM3, although the tyre size remained unchanged at 4.00 x 18in, and on the 750, the rear bevel box ratio was lowered. In an effort to improve handling, the rear suspension units were modified, and as a safety measure the prop-stand was exchanged for one which automatically sprang up, like a mouse-trap, as the dead weight of the motorcycle was removed. (This was to prove unpopular with several owners.)

There were also some cosmetic changes, and it was undoubtedly these that drew the most adverse comment. The capacity of the fuel tank was reduced to just over 3.85 gallons (17.5 litres), giving it a flatter appearance, and chromium-plated panels were added to its sides. The gap between the main and sub-frame tubes on each side was filled by chromed metal panels, while the twin grab-handles on the pillion seat were merged to loop around the rear. Neither the smaller tank nor, to a lesser

extent, the garish side panels, were popular, and for 1973 BMW was forced to return to the original 4.85-gallon (22-litre) tank (without the chrome panels) for most models sold, at least in Britain.

The first really major technical change also came for 1973, with the swinging arm being lengthened by 2in (50mm) to produce the so-called 'long-wheelbase' frame. This provided a cure for the previous tendency towards a see-sawing effect, which became apparent when opening or closing the throttle. At the same time, BMW engineers incorporated more space to fit a larger battery, as there had been complaints regarding the draining of the original battery, which seemed to happen all too easily with excessive use of the starter motor.

BMW-Puch Joint Venture

At this time, an almost entirely new range of smaller-capacity parallel twin BMWs was also planned. A proposed joint venture with the Austrian Puch company would have created a completely new range of 250

R90S

Classic Bike called the R90S 'Germany's sexiest superbike' in their September 1997 issue, an apt description of BMW's best-loved street bike of the post-war era. It was launched in a blaze of publicity on 2 October 1973, at the Paris show. The choice of venue was significant, for it was there that, 50 years before, BMW had presented to the public its very first motorcycle, the Max Friz-designed R32.

In 1973, the company had updated its existing models, totally replacing the Stroke 5 range by a Stroke 6 series, and had also hurled itself headlong into the superbike premier league with a brand-new pair of 900s. The R90S was the most glitzy and impressive, a potent-looking sportster, which *Motor Cycle News* immediately headlined 'BMWunderbike!'

The R90S used an 898cc (90 x 70.6mm) version of the famous Boxer engine and, as with all the Stroke 6 models, there was a switch from a four- to a five-speed gearbox. Compared with the standard R90, the 'S' variant produced 67bhp instead of 60bhp, at 7,000rpm against 6,500rpm. Weighing 440lb (200kg) dry, the R90S could top 125mph (200kph) in standard trim.

Its styling really represented a major milestone in BMW history, featuring a dual 'racing-style' seat, fairing cowl, twin hydraulically operated front discs (with German-made ATE calipers), and an exquisite airbrush custom paint job in smoked silver-grey (later also in orange) for the tank, seat and fairing. This not only took time but also meant that no two R90s models were identical. The fairing provided a surprising degree of protection for the rider, and also housed a more powerful quartz halogen Bosch headlamp, a voltmeter and electric clock. For the first time, BMW had employed a stylist – Hans Muth.

During its three-year life span (production ending in 1976), there were few changes to the bike. Perhaps the most noteworthy involved the twin disc front brakes. Originally plain, these were drilled for 1975, in an attempt to improve wet-weather performance, but by modern standards they still have a spongey feel. This is partly due to the 52-in (130cm) flexi hoses. Stainless-steel hoses provide a much firmer feel at the lever, and improved braking (although BMW's original stainless-steel discs suffer more than their fair share of grooving and cracking). After-market cast-iron discs provide more progressive braking and improve wet-weather performance, but the downside is rusty discs after a wet ride.

The R90S proved popular and led to success in sports production racing on both sides of the Atlantic, notably at Daytona and in the Isle of Man. Riders included Reg Pridmore and Ron Pierce in the USA, while, in Europe, Metzler tyre-tester Helmut Dahne made a big impression on the TT.

and 350cc overhead cam (chain-operated) models with vertical cylinders, very much in the style of similar small-capacity Japanese twins of the period.

The idea (as with the F650 Funduro of today) would have been to build these models in the Puch factory at Graz and market them as BMW-Puchs. Unlike BMW, Puch had spare production capacity, while BMW could easily accommodate the new machines within its substantial export and marketing divisions. It was also implied that Puch might be able to help solve the labour shortage at Spandau by manufacturing components for the flat-twins.

However, although prototypes were built and extensive testing was carried out, and despite the fact that both parties stated that production would start in either late 1972 or early 1973, with a planned output of some 25,000 per annum, the BMW-Puch parallel twins never entered production.

The Stroke 6 Series

On 2 October 1973, at the Paris Show, BMW made its next move in the evolution of its classic flat-twin design. The choice of Paris as a venue was no doubt deliberate, for it was there, almost exactly fifty years before to the day, that BMW had presented to the public its very first motorcycle, the R32.

The R90

Not only had BMW carried out a considerable amount of work in order to bring about the total replacement of the Stroke 5 series

by the Stroke 6 range, but it had also developed a new, larger model, the R90. This was to be built in two variants, the R90 touring model, and the R90S sportster (see Chapter 7 for the sportster).

The R90/6 tourer shared much the same styling and specification as the other two models, the R60/6 and R75/6. The R50 was discontinued with the advent of the Stroke 6 series, as a result of demand. A total of 38,370 R75/5s had been made, 22,721 of the R60/5, and only 7,865 of the smallest-engined model, the R50/5. In fact, BMW seemed finally to have axed the five-hundred (an engine size they had employed for half a century), simply because the current demand was for larger engine capacities.

In reality, the nine-hundred BMW was not really 'new' at all. As far back as July 1971, *Motor Cycle* had carried an article by Ernst Leverkus, a leading journalist and father of Germany's famous Elephant Rally. He reported that, despite non-committal comments by the factory, he had evidence that 900cc-class engines (rumoured for years) had been provided for

The BMW stand at the Cologne show in September 1974, presenting (foreground) the 1974 model of the R90S in the new orange colour scheme and with drilled front brake discs, (centre) the R75/6, and (background) the 1923 R23.

the factory trials stars Sebastian Nachtmann and Karl Ibschar. Although BMW knew nothing about it, Leverkus had actually tested a stock R75/5 fitted with just such an engine.

The R90/5, as Leverkus called it, displayed a significant increase in both power and torque. From a standstill, 62.5mph (100kph) was reached in a mere 4.2 seconds, 87mph (139kph) in 10 seconds, 100mph (160kph) in less than 15 seconds, and 112mph (179kph) in 25 seconds. This was achieved on stock R75/5 gearing, which under-geared the 900 to such an extent that it revved to 750rpm beyond the power peak of 6,000rpm, providing a maximum speed of 120mph (192kph) prone and 106mph (170kph) sitting bolt upright. Leverkus also posed several vital technical questions: with all that extra power and torque, should the bike have a longer wheelbase? How would the crankcase, the transmission and even the wheel spokes stand up? BMW showed that it had done its own comprehensive testing, and by the time the 900 finally entered production these criticisms had largely been addressed.

The Stroke 6s

All the Stroke 6 series (including the R90S) had crankcases with stronger internal webs to cope with the extra power and with the bore sizes; these made the 898cc (identical in dimensions to the prototype tested by Ernst Leverkus) very much a short-stroke, with 90 x 70.6mm bore and stroke sizes. BMW's project development engineer, Hans von der Marwitz, felt that if they had gone any bigger with the cylinder liner, it would have been too thin. The crankshafts were as before, but the 900 had heavier tungsten inserts in its counterweights. All the new models featured five-speed gearboxes,

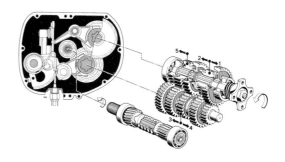

Stroke 7 featured a new, improved gearbox, with reinforced shift jaws, reinforced gear housing and optimized serration geometry.

another first on a production BMW motorcycle. Vents in the front of the engine casings on all the new models allowed more cooling air to reach the larger 280-watt alternator. They were also provided with larger batteries, up from 15 to 25 amp/hour.

Frames remained virtually the same, with a bolt-up rear section and just the addition of extra gussets at the steering head. Rear suspension was three-way adjustable, still incorporating a hand lever.

BMW fitted a single disc front brake to the R90/6 and R75/6, but the R60/6 retained the old 2LS drum front brake. (The R60/6 was now acting as the basic mount offered to fleet buyers for police forces around the world.) The drum brake on the rear (and that of the R60/6) no longer had the chrome trims which had graced the Stroke 5 models. Unusually, BMW's hydraulic brakes featured remote master cylinders hidden under the fuel tank and operated by a short cable from the handlebar lever. The calipers, mounted behind the fork leg, were also unusual in that they 'floated' on an adjustable pivot, rather than being rigidly mounted.

Other changes included new handlebar switches, an instrument panel with separate speedometer and tachometer, and new plastic side panels. Many more minor

A 1974 model R90/6, giving 60bhhp at 6,500rpm, with five speeds and a dry weight of 440lb (200kg).

refinements were part of an ongoing development programme in typical BMW fashion.

Changes and Improvements

For the 1975 model year, the most important change was a move to drilled discs. BMW claimed this much improved braking times in the wet; the early non-drilled discs had given a heart-stopping lag as the water was swept off the disc. However, braking power in dry conditions was no different, and considerable effort was still required in order to get maximum stopping power with the single-disc R75/6 and R90/6 models.

The front forks and fork spindles were beefed up, while the kickstart was finally axed as a standard fitment, but was still listed as an optional extra. At the same time, the starter motor was up-rated, to lessen the possibility of failure in sub-zero conditions. All models now featured Hella switchgear and 'dog-leg' Magura control levers, which were much appreciated by

The Stroke 6 machines featured separate instruments, with brake-failure, neutral, generator, oil and direction-indicator warning lights. Hand controls followed those of the Stroke 5 series.

those with smaller hands. The switches had tell-tale messages, as required by American law, but ergonomically they appeared to offer no real improvement.

In Britain, the new models were launched at the Donington Park race circuit, which had just re-opened, together with a museum adjacent to the track. The R60/6 was £1,244, the R75/6 £1,464 and the R90/6 £1,598.

#63 Racer

The name '#63' refers to a Stroke 6 racer developed in the USA during the mid-1970s, entered under the Butler & Smith banner, and ridden by Reg Pridmore. They also successfully campaigned an R90S in production class events, but #63 was an open class out-and-out racer which took on the likes of Harley-Davidson and the latest two-strokes, including the TZ700 Yamaha fours and TR750 Suzuki triples.

The B&S effort was very much American – based at the Butler & Smith warehouse and race shop in Compton, California – with virtually no input from the German factory, but the racer they developed was a potent and interesting motorcycle. The engine was based on the R75/6, tuned and modified, while the rest of the machine was virtually all new. The whole project was undertaken by just a handful of personnel.

The frame, based on the one successfully used by the BSA and Triumph triples, was built by Rob North, an Englishman living in San Diego. It was made of chrome-molybdenum steel fashioned into a full double-cradle design. The standard R75/6 driveshaft ran in an oil bath from the U-joint at the gearbox output rearward, but the added weight and complication of this arrangement was deemed unnecessary for the race bike, on which the joint ran exposed. The needle bearings in the U-joint required very little oil for efficient operation, so the B&S team periodically lubed this manually with a simple oil can!

BMW advised a maximum compression of 10.8:1, but #63 used a 12:1 piston made specially by Venolia. The crankshaft was basically stock, although it was lightened and finely balanced. Inlet passages on the stock BMW head were angled significantly to allow for clearance between the rider's feet and the carburettors; with rear set footrests this was no longer important, so the heads were totally re-worked by tuner Jerry Branch. Stock inlet valves on the R75/6 were 42mm in diameter, but the race bike used 2mm larger ones. The exhaust valve remained unchanged, and there were special valve springs (Norris, Erson and S & W were all used). Because of the larger inlet valves and extensive re-design of the ports, a larger, thicker valve seat was employed.

On the crankcase, cylinder barrel and basic hand castings, all the bore and stroke sizes were identical to those on the showroom bikes. The cylinder head to cylinder head span of the race bike was 28mm shorter, to give more ground clearance. Camshaft lift was the subject of much testing, and this was one area of great effort and improvement. Helmut Kern and Miles Rosstencher worked closely with camshaft specialist manufacturer Sig Erson.

Other areas of special attention were the pushrods (manufactured from chrome-molybdenum) and one-off titanium connecting rods. Each cylinder head employed twin spark plugs, fixed by an electronic Krober ignition system.

The transmission was a Kaiser-converted close-ratio five-speeder, while the clutch benefited from extensive re-working of the flywheel to minimize rotating weight. (This pre-dated BMW's own modifications in this area by some years).

Carburation was by Japanese Mikuni instruments. Originally, B&S tried 38mm units, before settling for 36mm.

Besides the Rob North chassis, the racer used triple Lockheed racing discs and calipers. The discs being made of low-nickel content cast iron and liberally drilled, not so much for lightness, but improved wet weather performance.

The front fork was a Ceriani GP type, with Betor yokes ('triple clamps' in the USA). These forks were to benefit from hours of work by Udo Giett, East Coast racing director of Butler and Smith. The rear shocks were special Girling double-acting (having both rebound and compression damper) twin shock absorbers, not normally available in the USA. The dynamics of the longitudinal crankshaft and shaft drive required heavy damping, yet gentle springing, so the shock absorbers featured rather light 60–80-lb weight springs.

Cast-magnesium wheels from Morris Industries were used both front and rear, with a Dunlop KR84 front tyre and a Goodyear slick of A4 compound for the rear. This seemingly strange combination suited the B&S BMW; to prove its unconventional nature, the BMW had been most unhappy at race speeds when fitted with a Goodyear slick up front!

Timed at 165mph, the #63 created great interest for both competitors and spectators; according to *Motorcyclist*'s February 1975 issue, 'Enthusiasts everywhere are treated to seeing and hearing one of motorcycling's most fascinating racing motorcycles.'

The Stroke 7 Series

The biennial Cologne Show in September 1976 witnessed the arrival of BMW's Stroke 7 series in 600, 750 and 1000cc engine sizes. It also saw, more significantly, the introduction of a completely new concept for BMW, the full-faired R100RS (see Chapter 8).

The R60/7 and R75/7 retained most of their mechanical internals, with the only real outward difference being new-style finning for the cylinder barrels, squared-off rocker covers and new crankcase badges. Internally, the valve gear had small changes, including the use of alloy tappets. The six-hundred at last was given a disc at the front in place of the old drum assembly.

The touring R100/7 had a lower 9:1 compression ratio than that of the R100RS motor, and smaller (32-mm) Bing carbs and smaller-diameter exhaust pipes than its more sporting brother. (For the full story, see Chapter 8.)

When the new 1978 model range was introduced, towards the end of 1977, there were nineteen improvements on the 1977 model range, several of them concerning the R100RS. One important change to the R100/7 was the addition of another disc at the front. Other changes or additions included improved gear-change linkages, re-designed instruments, a first aid kit, single-key locking and an audible warning for the direction indicators.

The R75/7 was dropped and replaced by the new 797cc (84.8 x 70.6mm) R80/7, costing £1899. *Motor Cycle News* considered it 'probably the best compromise of all the flat-twins: smooth power delivery, but plenty of low down torque'. *Motorcycling Monthly* asked whether the new 800 was 'an improvement or just a replacement for the 750?' However, for many the R80/7 was the best of all the stroke series models. Certainly, the late Fred Secker (for many years the driving force behind the British BMW Owners' Club) considered his R80/7 to be one of the best of a line of the German flat-twins he had been proud to own down the years.

Distinctive feature on the R90S were its Dell'Orto PHM 38mm pumper carbs.

The top-selling stroke series model was the R75/5, with 38,370 units sold, from 1969 through to 1973.

The last R100/7 model was built at the end of 1978, with the final R60/7s coming in 1980. Finally, in 1984, the R80/7 was replaced by the 'new' R80. By this time, BMW saw their future as lying with a combination of the new K-series with their three- and four-cylinder engines, and light-weight modern flat-twins, such as the R80 G/s enduro-style machine.

In 1976, the American importer Butler & Smith entered Steve Mclaughin and Reg Pridmore in the Superbike Production class at Daytona, scoring a highly publicized 1–2 for the German marque.

7 R100 and R80 Series

THE R100

The biennial Cologne Show of September 1976 saw the introduction of the Stroke 7 series (see Chapter 6), and the launch of a completely new concept for BMW – the fully-faired R100RS. A milestone in BMW motorcycle design because of its fairing, the R100RS represented a new era, not only for BMW, but also for motorcycling in general. This new feature certainly absorbed the lion's share of the machine's development budget. John Nutting of *The Motor Cycle* was enthusiastic after a 1977 road test:

> With the R100RS, the rider can now enjoy covering massive distances at 100mph [160kph] or more and still arrive at his destination fresh. In bad weather he remains dry and clean. Riding the bike is at first an uncanny experience. The streamlining is so well integrated that the rider never feels aware of it until he glances down at the speedo and realizes that he is travelling at 100mph [160kph] when he thought he was doing a relaxed 60mph [95kph].

Comprehensive fairings had been offered by manufacturers before, but the R100RS was to be the world's first truly successful series production motorcycle with full protection. This design evolution probably had a lot to do with BMW's concepts. The fairing was not made with increased speed

The 1976 Cologne show saw BMW launch an entirely new concept of their famous Boxer twins, the fully faired R100RS.

as a priority; had this been the aim, BMW would have used a much lower profile. What they wanted was to insulate the rider from wind pressure while maintaining the normal riding stance, and use the fairing to provide a degree of aerodynamic

To achieve the optimum shape for the R100RS's fairing, BMW hired the famous Italian Pininfarina wind tunnel.

downthrust to improve stability at high speeds.

To achieve the optimum shape for its particular requirements, BMW hired the well-known Pininfarina wind tunnel in Italy, at the extremely high cost of £2,500. Tufts of wool and strategically positioned electrodes allowed engineers to measure the airflow in the tunnel at speeds well over 100mph (160kph). As a result of these experiments, the fairing gained small spoilers level with the front mudguard, to enhance the downthrust on the front wheel, and a lip on the screen, which left the rider cocooned in a pocket of still air.

The larger capacity (also used on other R100 models of the era) had been achieved by boring out the cylinders even more than on the discontinued 900, to 94mm, giving 98cc. Compared with the R100/7 tourer introduced at the same time, the R100RS had a higher compression ratio (9.5:1 in place of 9:1), and also larger carbs (940mm as against 32mm). Larger-bore exhaust pipes were also used.

At the very top of BMW's range, the R100RS cost a cool £2,899. To give an idea of how expensive this was, it is worth comparing the prices of its major rivals: the Honda Goldwing was £1,600, the Moto Guzzi Le Mans £1,000, Benelli's six-cylinder 750 Sei £1,798, Kawasaki's Z900 £1,369, and a Dunstall Honda 900 £1,750, while Ducati's 860GTS seemed cheap at £1,499. Still, BMWs had always been expensive and, without doubt, the R100RS set new standards for the 'Ultimate Riding Machine'. Superlatives rather than brick-bats were the common response among the road testers.

Reviews

The January 1977 issue of *Motor Cycle Mechanics* called it 'quite simply, an outstanding bike'. Tester Bob Goddard found that, although 'the BMW is not perfect – in fact there are quite a few things wrong with it ... in all major requirements of a very serious motorcycle for a very serious (and wealthy) motorcyclist an R100RS is outstanding!' Goddard achieved 116mph (186kph) and an average fuel consumption of 47mpg over track testing and relatively

1977 R100RS

Engine:	Overhead-valve, flat-twin
Displacement:	980cc
Bore and stroke:	94 x 70.6mm
Maximum power:	70bhp at 7,250rpm
Carburation:	Twin 40-mm Bing CV type
Ignition:	Battery/coil
Lubrication:	Wet sump
Gearbox:	Five-speed, foot-operated
Clutch:	Single-plate, dry
Frame:	Twin tube
Suspension:	Front: telescopic fork
	Rear: swinging arm,
	twin shock absorbers
Brakes:	Twin discs front; drum rear;
	rear disc 1978 onwards
Tyres:	3.25 x 19 front; 4.00 x 18 rear
Weight:	463lb (210kg) dry
Maximum speed:	124mph (200kph)

The R100RS's larger capacity had been achieved by boring out the cylinders even more than the 900 it replaced, to 94mm, giving 980cc.

sedate touring. With the large $5\frac{1}{4}$-gallon (24-litre) fuel tank, the motorcycle provided a range well in excess of 200 miles (320km). Maximum power output was 70bhp at 7,250rpm. Bob Goddard considered the bike's star features to include the riding position and the superb level of protection offered by the injection-moulded fairing:

'You can cruise the R100RS at 100mph [160kph] plus all day without the strain of being buffeted by a hurricane.' The engine torque (greatly improved over the R90S) gave it a 'long-legged gait'. There was also praise for the 'superlative suspension and handling, instrumentation and dual Fiamm windtone horns', which let out enough noise 'to wake a sleeping policeman'.

However, as Goddard also revealed, for such an expensive machine there were quite

a few detail disappointments, including 'the screen edge trim, which peeled off during the test', and 'the headlamp window in the fairing, which leaked, allowing dirt-contaminated water to dirty the inside of the glass, where it reduced headlamp power and was impossible to clean'. As if to prove that not even top-of-the-range motorcycles are perfect, early models presented another problem for many owners: on the rubber bellows, which were intended to seal each fork leg to the fairing, resisted attempts to fix them in place, and responded to gravity by drooping down the fork leg. These annoyances were relatively minor, compared to the disappointing braking performance provided by the twin drilled discs at the front. These 'lacked bite and needed quite a lot of pressure to haul the bike down from high speeds in a hurry'. The seat also came in for harsh criticism. On the early R100RS models, there

The headlamp aperture for the Bosch H4 quartz halogen light unit on a 1977 R100RS.

A nice period shot of a 1978 model R100RS at a rally in the late 1970s.

was a massive hump at the rear, giving it very odd dimensions: 'It is big enough for one-and-a-half people, making it almost as unsuitable for solo use as with a pillion passenger cramped in behind.' It was also poorly padded – 'the edges of the seat pan were so thinly covered with sponge that they dug into the thighs when stopped at traffic lights, etc' – and, although the hump lifted to reveal a handy compartment and lift-out tray, this 'let water in'.

Owners' Comments

It is always interesting to compare the comments of testers and of owners, who have to live with the bike day in and day out. What appealed to most owners was the engine, with its long-legged flexible nature, weather protection, fuel consumption (*Motor Cycle* recorded an average 57.6mpg at

70mph) and, of course, that famous badge.

Once into top gear on the five-speed gearbox, there was rarely any need to change down, even in town, unless coming to a stop. Solid torque was delivered from 2,000rpm, but it was mid range where the R100RS scored best. This was best demonstrated with impressive top-gear acceleration at 50mph (80kph) and above. There were, however, a couple of vibration periods, which, although they did not detract from the overall enjoyment, annoyed the rider by making their presence felt. First, torque pulse vibes occurred when opening up at low engine revolutions, but could be minimized by very careful synchronization of the carburettors. There was also a period of resonance between 80 and 85mph (130-140kph), which rendered the mirrors completely useless, but on reaching 100mph (160kph), the mirrors became crystal clear once more.

A 1981 R100RS out on the road, with Brembo instead of ATE brake calipers. Rear disc and alloy wheels had been standard since the 1978 model year.

Except for colour, the 1982 R100RS (shown) differed little from the 1981 version, which had introduced several worthwhile mechanical improvements, most notably a lighter, more efficient clutch.

The gear change in the three higher ratios was silent and slick, but to get equally noiseless changes in the lower gears called for exact co-ordination of the controls, particularly in a congested urban environment.

The 1977 R100RS was a machine which much preferred travelling out of town. In fast going, over bumpy roads, the machine handled superbly, with an almost uncanny combination of ride quality and directional stability. Around town, it displayed its worst features, with excessive seal friction and heavy compression damping in the front forks virtually locking up the front suspension over short sharp bumps such as pot-holes and manhole covers. It was very much a bike that had to be ridden hard and fast in order to appreciate its full potential.

Improvements

When the 1978 model range was launched, at the end of 1977, there were several important improvements, most notably a proper dual seat and a hydraulically operated single rear disc to replace the long-serving drum. Another

was a foam cover over the handlebars to reduce injuries in the event of a head-on accident, re-designed instruments, improved gear-change linkages, a first aid kit, single-key locking, an audible warning for the direction indicators, and cast-alloy wheels. Later, these wheels would be the subject of an expensive warranty recall. Despite an additional 82cc, the R100S over the old R90S, owing to the use of new Bing carbs instead of Dell' Ortos. The R100S also heralded the reappearance of the already classic R90S fairing.

Compared with the two other R100 series models launched at the same time, the RS was a notable sales success, with a total of 33,648 machines being built between 1976 and 1984, compared with the R100/7 at 12,056, and the R100S at 9,657.

CHANGES AT BMW

A New Strategy

By the winter of 1978, BMW had launched the R100RT (a full-blown touring model with a massive fairing and 70bhp R100RS spec engine), and the similarly powered R100CS (with R90S-type mini-fairing). The company was also already planning a major change in models for its motorcycle division. As part of this strategy, extensive reconstruction of the plant and machinery at the Spandau facilities had been under way for much of the year; this was finally completed the following year. New three- and four-cylinder water-cooled engines were under development. For many years, stories had abounded concerning various new designs, included four-cylinder models. In 1978, the rumour was later proven to have been based on fact. In October 1978, BMW's chief executive Count Rudolf von der Schulenburg resigned, and was succeeded by Dr Eberhardt Sarfert. The former's departure was soon followed by a drastic bid to get the balance of the motorcycle division right, more staff were axed, the chief engineering, sales and financial directors were given transfers within the group, and new men placed in their seats.

Export

One of the major reasons for BMW to look at alternatives to its traditional flat-twins was diminishing sales in the lucrative North American market. A slump there had left some 7,000 BMW motorcycles unsold, from a budgeted 30,000. The German company had been the leading European marque in North America in 1977, but had slipped from sixth overall to eleventh behind the low-volume Swedish dirt bike specialists, Husqvarna. BMW was also faring badly in the home market, down to a lowly seventh in the league table, thanks in no small part to aggressive price-cutting by the Japanese importers.

Amid much gossip, BMW's press relations boss Michael Schimpke was forced publically to deny that the company was in dire straits. He did, however, admit that a problem existed, going on to say, 'It doesn't take a lot to see that it could have become very serious indeed if we had not been quick to make management changes.' He claimed that he was confident that BMW could 'redistribute' the 7,000 unsold bikes in the USA.

The main reason for this difficult situation in the USA was the weak US dollar in relation to the strong Deutschmark, which had prompted two price rises in 1978. The other reason was a conflict between BMW and its long-time Stateside concessionaires, Butler & Smith of New York City. The US company had known for some time that BMW would eventually attempt to dispense with their services, and had set up its own subsidiary. By the time the contract expired at the end of 1979, relations between the two companies were poor, and this had played a considerable part in the poor sales performance of BMW motorcycles in the USA of the late 1970s.

However, BMW's export fortunes were not uniformly bad. In fact, British sales of the flat-twins had never been better. In 1979, BMW Concessionaires GB Ltd increased their market share from 0.88 to 1.45 per cent – a rise of 61 per cent – with total sales of 2,518 machines (all twins). The massively increased use of BMWs as police machines had been a major reason behind this success. Forty-four of the fifty British constabularies that used motorcycles had BMWs in service. By then, the police and various British government departments had 1,262 BMWs on the road, and orders placed for another 322 machines.

Parts and accessories sales amounted to almost £1 million, and the motorcycle side of BMW concessionaires was looking increasingly profitable. The network had 86 dealers around the British Isles. In 1978, general manager Ian Watson had commented, 'We've had a superb year, latterly taking 27 per cent of the over-750cc market and plan on capitalizing and building on that success for 1979.' It was not clear exactly how this would be done, but at the same time an official denial was given regarding the likely replacement of the Boxers at the top of the market. Anton Hille, managing director of BMW Concessionaires, stated, 'BMW are not planning to introduce a new, shaft-driven water-cooled four-stroke triple or any other superbike in the foreseeable future.'

As in the USA, BMW's relationship with the British importers (in reality, a privately owned company called TKM) was not to last. Although TKM had held the concession for a decade, from 1 January 1980 a factory-controlled and financed operation took over. As Pat Myers, general manager of the new BMW (GB) Ltd explained, 'It's the policy of BMW in Germany to have its own subsidiaries to import their cars and motorcycles. As a sister company, we have a long-term commitment to BMW. Of course, we have to make profit, but it's the future we're interested in and that's why we plan to spend more on marketing. As far as the factory is concerned, they can take the overall view of their markets, and that helps them to control their production.'

BMW's wholly owned, multi-million pound headquarters in Bracknell, Berkshire, was a reflection of the German company's world-wide approach to marketing for the new decade.

New Models for the 1980s

BMW's ability to spend so much money on building a new headquarters was largely due to the world-wide success of its cars, and the profits they generated, rather than anything achieved by the motorcycle division. However, an indication of what could be achieved by BMW's two-wheel engineers came at the Cologne show in 1980, with the

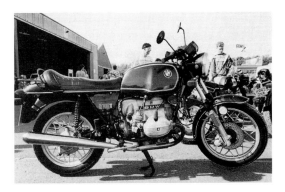

The unfaired R100T arrived in 1978 and ran through to 1984. A total of 21,928 were built.

presentation of the turbo-charged Futuro Boxer-engined project bike (see Chapter 11).

The measures adopted at the end of the 1970s had paid off, and BMW's motorcycle division was in a more stable and healthy condition than it had been for some time. The drastic fall in sales that was now taking its toll on the motorcycle industry around the world did not seem to be hurting BMW as much as it was hurting the Japanese, or the other European bike builders, including the British. By mid-1981, falling profits and subsequent redundancies were becoming common in an industry affected more than most by the massive downturn that was hitting the industrialized world. However, *Motor Cycle Weekly* was able to state, 'BMW GB is above its target for sales and registrations ... A lantern in the gloom.'

BMW had to have the right products to sell at the right time. Not only did the R100RS and R100RT models perform well, but also the smaller-engined R80RT, which arrived in 1982, using the 797cc (84.8 x 70.6mm) 50bhp R80/7 motor. Brand-new models such as the R45/65 (see Chapter 9) and R80 G/S (see Chapter 10) helped still further.

For the 1981 model year, all the twin-cylinder models adopted the new coated-alloy cylinder bores pioneered the previous

Built between late 1976 and the end of 1978, the R100S was built in much smaller numbers (9,657) than the R100RS.

year on the R80 G/S model, in place of the old cast liners. This allowed substantial reductions in piston/bore clearance, and a new type of piston ring was specified. The whole range also benefited from a re-designed clutch, which saw the operating parts reduced in weight by some 40 per cent, giving a lighter operation, and making the gear change far superior. The clutch design was very similar to that used on the K-series three- and four-cylinder machines.

Gone was the earlier-type clutch, with its 'dinner-plate' style flywheel, replaced by what was essentially a starter ring connected by a skeleton frame to a central boss. The basic dry single clutch plate remained, but in a re-designed form.

To improve lubrication, the oil passages were re-designed, and a deeper sump ensured that sloshing during heavy braking or acceleration would not starve the oil pick-up point. A Bosch transistorized ignition system finally replaced the twin contact breakers on the end of the crankshaft and a new type of electronic voltage regulator was employed. Also new was the air filter element and its box, which reduced intake noise, while throttle control was simplified so that a single cable operated a junction box

to feed both carbs. The choke moved from under the fuel tank to the handlebar, and the optional kickstarter was rehashed so that its gearing spun the engine over faster.

There was little alteration to the frame, apart from the modification that allowed easier removal of the battery, although some models had their swinging arms lengthened, while others received stronger driveshaft tubes to improve swinging-arm strength. A re-designed rear drive shell improved both cooling and torsional rigidity, as well as holding more lubricant.

The braking systems received much more attention, entailing changes of manufacturer and type. A new pad material was introduced, which contained no asbestos (by now recognized as a potential health risk), but which was claimed by BMW to provide as much as 40 per cent improvement in wet-weather braking performance.

The twins remained until the end of 1981, when BMW announced that it had begun to tool up for production of a new 1000cc water-cooled four. At the same time it was revealed that the company had set aside £35.5 million in a dramatic attempt to double its motor-cycle production by the mid-1980s, meaning in effect a sales target of 60,000 machines per year by 1985. In the event, the company actually achieved at total of 37,104.

Although the K-series of three- and four-cylinder went on to dominate BMW motor-cycle production in the mid- and late 1980s, they never succeeded in their intended role, which was actually to replace the Boxer twin. The flat-twin was, however, to make a stagger-ing comeback in the 1990s, effectively replacing the multi as BMW's main production type.

The R80 Series

At the Cologne show in September 1984, BMW announced an important development

---

Nivomat

The BMW Nivomat rear suspension unit (manufactured by the Boge concern) first appeared at the end of 1980. Although some R100RT models had it fitted as standard equipment, it is normally supplied as an accessory, and can be used on both twin-shock and monoshock models. It is designed to provide constant ride height, making it suitable for varying loads and terrain.

At the unit's heart is a combined air-spring unit with a concentric oil damper, with coil springs in case air pressure is lost. A pump tube runs from the top of the unit down into the damper body connected to the bottom half of the damper. This pump transfers oil from the low-pressure chamber into the high-pressure chamber (see page 126) until the required level is reached, when spill apertures stop the flow and the average height remains constant.

Allowance needs to be made over the first few hundred metres of riding until the suspension finds the level commensurate with the load aboard. Until that level is settled, the rear end can sit very low and upset steering geometry. Once the internal valves have found the optimum level, the suspension works normally.

It is important to realize that the Nivomat shock absorber cannot be dissembled. The only replacement parts are the rubber mounting bushings and rubber boot covering the spring in the lower section. The Nivomat is also non-adjustable.

---

in the twin-cylinder saga, with new R80 roadsters showing the direction in which the company was heading.

The R80 and R80RT (together with the R80 G/S on/off roader) were effectively the only twins available for the 1985 model year. Production of the R45, R65 and R100 series was stopped. There was, however, a new R65, originally for the home market only. (At first, this was built only in restricted form, but later a full-power 48bhp version was built for export.) The new R65 was very much based on the new R80, using a short-stroke 649cc motor from the old R65 range, different bore and stroke from the R80, and 2mm smaller valves.

The essence of the new R80 roadster series (and the new R65) was a modified Monolever swinging arm, together with new front forks and wheels similar to the K-series, and a new exhaust system. The only real difference to the engine was the use of revised rockers to reduce noise, and, for the first time, a capacity to run on unleaded fuel.

Limited Edition Flat-twins

Even though BMW had long been working towards entirely phasing out its roadster flat-twins, it found this far more difficult that it might have imagined. Such was the tide of feeling among BMW owners (and potential owners) around the world, that for the 1987 model year BMW built 'a new edition of the one-litre model (R100RS)', initially limited to 1,000 units. From 1988, together with a Stroke 7 version, this 'new edition' became a 'regular member' of the model range. Dubbed 'Limited Edition', the new versions of the R100RS and R100RT were based on the existing R80, using the Monolever rear suspension, and the same wheels, tanks and saddles. The only really visible differences were the fairing oil cooler and twin-disc front brakes.

Unfortunately for existing and potential customers, these machines were no longer the powerful 980cc models from the late 1970s and early 1980s, but a mere shadow of their former selves, strangled by strict noise and emission controls. (In common with all other BMW motorcycles, the R100RS/RT had to fulfil the ECE R48 European emissions limit, which took effect in 1988.) Power output was down from 70bhp at 7,250rpm to a meagre 60bhp at 6,500rpm. The performance potential of the bikes was effectively blunted by the use of lower compression pistons, smaller 32mm carbs (from the new R80), and the large expansion chamber on the exhaust system under the gearbox (also from the R80).

The engine and suspension of the new R100RT were identical to that of the new R100RS. However, whereas the R100RS was available in two different paint jobs (either mother-of-pearl white metallic with blue stripes, or Henna red with black stripes), the touring RT sported a Bermuda-blue finish, with dual silver lines and a black seat.

INTO THE 1990s

Emissions Technology

At the 1990 Cologne show, BMW became the world's first motorcycle manufacturer to announce the introduction of fully-controlled catalytic converter technology. The first models to use the technology were the four-cylinder K1 and K100RS machines, in May 1991. The twins were to employ the SAS (Secondary Air System) emission after-burning system as an optional extra on all R series models, from the 1991 model year onwards. This reduced HC (hydrocarbon)

The R100RT arrived at the end of 1978; its massive 'barn door' fairing gave it a level of protection which endeared it to long-distance touring riders.

emissions by about 30 per cent, and CO (carbon oxide) emissions by some 40 per cent. Its added advantage was that it had no influence on engine power, torque or fuel consumption. A disadvantage was that it could not be fitted to machines which had been originally supplied without the system; according to BMW, 'this operation would be too complicated in technical terms'. The system was not an optional extra in the USA and Switzerland, where it was compulsory.

From 1990, the R100RS was no longer available in all countries, even though the other R-series models continued to be offered.

R100R

At the end of 1991, it was announced that all BMW's Boxer roadsters would use Italian Marzocchi telescopic front forks (as on the GS models). The exception to this

1993 Two-Valve Twins Specifications

		R80	R80RT	R80R
Engine				
Cubic capacity	cc	798	798	798
Bore/stroke	mm	84/70.6	84/70.6	84.8/70.6
Max output	kW/bhp	37/50	37/50	37/50
at	/rpm	6,500	6,500	6,500
Max torque	Nm	58	58	61
at	/rpm	4,000	4,000	3,750
Design		flat-twin	flat-twin	flat-twin
No of cylinders		2	2	2
Compression ratio/fuel grade (also unleaded)		8.2/N	8.2/N	8.2/N
Valve control		OHV	OHV	OHV
Valves per cylinder		2	2	2
Intake/outlet dia	mm	42/38	42/38	42/40
Fuel supply		Bing carbs	Bing carbs	Bing carbs
No of carburettors/dia		2/32	2/32	2/32
Electrical System				
Ignition		Contactless transistorized coil ignition		
Alternator	W	240	240	240
Battery	V/Ah	12/25	12/25	12/25
Headlight	W	H 4 55/60 dia 180mm	H 4 55/60 dia 180mm	H 4 55/60 dia 180mm
Starter	kW	0.7	0.7	0.7
Transmission				
Gearbox		Five-speed gearbox with dog-type shift		
Gear ratios	I	4.40/3.20	4.40/3.36	4.40/3.20
	II	2.86/3.20	2.86/3.36	2.86/3.20
	III	2.07/3.20	2.07/3.36	2.07/3.20
	IV	1.67/3.20	1.67/3.36	1.67/3.20
	V	1.50/3.20	1.50/3.36	1.50/3.20
Suspension				
Rear-wheel drive		encapsulated driveshaft with universal joint and helical-gear follower plate, torsion damper in driveshaft BMW Paralever		
Clutch		Single-plate dry clutch with diaphragm springs		
Type of frame		Double-loop tubular steel frame with bolted-on tail section		

Spring travel front/rear	mm	175/121	175/121	135/140
Wheel castor	mm	120	120	101
Wheelbase	mm	1447	1447	1513
Brakes	Front	single-disc brake, dia 285mm	dual-disc brake, dia 285mm	single-disc brake, dia 285mm
	Rear	drum brake, dia 200mm	drum brake, dia 200mm	drum brake, dia 200mm
Wheels		Cast light-alloy	Cast light-alloy	Cross-spoke
	Front	MTH 2 2.50 x 18 E	MTH 2 2.50 x 18 E	2.50 x 18 MTH 2
	Rear	MTH 2 2.50 x 18 E	MTH 2 2.50 x 18 E	2.50 – 17 MTH 2
Tyres	Front	90/90 – 18H	90/90 – 18H	110/80 V 18
	Rear	120/90 – 18 H low-profile	120/90 – 18 H low-profile	140/80 V 17 low-profile

Dimensions and weights

Length, overall	mm	2175	2175	2210
Width with mirrors	mm	800	960	1000
Handlebar width without mirrors	mm	635	714	720
Seat height	mm	807	807	800
Weight, unladen with full tank	kg	210	227	217
Max permissible weight	kg	440	440	420
Fuel tank/reserve	ltr	22/2	22/2	24/4.7

Performance

Fuel consumption				
90km/h (56mph)	ltr	4.6	4.8	4.5
120 km/h (75mph)	ltr	6.3	7.2	5.5
Acceleration				
0–100 km/h (62mph)	sec	6.0	6.4	6.0
standing-start km	sec	27.6	29.0	28.3
Top speed	km/h	178	170	168

Model features

Fairing	Full fairing fixed positively to frame, adjustable windshield and integral stowage boxes (glass-fibre-reinforced plastic)
Standard features	Toolkit, repair kit	Toolkit, repair kit	Toolkit, repair kit, luggage rack

Specifications		R100R	R100RT
Engine			
Cubic capacity	cc	980	980
Bore/stroke	mm	94/70.6	94/70.6
Max output	kW/bhp	44/60	44/60
at		6500	6500
Max torque	Nm	76	74
at	rpm	3750	3500
Design		Flat-twin	Flat-twin
No of cylinders		2	2
Compression ratio/fuel grade		8.5/N	8.45/N
Valve control		OHV	OHV
Valves per cylinder		2	2
Intake/outlet dia	mm	42/40	42/40
Fuel supply		Bing carbs	Bing carbs
No of carburettors/dia		2/40	2/32
Electrical system			
Ignition		contactless transistorized coil ignition	
Alternator	W	240	240
Battery	V/Ah	12/30	12/30
Headlight	W	H 4 55/60	h 4 55/60
		dia 180mm	dia 180mm
Starter	kW	0.7	0.7
Power transmission, Gearbox			
Gearbox		5-speed gearbox with dog-type shift	
Gear ratios	I	4.40/3.09	4.40/3.0
	II	2.86/3.09	2.86/3.0
	III	2.07/3.09	2.07/3.0
	IV	1.67/3.09	1.67/3.0
	V	1.50/3.09	1.50/3.0
Suspension			
Rear-wheel drive		BMW Paralever	BMW Paralever
Clutch		Single-plate dry clutch with diaphragm springs	
Type of frame		Double-loop tubular steel frame with bolted-on tail section	
Spring travel front/rear	mm	135/140	175/121
Wheel castor	mm	101	120
Wheelbase	mm	1513	1447

Brakes	Front	single-disc brake; dia 285mm	dual-disc brake; dia 285mm
	Rear	drum brake, dia 200mm	drum brake; dia 200mm
Wheels		Cross-spoke	Cast light-alloy
	Front	MTH 2 2.50 x 18	MTH 2.50 x 18 E
	Rear	MTH 2 2.50 x 17	MTH 2.50 x 18 E
Tyres	Front	110/80 V 18	90/90 – 18 H
	Rear	140/80 V 17 low-profile	120/90 – 18 H low-profile

Dimensions and weights

Length, overall	mm	2210	2175
Width with mirrors	mm	1000	960
Handlebar width without mirrors	mm	720	714
Seat height	mm	800	807
Weight, unladen with full tank	kg	218	234
Max permissible weight	kg	420	440
Fuel tank/reserve	ltr	24/4.7	22/2
Performance			
Fuel consumption			
90km/h (56mph)	ltr/100km	4.9	4.4
120 km/h (75mph)	ltr/100km	6.1	6.6
Acceleration			
0–100 km/h (62mph)	sec	4.8	5.0
standing-start km	sec	26.5	26.0
Top speed	km/h	180	185

Model Features

Fairing	Glass-fibre-reinforced tourer fairing	
Standard features	Toolkit	Toolkit
	Repair kit	Repair kit
	Oil cooler	Oil cooler
	Luggage rack	Voltmeter
		Quartz clock
		Cases with standard lock

was the brand-new R100R (the second 'R' standing for roadster). This 'back to basics' machine would use Japanese-made Showa suspension instead, both front and rear.

Essentially, the R100R was a roadster version of the R100GS enduro, 'with the classic look of yesteryear', according to BMW's press pack that year. At its heart was the familiar two-valves-per-cylinder 980cc (94 x 70.6mm) engine, producing 60bhp at 6,500rpm and 56ft/lb (76Nm) of torque at 3,750rpm.

For the model's transition to a pure street bike, the oil cooler had been transferred from the cylinder protection bar, to the middle of the machine, in front of the engine protection cover. Unlike the GS models, the R100R came with the round muffler of the K100 model manufactured from stainless steel.

In common with the GS, the R100R featured 'wire' wheels, but with a 17-in at the front and an 18-in at the rear. The patented cross-spoke design (pioneering on the GS series) was fully suitable for modern tubeless tyres. Other features taken from the GS were the rear drum brake and the rear wheel single swinging arm with Paralever, helping to reduce driveshaft reactions to a minimum. An all-new feature was the gas-pressure spring strut adjusted to the shorter spring travel of 140mm. Its base spring was adjustable to six different positions, making the outward stroke-damping effect infinitely variable. A further innovation was the improved front fork with superior reaction; this was thanks to double-action hydraulic damping and a pro-gressive spring curve. Its spring travel was 135mm and its fork tube diameter 41mm. The R100R used the 285mm floating brake disc from the GS model, with the four-piston fixed caliper from the four-cylinder K models, providing more than adequate stopping power at the front.

To achieve a classic look, a chrome-plated headlamp shell (from the K75) was used for the round headlamp, while the instruments came from the GS.

Perhaps the star feature, though, was the use of round valve covers. First introduced no less than forty years before, on the legendary R68 sportster, they had last been seen on the stroke series that had been discontinued in 1976.

A 1982 model R80RT.

Buyers were able to specify (from March 1992) a special factory chrome kit com-prising the following components: fork stabilizer (brace), engine protection bar, valve cover, upper carburettor section, rear grab handle, tank cap, rear-view mirrors, exhaust fastening nut, instrument panel, direction indicator housings and handle-bar-end weights. Other features of the R100R that owed nothing to other models in the range were the handlebar cover, the battery and side panels, the passenger grab handle and the rear mudguard. As on the GS models, the handlebar console was based on that of the earlier R80ST, housing the controls and instruments of the K-series models, but without the automatic direction indicator cancellation.

The seat was much improved, with a new foam-plastic core (a feature later trans-ferred to other BMWs). The 5-gallon (24-litre) tank came from the GS and pro-vided a range of over 200 miles (320km).

The classic-style R100R was so successful, with 8,041 units sold by the end of 1992, that a smaller-engined R80R was launched for the 1993 model year. From 1994, it was made available with either 34 or 50bhp to meet new European novice-rider regu-lations. The R80R differed from its one-litre

The much-loved R80 series began with the Stroke 7, at the end of 1976. For 1978 onwards, cast wheels were specified in place of the original wire type. This is a 1979 machine.

brother only by not having an oil cooler, otherwise the two machines were identical.

In the spring of 1994, the R100R was produced in a limited edition, under the name 'Mystik'. The R100R Mystik had the following unique features:

• paintwork in Mystik red metallic;
• modified, chrome-plated headlight support;
• new metal cover for the instrument cluster, chrome-plated with new sign logos;
• new direction indicator supports, chrome-plated;
• new handlebar;
• new, improved style for seat, new tail section;
• new rear frame in black;
• new battery covers;
• new, shorter number-plate support;
• tailpipe to the inside by some 3cm along the side of pipe.

In late July 1994, production of all two-valve Boxers came to an end. This was too good an opportunity to miss for the BMW marketing men, who decided to stage a farewell party at the 1994 International Bicycle and Motorcycle Show in Cologne in October. Their aim was to celebrate four versions of what they referred to as BMW's Boxer Classic – R100R, R100R Mystic, R100RT, and the R100GS PD. This is an extract from the special brochure they produced to mark the occasion:

> After more than 70 years the time has come for a great farewell: BMW Boxer Classic. The ultimate edition. A long and winding road comes to an end. The BMW Boxer that has been known for decades will not be around much longer. After all, the successor is already on the road – and creates quite a stir with its new ideas. This is, however, no reason at all to just dismiss its successful predecessor. The 'old' Boxer has numerous friends and admirers throughout the world that love it just the way it is. That is why we have decided to name this particular edition.

In the final analysis, probably the biggest tribute to the two-valve flat-twins is the amazing mileages chalked up by their owners. The record was set by Carl

A special limited edition of the R100R, the Mystik, launched in 1994.

(Above Left) Clutch assembly (bottom) and fly-wheel only (top) of the type used from the beginning of the Stroke 5 series until the end of 1980.

(Above Right) The much lighter clutch introduced on the entire BMW twin-cylinder range for the 1981 model year. There was a weight reduction of some 40 per cent, compared with the type it replaced.

Nivomat, made for BMW by the Boge company, features an automatic self-levelling system, designed to provide optimum riding safety and comfort under all conditions, whether solo, or with a passenger or luggage.

Svobodn, who travelled more than 430,000 miles (688,000km) throughout the USA on his R60/6, named 'Windjammer'. This, more than any other achievement, acts as a lasting reminder to the greatness of the original BMW Boxer, the R32 of 1923. It is also an interesting fact that around 700,000 two-valve Boxers, of all shapes and sizes, were manufactured in just over seventy years, and BMW estimates that more than half of them are still on the road!

8 R45 and R65 Series

In the autumn of 1978, the German company made its most significant drive into the middleweight market with the announcement of the 473.4cc (70 x 612.5mm) R45, its smallest-ever flat-twin, and the 649.6cc (82 x 61.5mm) R65, which replaced the long-running six-hundred. There was also a third model, for the German domestic market only – the R45N, with its engine downgraded to 27bhp to take advantage of the significant insurance savings offered to German riders of bikes with lower power figures.

In 1978, the BMW twin-cylinder range was expanded, with the introduction of the R65 (left) and R45 middleweight models, shown here on test in southern Baveria.

The Late 1970s

Apart from the obvious differences in capacity, the R45/65 models were virtually identical, with a common stroke, the same 9.2:1 compression ratio, and 32mm exhaust valves. The smaller engine had 32-mm inlet valves, the R65 38-mm. The carbs were, respectively, 28 and 32 Bing CV (Constant Vacuum) instruments. Of the two machines, the R45 was smoother, but the R65 was much more relaxing to ride, because of its larger capacity and increased torque. Unfortunately, in the USA the newly introduced 55mph speed limit corre-

sponded almost exactly with the machine's vibration period. This plagued early models in the US market, as it was not something that the engineers in Germany had taken into consideration. The R45, meanwhile, was not affected by this problem, for the simple reason that it was never exported to North America.

Electrics were 12 volts with a 280-watt alternator. A new ignition system offered dynamic ignition advance and helped even out the already relatively smooth power delivery (not counting the R65's particular problem described above). An important feature of these engines was the addition of

The larger-capacity R65 was much nicer than the R45, its 649cc (82 x 61.5mm) engine producing a useful 45bhp at 7,250rpm. Maximum speed was a shade over 105mph (168kph).

Early R45/65 models had these fixed ATE calipers; later Italian Brembo equipment was specified.

1988 R65

Engine:	Overhead-valve, flat-twin
Displacement:	649cc
Bore and stroke:	82 x 61.5mm
Maximum power:	48bhp at 7,250rpm
Carburation:	Twin Bing CV type
Ignition:	Electronic
Lubrication:	Wet sump
Gearbox:	Five-speed, foot-operated
Clutch:	Single-plate, dry
Frame:	Twin tube
Suspension:	Front: telescopic fork
	Rear: single-sided swinging arm with single shock absorber
Brakes	Single 285-mm disc front, rear drum
Tyres:	90/90–18 51 H front, 120/90–18 65 H rear
Weight:	452lb (205kg) wet
Maximum speed:	108mph (173kph)

a torsion damper to the driveshaft, to smooth the ride during acceleration and braking. This virtually eliminated the previous bugbear of torque reaction from the flat-twin engine layout.

The frame on the smaller R models was argon-arc welded in the same gauge tubing as the Stroke 7s and to similar dimensions, although the main backbone was a single tube rather than double, as on the larger machines. The wheelbase was shorter, due to a shorter swinging arm, and there were new front forks, with the calipers mounted higher up the sliders and the spindle carried centrally rather than in front. Wheels were of the 'spider's web' variety, of pressure-cast alloy. Available as options on the Stroke 7 models, on which they proved prone to failure, these were standard on the smaller twins, although both were 18in diameter, with a 3.25 section front and 4.00 rear tyres.

The fuel tanks on both models now sported a sharper styling, but still offered a typically generous capacity of 4.8 gallons (22 litres). There was neater switch gear and a comprehensive console unit encasing the instruments and providing space for additional switches, and a clock. The Bosch headlamp was smaller, at 160-mm diameter, compared to the 180-mm unit specified for the larger bikes, but it was still powerful enough, being given the same H4 quartz halogen 60/55-watt bulb.

A 260-mm single hydraulically operated disc took care of the braking at the front, while a 200-mm rod-operated drum was specified at the rear.

Where it mattered – out on the road – the R65 proved to be an excellent all-rounder, but this was not something that could be said of its smaller brother. Even in de-restricted export guise, the R45 only managed 35bhp, and was to prove generally unpopular because of its poor acceleration and low top speed (around 95mph/150kph). As for the 27bhp restricted home-market N version, it was, frankly, one of the most gutless middleweights of its era, struggling to top 80mph (130kph) flat out. Its basic problem was its weight – the R65 and R45 weighed in at an identical 452lb (205kg) dry.

A particular technical problem which afflicted the early R45/65 models (those made in 1978 and 1979) centred around the valves. Valves with high mileage (over 40,000 miles/64,000km) should be replaced as a matter of course; above this mileage, detached heads and indented stem surface from rocker contact can occur. This is caused by gases affecting the welded section where the stem meets the head of the valve. From the beginning of 1980, BMW moved the position of the weld and thus cured the problem on these models.

Into the 1980s

For the 1981 model year, power output on the R65 was increased from 45 to 50bhp helped

by larger inlet valves. Both models had their contact breakers replaced by electronic ignition and their wheelbase increased to 1400mm. They also benefited from the latest clutch, with its reduced weight.

At the end of 1981, BMW announced a new six-fifty twin, the R65LS, basically a re-styled R65. It had a 'flow-line' treatment of the seat and tank, together with a small nose fairing, a new front mudguard and new cast-alloy wheels. Colours were much more flamboyant than for the standard model – red with white wheels, or all silver, with matt-black silencers and other parts. The handlebars were dropped weight, there were twin front discs, a new type of cast-alloy wheel and grab handles built into the seat, while the 50bhp motor performance was the same as that of the standard R65.

The whole of the flat-twin range, including the R45/65 series, continued essentially unchanged until 1985. Then the R45 was axed (28,158 had been manufactured), and the R65 was reissued in revised form based on the new R80 (see Chapter 7). 29,454 R65s had been built between 1978 and 1985.

The R45/65 used an argon-arc welded frame of the same gauge tubing as the Stroke 7's and to similar dimensions, although the main backbone had a single-thickness tube rather than the double type fitted to the larger twins.

Another 1981 improvement, on all the twins, was new clutch parts, shown here below their respective forerunners.

1980 R80 G/S

Engine:		Overhead-valve, flat-twin
Displacement:		79cc
Bore and stroke;		84.8 x 70.6mm
Maximum power:		50bhp at 6,400rpm
Carburation:		Twin 32-mm Bing CV type
Ignition:		Electronic
Lubrication:		Wet sump
Gearbox:		Five-speed, foot-operated
Clutch:		Single-plate, dry
Frame:		Twin tube
Suspension:	Front:	Telescopic fork
	Rear:	Single-sided swinging arm single shock absorber
Brakes:		Single disc front; drum rear
Tyres:		21-in front, 18-in rear
Weight:		380lb (173kg) dry
Maximum speed:		105mph (170kph)

The Reissued R65

Effectively, the R80-type R65 replaced three BMW models – the R45, the R65 and the R65LS. In common with the new R80, the 1985-onwards R65 featured the R80 G/S-derived Monolever rear suspension and swinging-arm layout. The R65 engine now also shared many features with the R80. This included the revised rocker gear to reduce noise. Valve sizes were 2mm smaller than the R80's, at 40mm and 36mm for the inlet and exhaust respectively.

BMW engineers wisely revised the power delivery of this latest version, to improve its mid-range pulling power. Peak power was reduced from 50bhp by reducing the compression ratio to 8.7:1, so that the torque peal was moved down the scale from 6,500rpm to a sub-basement 3,500rpm. The new engine needed much less thrashing than the one it replaced, although, compared with its bigger brother R80, it did demand more active use of the gearbox. The end result was much the same as the R80 although, in some respects, the R65 was smoother, mainly because the individual torque pulses from the engine were smaller so there were fewer mirror vibs at between

The 473cc (70 x 61.5mm) engine of the R45. It sold in two power versions – 35 and 27bhp, the latter to comply with learner laws in the home market.

131

Introduced late in 1981, the R65LS featured new styling with a cockpit fairing, styled seat and new tail-piece, new front mudguard, twin front discs, a new type of cast-alloy wheel, dropped handlebars, and grab rails built into the seat, plus black exhaust system.

3,000 and 5,000rpm. The only area where the R65 did match the R80 was, as one might expect, with a passenger.

The UK price of the R65 in November 1985 was £3,025, just £173 less than the R80, and, according to *Motorcycling Weekly*, 'an amount that hardly seems worth the trouble'.

Tester John Nutting was impressed enough to say the following about the R65: 'Everyone who rode the now smallest BMW available in the UK remarked on its willing and easy-going engine, precise roadholding, excellent equipment and sheer convenience.' He also commented, 'Personally, I'd choose a few of the BMW options to improve it: an extra front disc to give as much bite as on the K75 (three-cylinder), heated handlebar grips ('cos I'm getting soft in me old age) and the Nivomat self-adjusting rear shock.' He ended the test by saying, 'With all that fitted, the R65 becomes an attractive alternative to the new K75 with all the same conveniences and ease of

maintenance in a much smaller and more manageable package. With a fairing, it'd be just about the perfect bike for all-round use. Unless, of course, you want to make an impact everywhere you go!'

As for performance, the *Motorcycling Weekly* figures were as follows: top speed – 105mph (168kph) (two way); acceleration – 0 to 60mph in 6.8 secs; speeds in gears – 37mph, 57mph, 79mph, 98mph and 109mph at 7,250rpm; fuel consumption – 45mpg; tank range 220 miles (350km). At the end of December 1989, a total of 11,576 'new' R65 had been built. This was the last year this model was produced, as, after some twelve years, the curtain was brought down on BMW's modern range of middleweight twins. None of the models in the series had ever received the enthusiasm reserved for more glamorous or sporting models, but they had none the less played a vital role in BMW's motorcycle operation, bringing many thousands of first-time buyers to the established marque.

9 The G/S

THE G/S PROJECT

When it was presented to the international motorcycle press in autumn 1980, in the Pope's Palace at Avignon in the south of France, BMW's R80 G/S made a major impact. It was a new departure for the company's long-running flat-twin series, but was perhaps logical, given the German company's history in the sphere of off-road motorcycle sport. Although clearly aimed at the street, the new model did follow directly in the footsteps of BMW's success in European off-road championships and international six-day events in the 1970s.

In the G/S of the name, the 'G' stood for Gelände (off-road), and the 'S' for Straße, or road, symbolizing the dual purpose of this revolutionary machine.

Street Enduros

During the early 1970s, Honda launched their new XL250 four-valve single-cylinder machine, and achieved a breakthrough in a completely new market segment – the street enduro class. Yamaha followed with the legendary XT500 'Steamhammer' (so named because of its massive single

The R80 G/S was the first of a new breed, a larger-capacity enduro with more than one cylinder.

piston), setting the engine size limit at 500cc. Although before Honda and Yamaha there had been what the industry called 'street scramblers', these two machines created a new market for enduro-style bikes, which could be taken off road, but were none the less really aimed at the road rider.

At the time, market strategists in the motorcycle industry did not feel it appropriate or worthwhile to increase the engine size any further in the street enduro category. After all, an increase in engine size and a larger number of cylinders would mean not only more performance but also more weight, which is exactly what is not needed on an off-road mount. These fully street-legal machines were therefore considered to be restricted to a maximum of 500cc and one cylinder.

Despite these views, BMW's motorcycle division development department built a prototype using one of their flat-twin engines. This was shown to their colleagues in the marketing division during 1978, at the time strictly as a project bike only. The new management team of Dr Eberhardt Sarfert and Karl Gerlinger decided that this machine merited serious consideration for production, and in early 1979 they not only gave the go-ahead for the development

BMW presented the new R80 G/S enduro –styled 'on-off roadster' – to the international motorcycle press in the south of France during the autumn of 1980.

Engine weight of the 797cc (84.8 x 70.6mm) flat-twin had been cut by 15lb (6.8kg), mainly through use of aluminium cylinders and paring dead weight from the clutch assembly.

of the new K-series of multi-cylinder machines, and also for the project that was to be known as the R80 G/S.

Development of the G/S

The real start of the whole G/S project had been back in 1975, when suspension engineer Rüdiger Gutsche built his own private enduro machine based on an R75/5. In early 1978, Gutsche appeared with an improved machine, which caused quite a stir when he rode it as a marshal in the 1979 ISDT (held at Lager Stegskopf, West Germany). At around the same time, a number of his colleagues in the BMW development department had also constructed their own private enduros for participation in the annual Dolomite Rally in the Italian Alps.

Development of the R80 G/S proceeded apace. The technical highpoint of the new machine was the single-lever swinging arm; this was the BMW Monolever now patented all over the world and originally conceived for the K-series. Even before the K generation came along, BMW's engineers decided to introduce the Monolever for the first time on the R80 G/S. Its advantages included low weight, great torsional rigidity, reduction of the concept to one spring strut and easy changing of the rear wheel. This system was to prove such a success that in future years one BMW motorcycle after another would benefit from the technology.

The production G/S was not only radically styled (the project had been conceived with input from Italian bike-builders Laverda), but also presented a number of innovative departures from BMW's conventional roadster practice.

Tyre experts Metzeler had a challenging task at the time, facing the same difficulties as BMW's suspension and running-gear

R80 ST – A G/S for the Street

The R80 ST made its public bow at the Cologne Show in September 1982. Essentially it was a roadster conversion of the R80 G/S

When is a G/S not a G/S? When it's an ST! A direct development of the original R80G/S, the R80ST made its public debut at the Cologne show, in September 1982.

The R80ST was a successfully engineered roadster conversion of the G/S trial bike, which, although it was only manufactured for a relatively short period of time, was a popular mount. It retained the same single-shock Monolever rear suspension, tall chassis and hi-level siamesed exhaust system, but in place of the R80G/S's 12-in front wheel was a 19-in rim, carried in R100 stanchions, with R45/65 sliders so that the spindle was central rather than on the front of the forks. Wheel travel was also reduced, but the total effect combined to keep the trail and castor angle much the same as the G/S, retaining light but positive steering. At the rear, the shock absorber was shortened to give slightly less travel, but overall seat height remained a problem.

Most of the other changes from the G/S involved taking parts from the R45/65 series, to transform the bike into a true roadster. These included a close-fitting front mudguard, larger headlamp and the double instrument console, with a tacho as well as speedo, plus high handlebars from the American specification R65.

Power output and gearing remained the same as the G/S, although the ST was some 36lb (16kg) heavier at 404lb (184kg). Even so, it was a very light machine for its class.

Motor Cycling got a useful timed 103.65mph (around 166kph) with the rider prone, but perhaps the following extract from the October 1983 issue of *Motor Cycle Sport* provides a more accurate view of the ST: 'The rationale behind the R80ST has been to capture the handling qualities of the big trail bike in a roadster of almost equally light weight ... on the eve of the launch of the K-series, BMW's first venture beyond two pots, pushrods and some other elementals in motorcycle circles, we publish an appraisal of the company's most up-to-date twin. Ironically, the 80ST – light, a fine handler, relatively simple, powerful enough for most out of reach of the home country's autobahn – impresses as the most persuasive argument yet advanced by BMW in support of its policy of keeping the dizzier heights of Jap style hi-tech out of motorcycle design.'

specialists. After all, there was a fundamental contradiction in terms between the two objectives of the R80 G/S – good road-running characteristics on one hand, and an ability to perform equally satisfactorily off-road on the dirt on the other.

Weighing in at 441lb (200kg) wet, with 50bhp on tap, the R80 G/S could achieve 105mph (168kph). The machine's dual role presented further problems as officially enduro tyres were limited at the time to a maximum speed of 93mph (150kph). Metzeler responded by producing suitable tyres, and thereby began a trend that was later followed by other tyre manufacturers.

Specification

Engine weight of the 797cc (84.8 x 70.6mm) flat-twin had been cut by 15lb (6.8kg), helped by the use of aluminium cylinders with a Galnikal bore coating, and by paring dead weight from the single-plate diaphragm clutch assembly. This was reduced in diameter without reducing friction area, while the housing was trimmed and slotted for superior cooling. This not only lessened the effort of clutch operation, but also virtually eliminated noise when changing gear.

However, it was the single-sided swinging arm (comprising the rear drive and suspension layout) which made the G/S so distinctive among other production BMWs. The newly created Monolever had the swinging arm containing the driveshaft on the off side, with the wheel completely unsupported on the near side, effecting a considerable weight-saving. With no loss in structural rigidity, the Monolever strut proved a real boon, easing wheel removal and being largely responsible for the newcomer's excellent handling.

Other weight-saving features (compared

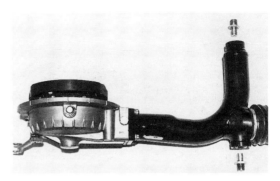

Monolever rear fork, on the first BMW to be equipped with this feature.

with the conventional BMW roadster range) included hi-level two-into-one exhaust, plastic mudguards, a simpler instrument console (without a rev counter), fibreglass seat pan, and a single perforated 260-mm front brake disc operated by a Brembo caliper and pads with a high metal content.

The G/S also benefited from other changes to the engine that BMW was making to their twins at this time. These included improvements to lubrication, by way of re-designed oil passages and a deeper sump, Bosch transitorized ignition, and a new type of electronic voltage regulator.

At a British price of £2449 in November 1980, the R80 G/S slotted squarely into the middle of the BMW price range.

After a development period of only twenty-one months, the R80 G/S debuted in autumn 1980 to much acclaim. Graham Sanderson's response was typical; on 15 November, he wrote, 'How's this for a sweeping statement? BMW's new 800cc R80 G/S trail bike is their best roadster and certainly the most memorable machine of the year.'

Publicity and Success

Shortly after the launch of the R80 G/S, BMW received considerable publicity, when

BMW Shaft Drive - From the Simple Shaft to the Paralever

From the very beginning of the motorcycle, the motorcycle driveshaft was associated with Munich. It started in 1896, long before the foundation of BMW, before the term 'motorcycle' was even known – Alois Wolfmüller from Munich coined the name a year later, and had it patented. One of his employees – Ludwig Rüb, a part-time employee of the Hildebrand & Wolfmüller motorcycle works – had the idea to use a driveshaft. Rüb provided the first design of a motorcycle with driveshaft in 1896, and completed a second design in 1897, paving the way for BMW's subsequent designs with a longitudinally fitted driveshaft.

Rüb's designs, which never went any further than the drawing board, were based on the Belgian FN shaft-drive bicycles. Indeed, at the beginning of the 20th century, FN became the first manufacturer successfully to apply the shaft-drive concept (which had never really made it with the bicycle) to motorcycles.

In 1922, the driveshaft concept returned to Munich, the city where it had been born. BMW's chief, Franz Josef Popp, took the historical decision to build more than just horizontally opposed engines for aircraft, small cars and motorcycles. Having experienced complaints from annoyed customers, he decided to take over motorcycle production entirely, and gave Max Friz the order to design the first BMW machine. Friz wrote motorcycle history on the drawing board, developing the concept of the BMW flat-twin with shaft-drive, and coming up with the idea of the straight drive train, with the crankshaft, transmission shaft and propeller shaft aligned in a row, facing towards the rear-wheel drive.

This early drive concept, with its shaft to the rear wheel, was referred to as the 'cardan drive'.

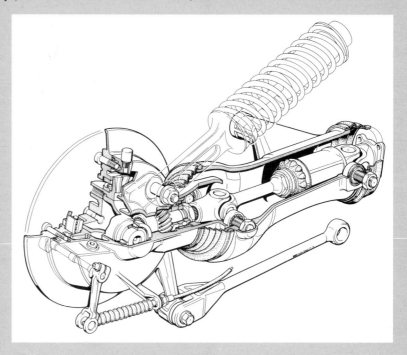

*Patented BMW
Paralever system –
unique and effective.*

Originally inspired by Italian scholar Geronimo Cardano (1501-76), this type of power transmission had never been considered in the context of the motor-cycle. Cardano had invented the 'cardan suspension' for compasses, and the same principle was subsequently used for driveshaft joints. BMW's early machines, such as the R32, did not require such joints because they had rigid frames without any rear-wheel suspension. A rubber disc ('hardy disc') was quite sufficient as a shock absorber.

Fourteen years after the R32, the flow of power to the rear wheel did require the use of a joint. BMW's racing machines already featured the vertical shaft engine with compressor, which had become so powerful that it could no longer be controlled, even by a skilled rider, without the help of a genuine rear-wheel suspension. In 1937, therefore, BMW's works racing machines were fitted with a suspension featuring straight guide sleeves on vertical tubes. The driveshaft now required for the rear wheel was equipped for the first time with a universal joint. In 1938, BMW also introduced this rear-wheel suspension on the R51, R61, R66 and R71 production models. This design principle, with straight guide sleeves and short spring travel, was retained until 1955, at least on BMW's standard production machines.

The first ideas for further refining the BMW concept evolved in the design offices during the early 1950s. At the time, the trend in motorcycle engineering was to move away from the wear-prone straight-travel rear-wheel suspension towards the swinging arm, which offered less friction and longer spring travel. Even then, however, BMW's engineers realized that this principle, applied very successfully with chain-drive machines, is subject to physical limits when combined with a drive-shaft. The drive forces create a certain lifting action when starting off and accelerating, causing the rear wheel to move up and hardening the suspension. Quite logically, this effect becomes greater with increasing engine power and spring travel.

In 1954, Dipl. Ing. Alex von Falkenhausen, the designer of the first rear-wheel suspension in 1936, and later the creator of BMW's successful car engines, took up a proposal made by motorcycle specialist Helmut Werner Bönsch. He patented a pivoted rear-wheel drive housing with a driving force support. Soon, von Falkenhausen's idea became reality, proving absolutely essential on BMW's racing machines. The works version of the BMW RS used by Walter Zeller in the World Championships from 1955 had a correspondingly modified drive system, with two driveshafts for conveying the power of the RS engine.

For 1955, BMW's standard production machines were equipped with a swinging-arm suspension based on that of the RS racing machine. The housing of the driveshaft leading to the rear wheel was fitted positively to the swinging arm. With engine power still quite modest at the time (the R69S developed 24bhp), and with spring travel on the rear wheel relatively short (80mm), there was no reason to make any efforts.

Providing more power and longer spring travel, the next generation of BMW motorcycles, launched in 1969, started to show a greater reaction of the driveshaft than before. Applying full throttle on the 50-bhp R75, and later on the 70-bhp R100, the rider really had the feeling of going up in a lift – the machines rose up a bit when accelerating - but most regarded this more as a typical characteristic than as a shortcoming.

Off-road riders were not so happy about the 'lift action', although they certainly appreciated the long spring travel and, soon, the superior power of BMW's enduros. The problem with the enduros was that the rear wheel rose up, largely eliminating the spring travel whenever the rider really opened up the throttle.

When BMW launched its first white-and-blue standard production enduro, the R80 G/S, in 1980, the existing concept with one joint started approaching its limit, although the remaining margin was still quite sufficient. While the 50bhp of the standard model allowed a reasonable compromise, it was obvious that any further increase in engine output would start to create problems. This was precisely the experience of the enthusiasts who, more or less secretly, converted their R80 G/Ss into 1000cc machines. BMW also had to learn this lesson with the factory competition machines raced in the Paris-Dakar Rally. Despite their longer swinging arm, the physically induced lift forces presented certain problems (although this did not stop BMW from winning the rally four times).

The first plans to introduce a new and even better concept date back to 1981, and inevitably resulted in the reinstatement of the pivoting swinging arm. This time, thirty years on from von Falkenhausen's design, with the introduction of the R80G/S, BMW once again revolutionized the driveshaft concept, introducing the Monolever single swinging arm. The task had been to fit the swinging arm with a joint able to work efficiently without play and distortion, even under the toughest off-road conditions. Developments carried out along these lines by BMW suspension engineers René Hinsberg and Horst Brenner were reflected by a patent registered in November 1983. The final design was a direct consequence of these developments. The Paralever double-joint swinging arm is made of cast aluminium, as on the four-cylinder K100. Despite its more sophisticated design, it is hardly heavier than the steel-tube version.

The new, refined version of the driveshaft concept debuted in 1987. Just as the R80G/S had been BMW's first model with the Monolever in 1980, the new enduro models R80GS and R100GS marked progress, with the new Paralever. The K1 was the first K-series machine to feature this unique technology, and was followed by the K100RS.

French rider Hubert Auriol won the prestigious Paris–Dakar Rally on a competition version of the bike in early 1981. The R80 G/S quickly made a name for itself in other areas, too. An increasing number of riders soon found out that it was the ideal tool for long-distance adventure journeys. Strong and robust, rugged and reliable, and easy to handle, the G/S could tackle almost anything, even with a passenger and lots of luggage. All kinds of roads, and even the harshest terrain could be attempted on this genuinely multi-purpose bike; it was truly 'a bike for all seasons', as they would say in the USA. Whether it was used for crossing African deserts or the Brazilian rain forest, for ultra-long tours from Alaska to Tierra del Fuego, or for crossing passes in the Himalaya all the way to China, BMW's flat-twin enduro did not take long to become the first choice of motorcycle globetrotters of the 1980s.

The R80 ST road version (see page 136), launched in 1982, was supplemented in 1984 by the limited-production Paris-Dakar model featuring a 7-gallon (32-litre) fuel tank. Sales of the R80 G/S (including the R80 ST and the Paris-Dakar) ranged from 3,156 to 5,213 units per year between 1981 and 1986, the main markets being the European Alpine countries. During this period, the R80 G/S carved out its own niche, having no competition in the road

BMW built small numbers of the special R80 G/S Paris–Dakar model from late 1984 to celebrate the company's success in the famous desert endurance race. There was also a retro-fitting kit of parts for anyone with a standard model.

enduro scene, both in terms of engine size or in number of cylinders.

When BMW's competitors finally entered the arena, enlarging the engine of their existing single-cylinder models (Yamaha's Teneré, for example), and upgrading their machines in some cases to two cylinders, an entirely new market segment was created for the large, long-distance enduro (or trail) bike. BMW responded instantly to this new challenge. Having built some 28,000 R80 G/S models (including the ST and Paris/Dakar variants) in seven years, the company now took the decision to create a new generation of GS models, this time without the stroke between the 'G' and the 'S'.

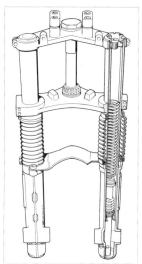

Italian Marzocchi front forks were fitted to the GS for the 1988 model year. Marzocchi had previously supplied BMW with forks for its Paris–Dakar racing models.

THE SECOND GENERATION

BMW's two second-generation enduros were launched in Florence during the autumn of 1987. They had one all-important task – to continue the successful career of the former model. Coded R80 GS and R100 GS, just about everything on these motorcycles was new, with hardly any unchanged components taken from the original model. Two of these were the headlight with all its interior fittings, and the handlebar,

including the levers and switches.

Once again, it was the suspension that featured the most dramatic and eye-catching modifications. The frame had also received special treatment, with the oval tubes inside the tank tunnel being reinforced for greater rigidity. The rear frame section supporting the seat and the built-in luggage rack had also been increased in strength.

Unlike the R80 G/S, the new machines used an Italian-made set of front forks. Manufactured by suspension specialists

The BMW Paralever: Idea and Effect

Drive forces conveyed to the wheels inevitably cause a certain reaction, both in motorcycles and cars. An effect of this kind will always occur when all the wheels are unsprung, in which case there is a dynamic shift in wheel load. Sprung wheels, on the other hand, react additionally to the drive forces, the extent of this reaction depending on the geometric arrangement of the suspension components. It is therefore possible, both in theory and in practice, to compensate both drive and brake forces, either in full or in part.

With motorcycles, this reaction of the suspension depends on the type of drive system. Machines with chain drive tend to move down to the rear on the sprung wheel when starting off. Machines with a driveshaft, on the other hand, have exactly the opposite reaction, and the rear wheel will move up.

The simplest and most obvious way of compensating for this effect is to use a longer rear-wheel swinging arm, but even this provides only a partial solution. On a BMW, the swinging arm necessary to compensate fully would have to be 1700mm long, longer than the bike's wheelbase. A double-joint swinging arm, on the other hand, provides the same effect as an extremely long single unit, but takes up much less space. This is because the parallelogram arrangement increases the radius of the wheel elevation curve.

BMW's Paralever provides the same effect as a swinging arm measuring 1400mm in length, providing compensation of 70 per cent. This is enough to reduce the effects of acceleration forces to an insignificant minimum and also ensures that, when decelerating, there is no significant brake dive. Indeed, the Paralever substantially improves the motorcycle's braking characteristics, totally eliminating the otherwise hardly avoidable judder effect of the rear wheel when braking hard or shifting down suddenly.

Marzocchi, who already provided BMW with the forks for their Paris-Dakar racing models, the new fork assembly was specially developed for the new machines. Among other features, there was a particularly hard-wearing anti-friction surface between the inner and outer tubes. This surface consisted of sleeves, with a multi-layer metal bearing and Teflon coating providing perfect conditions for smooth and consistent action of the light-alloy sliders. Spring travel of the Marzocchi fork was 225mm, with the diameter of the main tubes (stanchions) 40mm. This compared with the old model's figures of 200mm and 36mm.

The damper units inside the fork operated with a larger oil volume, a higher oil throughput and larger holes and cross-sections. This ensured an active damping effect, even under extreme off-road conditions. The new fork assembly was equipped as standard, with a fork brace. The front axle had the same dimensions as that of the K-series, 25mm, and was hollow to save weight.

Being much sturdier, the new fork largely prevented the machine from pulling to one side when braking, even though the forces acting at the front were greater than before. The diameter of the brake disc was increased to 285mm, and the Brembo

The new large-bore GS certainly had enough 'go' to perform more than the odd wheelie.

Patented cross-spoke wheels, which provided a closed, self-contained rim base and, accordingly, allowed the use of tubeless tyres.

caliper was now one size larger than on the old model. The hydraulic operation of the brake had been modified to ensure lower operating forces. Now the rider needed only a moderate effort on the road to brake the machine up to the point where the wheels would lock. Off road, the rider only needed one or two fingers to apply the brakes smoothly and efficiently.

The rear swinging arm was also brand new. Patented as the BMW Paralever, it replaced the Monolever. It was the most significant innovation of the new GS models, and is described in detail on page 142.

Like the front wheel, the rear assembly also had longer spring travel than before – increased to 180mm from the earlier model's 170mm. The inclined monoshock featured a Boge gas pressure shock, which was adjustable in four different settings and now rested directly on the final drive housing. The wheels of the second-generation GS stood out immediately, thanks to their entirely new cross-spoke styling. This new, patented solution offered several benefits:

1. The position of the spokes running through the rim hump provided a closed, self-contained rim base and, accordingly, allowed the use of tubeless tyres;

For 1989, BMW offered the R100GS Paris–Dakar. The individual parts, such as the 7-gallon (35-litre) fuel tank or the fairing, were also available, as was a kit to fit to an existing machine.

2. The threaded end on the spokes of the hub allowed the spokes to be replaced both with the tyre and the wheel fitted in position;

3. The crosswise arrangement of the spokes enhanced the torsional rigidity of the wheel, giving it the same strength and stability as even the best of cast wheels;

4. The tubeless tyres could easily be exchanged using normal tyre-changing tools. There was a wider rear rim so a 130/80–17 tyre could be fitted (replacing the former 4.00–18). As before, the new wheel was extremely easy to change – the only difference being that now there were four bolts instead of three.

Although the power of the smaller model remained unchanged from that of its predecessor, at 50bhp, the top-of-the-range R100GS put out 10 more bhp, making 60 in all. The torque was also up to 56ft/lb (76Nm) at 3,750rpm.

On its way to becoming an enduro, the one-litre flat-twin was re-born in the R100RS, and had the benefit of various design improvements. For a start, there were two 40-mm Bing constant-depression carbs. These instruments had already proved their worth in the factory's Paris–Dakar racers. With an improved rocker arm guide, the valve-train of the flat-twin was both smoother and more reliable. Reflecting the signs of the times, modifications to the valve seals enabled the engine to run on unleaded fuel (even though at that stage, this was not obligatory). Like the R100RS and R100RT roadsters, the R100GS was equipped with an oil cooler.

Another new feature of the engine was the starter. As with the K-series, this was a so-called layshaft starter, which weighed 4.4lb (2kg) less, because of its smaller electric motor, but nevertheless provided the same torque by way of the intermediate transmission. While the starter required less power when starting the engine, the GS was now fitted with a higher-output 25 amp/hr battery.

The exhaust collector box beneath the gearbox was of increased capacity, but virtually no heavier than before. With a volume of three-quarters of a gallon (3.8 litres), compared with one-third of a gallon (1.5 litres), it not only reduced the noise level but also served to improve the torque curve. The new models sported a 5.75 gallon (26-litre) fuel tank, larger than that on the R80 G/S. Without fuel, oil and tools, the new R80GS and R100GS weighed in at 418lb (187kg).

The seat had been re-styled, and also offered improved qualities. It was longer and wider, and more comfortable. The seat upholstery had been improved by using polyurethane and latex foam, in a sandwich arrangement. Standard seat height was 850mm, but a higher seat, giving 880mm, was available for the taller rider. A small windshield encompassing the cockpit and helping reduce wind pressure at speed was standard on the larger model, and available as a retro-fittable option for the smaller bike.

BMW's objective in developing the new GS models had been met, with the Paralever system eliminating undesired problems with the driveshaft and its reaction to a change in load. They had succeeded in providing a higher standard, both in riding safety and suspension comfort. The reinforced frame, the new forks and wheels, and the new-generation tyres certified for speeds up to 118mph (190kph), all helped.

The one-litre power-plant gave a higher top speed (112mph/181kph) and superior torque, which was particularly helpful for those riders wishing to travel long distances with a passenger and lots of luggage.

At the end of 1989, there were further

The first the public saw of the new generation GS – the four-valve 1100 – was at the Frankfurt Show, in September 1993. It went on sale in the spring of 1994.

1998 R1100GS

Engine:	Overhead-valve high camshaft four-valves-per-cylinder flat-twin
Displacement:	1085cc
Bore and Stroke:	99 x 70.5mm
Maximum power:	80bhp at 6,750rpm
Maximum torque:	97Nm at 5,250rpm
Fuel supply:	Bosch Motronic MA 2.2
Alternator:	700w
Battery:	12v, 19amp hour
Gearbox:	1st 4.16/3.00; 2nd 2.91/3.00;
	3rd 2.13/3.00; 4th 1.74/3.00;
	5th 1.45/3.00
Rear wheel drive:	Paralever
Clutch:	Single-plate, dry
Frame:	Tubular space type; engine serving as load-bearing component
Front suspension:	Telelever system
Spring travel front/rear:	190/200mm
Wheel castor:	115mm
Wheelbase:	1509mm
Steering assembly angle:	64 degrees
Brakes:	Front: dual-disc 305mm
	Rear: single-disc 276mm
Wheels:	Front 110/80 H19TL; rear 150/70 H 17 TL
Seat height:	840/860mm, adjustable
Weight:	536lb (243kg), unladen with full tank
Maximum speed:	119mph (195kph)

Note: Motor Cycle News *test 6 April 1994, electronically timed 133mph (214kph)*

developments in the GS story. For the 1990 model year there was a newly developed Paris–Dakar version of the R100GS. All the special components on this model were also made available individually, or as a kit to be fitted on both the R100GS and R80GS. There was also a sports suspension conver-sion kit for GS models, in a joint venture by BMW and the Dutch company, White Power. The kit consisted of a complete set of long progressive-action telescopic springs with improved load-bearing capacity, plus a sports-tuned rear-wheel spring strut adjustable to several different settings.

Planning for the new generation GS, using the four-valve high camshaft flat-twin engine, began back in 1992 with a series of sketches; this shows the one that was selected for development.

All the 1990 flat-twins featured an improved drum rear brake, the brake shoe width having been increased from 25 to 27.5mm.

Finally, a special model for the German home market was developed, in the shape of a 27-horsepower R65GS. Except for its engine, which was virtually the same specification as on the standard R65, this entry-level enduro was essentially the old R80 G/S in terms of suspension, running gear and styling.

From 1990 until the autumn of 1993 there were no further changes. Between the first R80 G/S appearing in 1980 and September 1993, a total of over 62,000 of the various models were manufactured.

Four-Valve GS 1100

In spring 1993, BMW launched their next-generation flat-twin, with four valves per cylinder, high camshaft control and 1085cc (99 x 70.5mm) Motronic fuel-injection engine (for a technical description of this engine, see Chapter 12).

During the planning of BMW's new generation of Boxers, it was predictable from the beginning that there would once again be a GS version. It would have to be a motorcycle with even more power and torque, even greater fuel economy ensured by DME (digital motor electronics), improved environmental friendliness, owing to a fully controlled catalytic converter, and extra riding safety, provided by the combination of Telelever and ABS.

The first the public saw of this second model in the new generation of Boxers was when the R1100GS made its debut at the Frankfurt Motor Show in September 1993. BMW announced that the motorcycle would go on sale at their dealerships in spring 1994, at precisely the right time to maximize sales for the new season.

The engine of the R1100RS had been modified for its new task, and gave less power and more torque. Even so, it was considerably up on the old two-valve motor, giving 80bhp at 6,750rpm, and maximum torque of 72ft/lb (97Nm) at 5,250rpm. This made the newcomer not only the largest enduro

on the market, but also the most powerful in terms of torque. This modification of the model's torque and power was made possible by an adjustment to the Bosch-made Motronic MA 2.2 engine management system, modified camshafts, different valve timing, modified exhaust manifolds and silencer (now manufactured in stainless steel), lower-compression pistons (down from 10.7 to 10.3:1), and a final drive ratio of 1:3.00 instead of 1:2.81 (the ratio used on the R1100RS from the 1994 model year).

Like the R1100RS, the big GS came with a three-piece frame concept on the same scale as before, the engine and transmission housing forming one load-bearing unit. Front-wheel suspension technology also came from the R1100RS, with the use of BMW's novel Telelever with its control sprint strut (see Chapter 11). Because of the enormous variety of conditions under which an off-road machine must prove itself, the front, centrally mounted spring strut, with 190mm spring travel, allowed spring pre-tension to be adjusted to five

different levels by means of a hook spanner provided in the motorcycle's toolkit.

The 33-in (820-mm) handlebar of the R1100GS was mounted separately, the fork bridge and handlebar being connected with the fixed-position tubes of the Telelever through two ball joints in the fork bridge, thus not following any tilt motion of the Telelever. With the sports-style handlebar of the R1100RS, which, unlike the handlebar of the GS model, did not rise upwards at such a steep angle, such tilt or swivel motions were hardly perceptible, and it did not need to be mounted separately. Like its RS counterpart, the four-valve-per-cylinder GS came with its rear wheel running in a Paralever swinging arm with central spring strut and 200mm spring travel. Spring pre-tension was infinitely adjustable by way of a hydraulic adjustable wheel, while outward-stroke damping was also infinitely adjustable, by means of a setting bolt.

The R1100GS continued the previous models' patented cross-spoke 'wire' wheels, with a 110/80–19 front tyre, and 150/70–17

The R1100GS, an aggressive-looking chunk of machinery, is surprisingly capable on or off road in the right hands.

at the rear. While the front wheel employed the double disc brakes of the R1100RS, with four-piston fixed calipers and floating stainless steel 305-mm discs, the brake system of the rear wheel had to be modified due to the fitment of a cross-spoke wheel. The GS featured a single 276-mm disc equipped with a two-piston floating caliper. As an option, the R1100GS is available with BMW's improved ABS II (see Chapter 11), already featured on the R1100RS. On the GS, the ABS system can be deactivated by the off-road rider, by pressing the ABS deactivation switch and firing the ignition at the same time, but this can only be done before setting out. The rider is then informed by the ABS warning light that the anti-lock brake system is currently not in operation. To re-activate the system, all the rider had to do was switch off the ignition and then switch it on again.

The R1100GS came with a 5-gallon (25-litre) plastic fuel tank. The upper front mudguard was integral with the cockpit fairing giving the machine a unique look, either

loved or hated! The second (lower) front mudguard was fitted to the lower fork bridge (brace), thus following the steering. The rear wheel was equipped with a plastic guard, fitted directly to the rear-wheel drive.

Like the R1100RS, the R1100GS was equipped with a special ergonomics package. This included a windshield which could be adjusted by 13 degrees (using the toolkit), and a two-piece seat, which could be set at a height of either 860mm or 840mm, the latter being remarkably low for a large-capacity enduro-type machine. Again, seat height can be varied easily, simply by fitting the seat into fixed supports at various levels.

Another feature common to the R1100RS roadster was the integrated ignition and handlebar lock, allowing the rider to lock the handlebar in both right or left positions. The ignition key also locked the tank cap, seat and helmet-fastening catch.

The instruments, controls and switches, with the exception of the rider information display, were the same as on the RS. Again, as on the RS, the front brake lever could be set to four different positions. Further standard features were the main and side stands (the latter with the safety device starter interrupter function), the plastic cylinder protector, the aluminium protection plate (or 'sump bash-plate'!) beneath the engine, hazard warning flasher and luggage rack. A special feature was that the rider could enlarge the luggage rack, by removing the rear half of the two-piece passenger seat. The grab handle for the passenger could also be removed, and there was a separate box for the on-board toolkit beneath the luggage rack.

The only change for the 1995 model year was a new lower front mudguard, extended to the front by an additional 7in (192mm), to provide more adequate protection.

By July 1995, more than 14,600 units had been built, and the R1100GS had been in the number one spot in Germany's over-750cc enduro market segment from the very first year. A year later, the sales figure had risen to over 22,000.

Reflecting BMW's usual philosophy, the R1100GS is available with a wide range of options and accessories. Besides the factory-fitted ABS II and fully controlled catalytic converter (standard in some countries, including Germany and Switzerland), there are also a rider information display, heated handlebar grips, various cases and panniers, an anti-theft warning system, soft-form handlebar grips, hand protectors, a handlebar impact protector, cylinder crash bars, and much, much more. As with the original R80 G/S model back in 1980s, BMW Geländé concept has proved a surefire winner, which shows no sign of diminishing in the approach to the new millennium.

10 Specials

BMW twins have always found favour with the touring fraternity, but they have also proved of interest to the more sporting rider, and this enthusiastic following has led to a number of special machines being built, both for competition and street use. The factory, specialist dealers and private individuals have all played their part in this important sub-plot in the BMW story.

This pictorial guide covers a selection of the most unusual and technically interesting examples.

To mark their star rider's retirement from racing, BMW presented Walter Zeller with this unique sports roadster, in November 1958.

For many years, companies such as Ernst Hoske and Schorsch Meier offered hand-made, large-capacity fuel tanks for BMW twins. This is an example of an R69S kitted out with a Meier tank. Note also the telescopic forks in place of the usual Earles-type, and more sporting silencers.

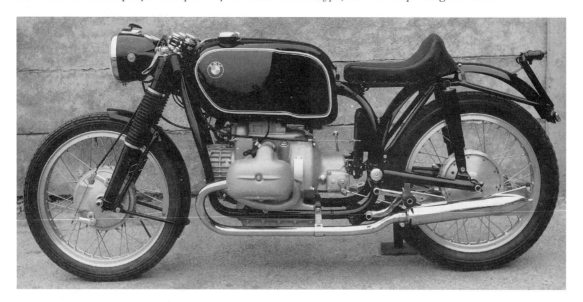

Zeller's roadster was hand-built, using the best materials available. Very much the ultimate BMW sportster, with its supercharged 600cc motor, minimum weight and tucked-in exhaust, it was almost too good to ride.

London BMW dealership Gus Kuhn, under Vincent Davey (seated left), did much to raise the company's profile by racing the flat-twins.

(Below) Martin Sharpe, during the 1975 Isle of Man Production TT at Union Mills, in action aboard the Gus Kuhn-entered BMW R90S.

Former MV Agusta racing team manager Arturo Magni launched his MB2, using a R100RS engine, at the Cologne Show in September 1982. It was built in small numbers over the next few years.

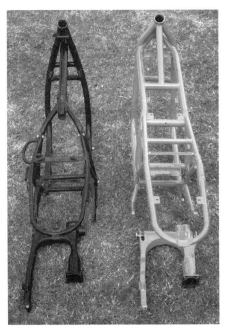

Standard BMW R100 frame (left); Magni MB2 version (right). The advantages of the Italian-made chassis are evident.

Close-up of Krauser four-valve technology, sharing rocker arms.

Krauser four-valve kit comprising complete cylinder-head assemblies, pushrods, through-bolts, head gaskets, plug leads, special forged Mahle piston assemblies and other components.

Mike Krauser also built limited quantities – around 200 – of the MKM 1000 roadster, using a combination of standard production BMW components fitted into a triangulated chassis developed from the 1976 endurance racer. They were sold through selected dealers, with the standard BMW guarantee.

Krauser MKM 1000 frame assembly, including swinging arm, shaft drive and bevel box; plus twin rear shock absorbers. The trellis design is similar to that used on modern Ducatis, such as the 916 and 748 V-twins.

Kidge Elder's immaculately turned out and very trick Krauser-R90S, Silverstone, October 1984 – cast-alloy wheels, leading link front forks and Krauser eight-valve engine.

The German Krauser firm was well known for not only its luggage equipment, but also by way of racing, in particular 80cc solos and sidecar engines. They were also heavily committed to BMW. This is a prototype Krauser endurance racer (using a modified Stroke 6 roadster engine). Ridden in 1976 by the likes of Freddie Habfield and Peter Zettelmeyer it handled well, but was not fast enough to challenge the likes of Honda or Kawasaki at the top level.

Paul Iddon ready for the off at Brands Hatch March 1984, for his first ride on the L&C of Tunbridge Krauser BMW racer. This potent machine used both the trellis frame and four-valve cylinder heads.

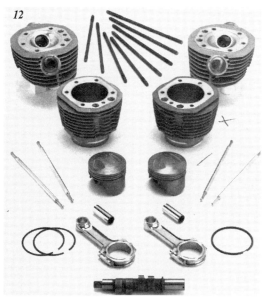

Fallert tuning kit for the late 1970s R100 series engine, which bumped the power output up to 91bhp. The kit comprised heads, barrels, pistons, con-rods, camshaft, pushrods and studs.

Fallert Motor GmbH of Achern, Germany not only manufactured a range of tuning parts for standard production BMWs, but also their own overhead camshaft engine.

This desmodronic BMW was built by an Austrian enthusiast and displayed at Salzburgring in July 1986. Besides the Ducati-type 'desmo' valve gear, it also featured ohc. Other details included clip-ons, and a single seat and Conti silencers from a bevel 900SS Ducati V-twin.

The Futuro Project Bike

At the Cologne Show in September 1980, BMW showed what was possible with the classic flat-twin Boxer layout. If this had been a four-wheel vehicle, it would have been described as a 'concept car'; BMW called it the Futuro.

The Futuro was very much a one-off engineering showcase, with a turbo-charged 800cc engine, which BMW said would achieve 125mph (200kph) from its 75bhp output. This speed was assisted by aerodynamics of the carbon-fibre reinforced plastic fairing. The designers had also gone to considerable lengths to pare weight from the running gear, including spun aluminium solid disc wheels, alloy disc brakes and frame in a mixture of tube and alloy sheet. Although intended as a design exercise rather than as a future production model, the Futuro gave an interesting insight into the wide range of technical features under consideration within the BMW research department of the 1980s.

The turbo system closely followed similar work being carried out by the Japanese. Perhaps BMW was fortunate, from a financial point of view, that the Futuro project never reached production; corporate chiefs of the Big Four Japanese makers would agree, with the benefit of hindsight, following their embarrassing failure in production-turbo sales.

The Futuro's boost pressure was controlled by a microprocessor which took full account of the engine's revolutions and running temperature. The fuel injection by Bosch LH Jetronic system featured hot-wire air metering to register the airflow into the engine. BMW engineers claimed that this provided the smoothest possible torque curve, with the lowest fuel consumption.

Other features of this unique prototype included digital instrumentation, a horizontal single rear shock absorber, triangulated swinging arm, triple Brembo brake calipers, a hydraulic steering damper, and shortened telescopic front forks with clip-on handlebars.

In common with the later Kawasaki 750 Turbo, the Futuro had its turbo-charge unit located at the front of the engine unit, next to the exhaust pipes. This was intended to minimize the turbo lag experienced by both the Honda and Yamaha turbo production models.

The Futuro's turbo system closely followed similar work being carried out by the Japanese at the time. Its boost pressure was controlled by a microprocessor, with fuel injection by the Bosch LH Jetronic system.

Computers controlled the Futuro instrumentation.

One of the stars of the 1980 Cologne Show was the Futuro concept bike, powered by a turbocharged 800cc flat-twin engine and capable of over 125mph (200kph) from 75bhp.

159

Le Mans 24 Hours, May 1985. The engine was Michel-tuned, while the new frame was the work of Piet Mantel. Besides endurance events, the Struik BMW was also campaigned in the Dutch Battle of the Twins series.

For the Bol d'Or in September 1983, the same R100-based Struik racer was converted to chain final drive.

BMW R100 modified by the Dutch-based Struik endurance-racing team and ridden in the 1983 Le Mans 24 Hours.

Italian TAG Moto GS1000 special on display at the 1987 Milan Show.

11 The Arrival of the Four-Valves

A NEW BOXER ENGINE

One of the most exciting and significant chapters in the long-running history of BMW's flat-twin family of motorcycles was added in the spring of 1993, when the German marque unveiled its long-awaited replacement for the conventional air-cooled, pushrod, two-valves-per-cylinder Boxer.

The members of BMW's faithful following around the world held their breath on this occasion, which was tinged with mixed feelings. While it had long been clear that, in its existing form, the horizontally opposed engine had reached its sell-by date, the speculative pre-launch illustrations of its replacement showed a machine that, frankly, lacked the 'elegance of its forefathers' (according to Bruce Preston, in an issue of respected enthusiast journal, *Motorcycle Sport*).

Exactly a decade earlier, in 1983, the first of the K-series (the K100 four-cylinder) had

Seventy years separated BMW's original flat-twin, the R32, and the brand-new four-valve Boxer, the R1100RS, when it hit the streets in 1993.

The R1100RS was to be the first in an entirely new series of modern Boxers ready for the 21st century.

been launched. It was generally well received by both press and public, and was undoubtedly a good bike, but it never really replaced the famous Boxer. And BMW certainly tried hard enough, with a whole range of K100 derivatives, as well as the smaller K75 three-cylinder models. In the end, they had to admit defeat, and re-introduced the R100 two-valver in various forms, including the RS and RT, during the late 1980s. However, even the factory realized that this was only a temporary measure. The enthusiasm for the classic Boxer layout was still there, and it would have to be satisfied by more than a re-hash of an outmoded model, however long-serving and excellent that model had been.

The demand led to project R259, the new Boxer engine. Its history can be traced back to the mid-1980s, when BMW's motorcycle managers and engineers had realized that its customer base wanted a new range of Boxers, and an engine of entirely new design.

It was obvious to everyone involved that this new Boxer had to offer more power and more torque than its predecessor. Accordingly, there was no doubt that it had to have four – and no longer two – valves per cylinder. Top priority was also given to the improvement of fuel economy, the minimizing of exhaust emissions and engine noise, as well as the ease of maintenance (even though in future this would be aimed at the dealer rather than the individual).

The development of the new Boxer engine technology was the most significant advance made by BMW since Max Friz's original R32 of 1923. The first production version of the new R259-engined model made its debut in 1993, so no less than seventy years separated these two enormously significant events!

THE NEW R259 BOXER ENGINE

The Engine Housing (Crankcase)

The engine housing (crankcase) consists of two cast-aluminium shells joined together in the middle. BMW's engineering team decided not to use a single-piece tunnel housing, as on the old Boxers, since the two shells can be cast more economically and with maximum efficiency.

The shells are almost identical, the only difference being that on the off side there is a flange for the oil-pressure check valve, while the oil-level inspection window is on the near side. The shells are sealed by an elastic, silicon-based compound, offering the advantages of being temperature-resistant and easy to remove. The oil sump is integrated into both halves of the two-piece housing and has a capacity of 1 gallon (4.5 litres).

By opting for this design, BMW's engineering team solved the possible problem of oil leakage, which might have presented itself if the oil sump had simply been connected to the engine block. The middle-pressure aluminium casting process was chosen over the

Following its car technology, BMW intentionally fractures the connecting rod boss of the four-valve Boxer engine, a world first in motorcycling.

time-consuming chill-casting procedure with sand moulds, because of the substantially reduced reject rate of the former.

Drive Unit

As the drive unit is the motorcycle's main load-bearing component – BMW called it the 'backbone' – the engine and transmission components were designed for optimum strength and rigidity, with the help of the computer-based finite-element method (FEM). The front end of the engine is sealed off by the alternator cover, manufactured of pressure-cast light alloy and housing the alternator, itself driven by a poly-V belt. Another cover comes right at the end, integrating the engine and alternator, and forming the final section at the front.

Four Valves per Cylinder

The new engine was required to fulfil demanding standards, and there was no

The main components of the four-valve Boxer engine – modern in every way, but holding true to BMW's flat-twin heritage.

Details of the four-valve Boxer engine include 1085cc (99 x 70.5mm), 90bhp at 7,250rpm and 95Nm of torque at 5,500rpm. Note how well the exhaust pipes are tucked away, the cylinder of aluminium with hard-wearing Gilnisil coating, and the special attention paid to the design of the cylinder/head finning.

doubt from the very beginning that only a four-valve power unit would suffice. Two inlet valves in each cylinder guarantee an optimum cylinder charge and fuel/air flow. Because of the symmetrical arrangement of the two exhaust valves, the spark plugs with their three electrodes have ample room in the middle of the cylinder head. Featuring specially contoured pressure edges at the sides, the roof-shaped combustion chambers are very compact. BMW found that, although they exhaustively tested two-, three- and five-valve layouts, the four-valve type proved the best at providing an all-round mix of fuel economy, performance, torque, and efficient running.

Oil Cooling

To ensure maximum cooling without reverting to a liquid-type, the engineering team looked particularly at the hot exhaust section; the exhaust valves in the cylinder

The engine housing crankcase consists of two sections split vertically, rather than one unit, as on the old two-valve Boxers. They also serve a load-bearing function.

head of the R259/series engine are tilted to the front, in the direction of travel, giving the full benefit of the air flowing around the cylinders. For even greater efficiency, the cylinder bank, which develops temperatures of up to 570°F (300°C) is cooled by oil flowing between the two exhaust valves.

Valve Adjustment Intervals

The advantage of this additional oil cooling is that both the valve and the valve seat have a much longer service life. In addition, the intervals between valve adjustments are longer, up from 4,660 miles (7500km) to 6,200 miles (10,000km). To avoid coking along the hot cooling ducts after switching off the ignition, the ducts are designed to remain fitted with cooling oil at all times.

Owing to this combination of air and oil cooling, the engine is more resistant to high temperatures and hot weather, runs more quietly, and offers longer service life.

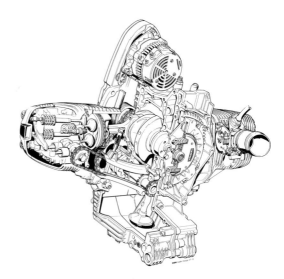

The R259 engine, with its four valves per cylinder, high camshafts (chain-driven to short pushrods), and air/oil cooling.

Valve Control

Since the valve control system used on the old two-valve Boxer (featuring a central camshaft, tappets, very long pushrods and rocker arms) would not have been strong enough or stiff enough for a four-valve power unit, BMW's engineers had to take a new approach in designing the valve drive system.

Classic valve drive systems with sohc or dohc and bucket tappets, as used on BMW's K-series engines, had to be ruled out from the start, since they would have increased the width of the Boxer engine by some 1in (4cm). This would have made it quite impossible for the rider to negotiate bends at an angle of up to 49 degrees, as required by BMW's own specifications. A further drawback is that a valve control system of this kind would have made it impossible to air-cool the exhaust section of the cylinder head. A vertical driveshaft would have been too elaborate, difficult to service and expensive. BMW's engineers opted for the following solution: via a chain, an auxiliary shaft with a reduced ratio of 2:1 is driven directly from the crankshaft; located deep within the engine

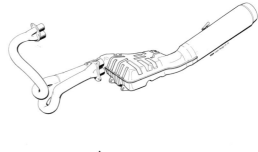

The stainless-steel exhaust assembly (top) of the four-valve Boxer engine, and the optional catalytic converter.

beneath the crankshaft, this auxiliary shaft, running at half crankshaft speed, incorporates a further chain on either side driving the respective camshafts running within the near- and offside cylinder heads at the back next to the inlet valves. The decision to use chains for this purpose was a wise one, given the failure rate of toothed belts on many modern overhead camshaft car engines.

Using an auxiliary shaft offers one advantage – the sprocket within the cylinder head is smaller than usual and, therefore, the cylinder head is kept slender (even so, space within the cylinder head is very limited). A light-alloy sub-frame is bolted directly to the cylinder head, to accommodate the valve drive.

Camshaft

The camshaft and rocker arms run directly on the sub-frame. Unlike the conventional design, the camshaft is no longer made in one single piece. Instead, the cams are sintered and forced on to the specially hardened and heat-treated steel shaft.

Working against the bucket tappets, the rotating cams transmit the forces converted from a rotary to an up-and-down motion via pushrods to the forged rocker arms. The rocker arms, in turn, transmit this drive force to the valves to be opened, with a pressure of 59lb (27kg). They also feature adjustable bolts for the pivoting slides driving the valves in pairs.

This type of camshaft drive is referred to as the high-camshaft design.

Cylinder Cooling Fins

The two typical Boxer cylinders sticking out on either side are manufactured of cast light alloy. To obtain a larger outside surface, and thus dissipate heat more efficiently, they feature cooling fins specially designed to prevent the hissing noise such fins often cause on other air-cooled motorcycles. Usually, manufacturers fit rubber silencing blocks. The fins and connection pieces are as long as necessary to provide optimum heat dissipation, at the same time preventing vibrations and eigenfrequencies audible as a distinct noise around the engine.

Gilnisil Cylinder Coating

Inside, the cylinders are finished with a high-strength, low-wear layer of Gilnisil, a special nickel silicon coating, which minimizes frictional losses on metal surfaces running against each other. (The 'Gil' in the name represents the Italian specialist company Gilardoni.) Further advantages of this design are minimum oil consumption (although this is a particular problem in the early stages of the R259 series engines, see page 187), high strength and closer operating tolerances, which all combine to offer a longer service life.

Piston Design

Each piston features three rings (one for removing the oil, two for compression and sealing), and the two pistons are manufactured of cast light alloy. Measuring 99mm in diameter, the pistons weigh almost one-third less than the type used in the two-valve engines. This lighter weight reduces mass forces and allows higher running speeds, and other side-effect is less vibration.

The low weight of the pistons also results from their modern sectional structure, with a much shorter piston skirt. While the gudgeon pin used to be supported by a reinforced skirt, the new design of pin, reduced in length, is held in position by two pins.

Connecting Rods

The connecting rods are made of sintered and forged steel. Compared to the old steel con-rods, which were merely forged but not sintered, the new rods have more accurate dimensions, superior surface contour and a higher quality.

The sintered con-rods' biggest advantage is that they all have virtually the same weight following production, without deviation from one rod to another. While the old steel components had to be subsequently machined and then categorized into no less than seven weight groups, the new sintered rods are all in one weight group.

Con-Rod Boss

Amazingly, in a world's first on motorcycles, the connecting rods of the four-valve Boxer are made using the fracture (or 'crack technology') first introduced on BMW cars. The large con-rod boss (eye) encompassing the crankshaft is intentionally fractured, and not simply sawn in half.

The advantage is that both surfaces along this intentional fracture fit together perfectly when subsequently re-joined. Indeed, when subsequently bolted together, the fracture lines provided form a larger common surface with superior alignment of the two halves than with the conventional joining process. It is such a simple technology, yet so efficient!

Crankshaft

The crankshaft is the very centre of any engine. On the new four-valve Boxer it is a one-piece construction made of top-quality heat-treated steel, running in two slide bearings, the rear bearing being of double collar design. The advantage in the event of repairs is that there is no need for time-consuming

The chassis of the R1100RS, and the four-valve Boxer's frame and suspension systems are alien to conventional motorcycle practice.

alignment of the bearing and crankshaft. BMW's engineering team deliberately dispensed with a third crank bearing, since this would have required the two pistons opposite each other to be moved too far to the side.

The crankshaft drives the alternator and the layshaft controlling the valves and the two oil pumps, and extends directly into the five-speed gearbox.

Lubrication

The two inner-serrated oil pumps are housed in a separate unit at the front end of the layshaft, the cooling oil pump at the front, and the lubrication oil pump at the rear. The circulation of lubricant is controlled by a pressure valve fitted directly behind the pump; compressed oil flows first through the oil filter and then up the distributor chamber with its various ducts and connection pipes. Here, in the pre-cast main oil duct, the lubricant flows past the oil-pressure switch and is siphoned off for lubricating of the layshaft bearings and the nearside cylinder head.

Another duct inside the chamber leads to the front and rear main bearings for the crankshaft. One hole is sufficient in each

The bodywork of the R1100RS benefited from wind tunnel testing.

bearing to ensure ample lubrication. From the main bearings of the crankshaft, the oil flows through additional ducts to the con-rod bearings also requiring lubrication. To lubricate the cylinder head on the off side, oil is siphoned off through a set bolt duct from the main oil stream, flowing to the rear main crankshaft bearing and then being forced through the control sub-frame into the hollow-drilled rocker arms and camshaft. The bucket tappets are lubricated by splash.

Cooling Oil

The cooling-oil pump features an open circuit, its task being to turn around as much oil as possible and circulate it into the system. Accordingly, it is a volume pump, and not a pressure pump. Flowing through a distributor pipe, the cooling oil is fed into the drilled riser pipes of both cylinders and flows to the cylinder heads. In the cooling duct itself, the oil flows round the exhaust valve seat and from there runs back into the housing, from where the two oil streams from the near end offside cylinder meet once again. The re-flow pipe enters the housing on the near side, below the surface of the oil.

The Environment

Efficient extraction of air from the crankcase is vital to engine performance, as it helps to minimize oil consumption.

Each time the pistons move down to their bottom dead centre, either on the intake or compression stroke, the air in the housing beneath the pistons is forced out. This air is enriched by blowby gases – exhaust gases forced into the crankcase between the walls of the cylinders and the pistons and past the compression rings. This exhaust gas is contaminated by oil residues, which have to be collected and removed. This is done first by a labyrinth integrated in the crankcase, and then by an external oil separator further downstream, where even the last

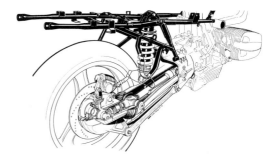

The rear drive, sub frame, and BMW's patented Paralever on the R1100RS.

traces of oil contained in the exhaust gas are retained. Oil particles in the blowby gas oil mist impinge on the walls of the cyclone separator, and are removed from the gas by means of centrifugal forces.

The oil 'washed' in this way flows back into the engine through an external pipe leading out of the oil separator. The gas is fed into the intake silencer, from where (mixed with air) it flows back into the combustion chambers. This sophisticated process minimizes oil consumption throughout the engine's entire

The Bosch-made Motronic fuel and ignition systems play a large part in improving both performance and fuel economy in the four-valve Boxer engine.

One of the outstanding innovations on the R1100RS is the ergonomics package, fitted as standard, and comprising adjustable fairing windshield, adjustable handlebar, and an adjustable seat.

running life (although, in practice, during the initial break-in period this does not quite apply).

Intake System

Through a snorkel beneath the tank, fresh air is drawn into the intake system air chamber, where it is cleaned by a paper filter. From the pure air chamber downstream of the filter, the air flows on through two specially designed intake manifolds, via the inlet valves, into the two combustion chambers. In their length and shape, the inlet manifolds are designed to provide superior output and an optimum torque curve, thanks to the resonance within the intake system.

Digital Motor Electronics

To enhance engine output and torque further, while at the same time reducing fuel consumption and exhaust emissions, it

Café Racer – Concept or Production Model?

Ever since 1994 when the factory displayed a non-running streetracer-style bike (in bright orange!) at shows around Europe, rumour and counter rumour have abounded concerning BMWs intention of launching a café racer version of its 4-valves-per-cylinder Boxer.

In their 27 September 1995 issue *Motor Cycle News* went as far as saying, 'Now inside sources at BMW's Berlin factory have told MCN that a full production model, will be ready to break cover in the spring'. There was even a full-page colour artists impression of how MCN expected the promised newcomer to look.

In creating a more sporty version, BMW's management will have had to make a decision on whether to go for the latest styling to match the modern mechanical features of the basic machine, or whether to plump instead for a retro or even classic style. Certainly the concept bike displayed back in 1994 was very much a café racer of the traditional variety, complete with wire wheels, rearset footpegs, drop handlebars and that wacky one-piece set of bright orange bodywork.

Another question to have been answered was whether to simply offer a styling exercise, or to provide potential buyers with a real sportster including up-rated engine and more race-worthy running gear, complete with additional stopping power and a firmer ride.

Finally, now that the custom R1200C has appeared with more cubes, will the long promised café racer come as an 1100 or 1200?

As this book was being compiled (spring 1998) there were strong rumours once more that such a machine would be launched at the Munich Show later in the year.

---

was necessary to equip the engine with an electronic management system. This proved to be a relatively easy task, with BMW's engineers simply turning to the digital motor electronics (Bosch Motronic) already featured in the K-series.

Compared with the old Boxer, equipped with a pair of Bing carburettors, the advantages of the new R259 engine with electronic fuel injection include:

• improved performance through the design of the intake system;
• superior engine response ensured by the significant reduction of flow losses with the inlet manifold;
• improved economy and reduction of fuel consumption; whenever the throttle butter-fly is closed, and when the engine is in overrun above 2,000rpm, the supply of fuel is totally interrupted;
• grid control for extra smoothness and refinement;
• superior level of (dealer) service, provided by a diagnostic chip memorizing any defects and subsequently read by the BMW diagnostic tester;
• improved reliability and failsafe functions built into the Motronic system, allowing further (albeit restricted) operation of the engine in the event of a deficiency;
• no wear of electronic systems (although these could fail at some stage);
• ideal conditions for using a fully controlled catalytic converter.

The R1100RS is available both with the standard 'three-quarter' fairing, or with full fairing, as seen here (at extra cost).

(Inset) The R1100R's powerplant, displacing 1085cc, is most closely related to that of the softer-tuned R1100GS. Like the GS, the R's engine is designed not so much for maximum power, but for grunty, low-down torque.

In all a highly competent, modern engineering package.

MOTRONIC AND ITS SYSTEM

The Fuel Supply System

Housed in the fuel tank, the electronic fuel pump transmits fuel to the electromagnetic injection valves with the throttle butterfly manifold, a regulator keeping the pressure required for the injection process consistent. Fuel is discharged into the two inlet manifolds through the pair of electronically controlled inlet valves. The compression ratio of 10.7:1 (R1100RS) requires unleaded premium fuel (95 RON).

The Ignition

The ignition system consists of the terminal stage and coils. The ignition angle specified by the control unit is communicated by the system as a high-voltage pulse to both spark plugs.

The Control Unit and its Sensors

The sensors determine the engine's current operating conditions. The information obtained in this way is fed into the control unit, where it is compared with the data stored in the EPROM of the CPU (Central Processing Unit). This comparison of data shows the exact amount of fuel required and the duration of the injection period.

The Supply of Data

The following sensors serve to supply the data required to the Motronic Central Processing Unit:

1.   Throttle butterfly angle.

To determine the engine's current lead conditions, throttle butterfly angle alpha is measured by a potentiometer located on the throttle butterfly shaft and serving to determine dynamic driving conditions (any change in the position of the throttle butterfly). Applying the throttle butterfly angle and speed signals, the Motronic determines the basic data for the ignition angle and injection period, subsequently

The naked R1100R and R850R both utilized the pioneering Telelever front suspension; a hydraulic steering damper was fitted to both 'R' models as standard equipment.

adjusted by additional consideration of the intake air and engine oil temperature.

The next of the new four-valve Boxers after the R1100RS was the GS version (see Chapter 9). The third model, the unfaired R1100R, arrived in the autumn of 1994, together with the virtually identical smaller-engined R850R.

A 1997 R850R. It used a smaller-bore (87.5mm) version of the R1100R engine (the stroke remaining unchanged), producing 70bhp at 7,000rpm, with maximum torque of 57ft/lb (77Nm) at 5,500rpm.

A 1998 model year R1100R out on the road. The 1997 update improved its rather 'frumpy' appearance.

2. Engine speed.

Two Hall detectors on the crankcase also serve as sensors providing data to the Motronic Management System. They incorporate two magnets determining the rotational speed of the crankshaft without direct contact.

3. Intake air temperature.

The temperature of the fresh intake air is measured in the air-filter housing, the sensor changing its electrical resistance as a function of temperature.

4. Oil temperature.

The oil-temperature sensor is fitted at the outlet from the cooling-oil circuit to the oil cooler itself. It records the information required and passes on this information to the Motronic control unit and, if fitted, to the oil-temperature gauge.

5. Air pressure.

The air-pressure sensor (a pressure socket incorporating a diaphragm measuring air pressure on a piezo-crystal via a vacuum),

measures ambient air pressure, and makes any adjustments required depending on the elevation at which the motorcycle is travelling. This system is only required, however, on models with a basic catalytic converter without electronic control, since the oxygen sensor takes over this function on machines fitted with a three-way catalytic converter.

Three-Way Catalytic Converter

BMW was the first manufacturer in the world to build motorcycles with a fully controlled three-way 'cat' (on the K100 series), and has continued this active policy in its range of new Boxer twins.

The process of conversion, reduction and oxidation are only possible as long as the Lambda 1 engine data are strictly observed. The stochiometric ratio between the amount of fuel actually supplied and the amount of fuel theoretically required is

In the spring of 1997, both the R1100R and the R850R received a mini-facelift, which included a re-designed instrument console, an all-new instrument support, and chrome-plating of items such as the headlamp shell, instead of the previous silver-painted finish.

based on an air/fuel mixture of 14:1. To maintain this mixture, regardless of running conditions, the oxygen sensor (sometimes also referred to as the Lambda probe) measures the amount of oxygen in the exhaust gas emitted by the engine.

In the three-way catalytic converter used on the R259 series engine, the expensive metals required for oxidation (platinum and palladium) and reduction (rhodium) are applied to a metal substrate. Oxidation converts carbon monoxides into carbon dioxide, and hydrocarbons into carbon dioxide and water. The withdrawal of oxygen then allows the breakdown of nitric oxides into nitrogen and carbon dioxide. Compared with a ceramic-based catalytic converter, the metallic converter offers advantages in terms of both space and time. It is smaller and responds more quickly, since the metal substrate is more efficient in absorbing the heat from the exhaust gas.

BMW offers the three-way catalytic converter as an option. The R259 series engine also comes in a version prepared for subsequent installation of the 'cat', with all

This drawing shows the main components of the R1100R, certainly no retro bike, like the Kawasaki Zephyr, but one that very much goes its own way.

technical modifications already made for relatively easy retro-fitting.

At the end of its working life, the catalytic converter is recyclable; this is best left in the hands of a BMW service outlet.

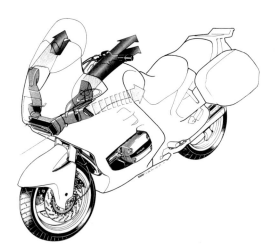

The fairing of the R1100RT features ducts to supply cool air in summer, and a special warm air supply supplied via the oil cooler. These operations are controlled by a switch.

The fourth of BMW's four-valve 1100s is the RT version, which made its world premier at the Frankfurt Show in September 1995. For many it is the finest of the de luxe tourers, with best use of the design's strong points.

Rider's-eye view of the RT's 'cockpit'.

Oxygen Sensor

On the K100 models, the oxygen sensor is fitted downstream of the converter, while on the R259 series engine it is upstream of the catalytic converter, and is therefore activated quickly and efficiently. The optimum operating temperature of the ceramic probe is 1112°F (600°C), and temperatures in the region of 656°F (300°C) ensure that the sensor will be activated within seconds. To provide an even faster response, the sensor is heated by a 12-watt heating system.

Immediately after the engine has been started, the oxygen sensor is switched off until the engine reaches its normal operating temperature, the fuel/air mixture being enriched in this start or warm-up phase in order to make the engine rum smoothly. When the engine is in this operating condition, engine speed is increased by the choke adjusting the position of the throttle butterfly. As soon as the engine has reached its normal operating temperature,

this assistance is of course no longer required.

Fuel Enrichment

The oxygen sensor control system is also deactivated whenever the engine is enriched during acceleration. This is essential, in order to compensate for the leaner fuel/air mixture during acceleration, and allows the engine to run not only at its most efficient, but also at its maximum smoothness.

Monitoring the throttle butterfly angle, the rate at which the throttle butterfly angle

Where shall we go?

changes, the absolute change of angle, engine temperature, and engine speed, the computer is able to determine any sudden need for power. A quick twist of the throttle twistgrip by the rider leads to a complicated calculation process within the computer.

To obtain spontaneous engine power without the slightest delay, the injection period required by the electronic control system is 'bridged' by short, interim bursts of fuel enriching the mixture injected. This power-enhancement process starts immediately after any change in engine load.

Overrun Control

Overrun control serves to reduce both emissions and fuel consumption. It is activated

at engine speeds above 2,000 rpm, as long as the throttle butterfly is closed.

To avoid engine damage, the injection signals are interrupted at approximately 8,000rpm; this speed-governing function reliably ensures that the engine will not be over-revved.

Exhaust System

Manufactured completely of stainless steel, the exhaust system is extremely resistant to corrosion. The two manifolds are expressly designed to act as a resonance pipe for the exhaust gases, providing maximum torque and output. They come together upstream of the silencer.

On models fitted with a catalytic converter, the oxygen sensor is located directly at the point leading into the silencer, ensuring maximum efficiency.

In the standard version of the silencer, with a volume of 0.35 cu ft (10 litres), the exhaust gas flows through an intake pipe with a special absorber. On the catalytic converter model this absorber is replaced by the metallic substrate.

Measured according to the latest EC

Long-distance touring is what the R1100RT is all about, its large fairing with adjustable screen providing a level of protection unmatched by any other motorcycle.

177

Telelever

The progressive design of the four-valves-per-cylinder Boxer's running gear is hardly visible from the front, but stands out clearly from the side. The first feature to catch the eye is the BMW patented Telelever, an all-new front-wheel alignment and bearing system, providing a synthesis of the telescopic fork and swinging arm.

Design

With its main tube measuring only 35mm in diameter, the telescopic fork pivots on a ball joint in a slide tube, on the longitudinal control arm at the bottom, and a fork bridge within the frame of the motorcycle at the top. A central spring strut providing 120mm spring travel, measured perpendicular to the road, connects the longitudinal control arm with the front section of the frame. From the 1997 model year, the spring strut is infinitely adjustable on the output stroke by way of a bolt.

The telescopic fork shafts contain only fluid to lubricate the two tubes running inside one another, and no longer comprise any spring or damper components. As a result, the response of the telescopic fork to road and riding conditions is particularly smooth and soft, the fixed tubes running in slide bushes with Teflon coating for minimum friction.

The maintenance-free ball joints, running without any play within the slide tube and fork bridge, efficiently transmit the steering movements on the telescopic fork. The other ball joint bolted on to the longitudinal control arm feeds most of the forces generated when applying the brakes into the stable engine housing. The longitudinal control arm, in turn, is fitted on a swivel mount on either side of the engine housing; the telescopic fork on the BMW Telelever system is, therefore, only required for guiding the front wheel and for steering (the maximum lock angle is 32 degrees on each side).

Advantages

Compared with conventional wheel-guidance systems, the wheel-alignment geometry achieved substantially reduces the dive effect of the telescopic fork. It works like a mechanical anti-dive system, ensuring that spring travel remains adequate, even when braking in an extreme situation.

Even with the springs strongly compressed, the wheelbase and castor remain largely

Telelever keeps castor and wheelbase more or less constant over the entire suspension travel, even when the brakes are applied. Thus, the nose does not dive, as it does with conventional telescopic front forks.

unchanged throughout the motorcycle's spring travel. This guarantees superior stability in all situations, such as when applying the brakes in a bend.

The substantial overlap of the fixed-position tubes and long slide tubes further enhances the Telelever's outstanding stability.

The absence of fork springs helps to minimize frictional forces and ensures an excellent response of the telescopic fork.

Compared with a conventional telescopic fork, the centrally mounted spring strut allows greater flexibility in tuning the springs and dampers, and provides aprogressive kinematic response of the entire spring and damper system.

With its anti-dive and superior longitudinal rigidity, the BMW Telelever offers ideal conditions for anti-lock brakes and excellent ABS control.

Since the space between the front wheel and the engine is smaller than with a conventional telescopic fork, the entire power unit has been moved further to the front, providing optimum front-to-rear weight distribution (52.7 per cent at the front, 47.3 per cent at the rear).

The entire Telelever system requires no maintenance or oil change. Only the ball joints have to be checked after just over 62,000 miles (100,000km).

---

standard, the new four-valve-per-cylinder engine develops a noise level of 79dBA, the current limit being 80dBA.

Clutch and Gearbox

The clutch is a single-plate dry type with the lowest possible inertia for the maximum smoothness and case of gearshift. Made of metal plate, the flywheel incorporates the starter crown gear.

The dog-shift five-speed gearbox is derived from the type that has already proved itself in the K-series.

700W Alternator

The new generation of Boxer flat-twins comes with an alternator offering particularly high output. Operating with a regulator voltage of 14V, the new unit develops 50 amps equal to an output of no less than 700 watts. A particularly important point is that the new alternator generates a surplus output of up to 70 watts, even at idling speed, ensuring a very good battery charge at all times. This, in turn, makes sure that the motorcycle will always start easily, and at the same time gives the battery an extended service life.

THE CHASSIS

The chassis or 'running gear' on the new bikes was as interesting as the engine assembly. When the first model in the R259 line, the R1100RS, made its debut on the island of Lanzarote at the beginning of 1993, there were some real surprises in the area of the chassis.

At the time, the chassis design was totally different from that of other motorcycles. The flat-twin engine no longer has the traditional one-piece crankcase – the crankcases are vertically split in the

Endurance Racing an R1100RS

In 1997, an R1100RS finished second in the Twins/Triples/Single class of the British Endurance Racing Championship. Entered by the G-Force BMW Team, it was the brainchild of Pat Keenan, then working as a technician for dealers Heathrow BMW. Other like-minded individuals were recruited – Paul Kemp, service manager at Heathrow BMW, Nick Horley, managing director of London-based PR company Buffalo Communications, and George Mackintosh, managing director of Geoconference of Aberdeen and London. The team was formed in

G-Force Racing confounded the pundits by campaigning a R1100RS, scooping runner-up spot in their class in the five-round 1997 British Endurance Racing Series. Riders and pit crew after victory at one of the two Snetterton rounds.

September 1996, and all its members shared a burning desire to see the BMW marque back on the race circuit. All liked the concept of endurance racing, and BMW could boast a proud record in this sport. Keenan convinced the others that the R1100RS would be the most suitable of BMW's product range for this type of competition.

A start was made by purchasing a crashed R1100RS, with cosmetic damage only. Several companies, including BMW GB, came up with significant financial help in the form of sponsorship. Some of this money was spent on a performance-orientated 2–1–2 exhaust system, a one-off 35l aluminium fuel tank, and a programmable management system. Other items included a Premier refuelling kit (which proved a great asset), and a pair of beautifully crafted Harrison Six-Pot brake calipers. A special rear sub-frame was built, and this was mated to a fibreglass seat unit adapted to suit the sub-frame and the standard RS's original fairing (which BMW insisted the team retain, in order to keep the machine's identity). The original fuel tank had its base cut away and fitted over the new alloy component. The ABS system was removed to shed weight, and the original battery was dumped in favour of a smaller, lighter one, which was re-located under the seat tail-piece to ensure it was readily accessible.

The standard headlight was removed and its place used to house the Emerald programmable fuel and ignition ECU, and the fuel pump, fuses, and so on. This 'compartment' was then covered by the regulation race number-plate. This was quickly detachable to gain access to the vital parts, such as the ECU's communications lead, which provided an array of settings for fuel and ignition, allowing the bike to be tailored to individual tracks or weather conditions. This was the first time an Emerald system – originally designed for car racing – had been used on two wheels. Dave Emerald himself attended the meetings, to ensure everything went smoothly.

Pat Keenan leading a couple of other competitors accelerating away from Russells Corner, Snetterton, on the G-Force R1100RS.

Also of great service to the team were Ben Parry, a development engineer with Lotus Cars, and John Leon, who assisted Keenan in the meticulous rebuilding of the motorcycle prior to the season's racing.

After testing and dyno work, the initial target of 100bhp was achieved. No race circuits were available for track testing, so Bruntingthorpe Proving Ground was used for speed runs, and to ensure everything would hold together.

The G-Force team completed all five rounds of the championship – thirty-two hours in all. Their R1100RS won the first round (class), was winner of the BestPrepared Bike award at the next, and was awarded the prize for Exceptional Achievement of the Series. Had it not been for the need for a gearbox change (due to a bent selector) during the last round, the team would have won its class D category; instead of finishing runner-up. The season was a notable achievement for a remarkable near-standard sports tourer, not a race replica.

middle, and in two die-cast sections. The engine, coupled with the bolted-on gearbox serves as the main stressed section of the chassis, with no central frame section necessary. The entire front end of the frame is made of chill-cast aluminium for extra stability. Securely fastened to the engine housing, the front sub-frame holds the central spring strut of the Telelever in place. A rather basic tubular steel structure carries the seat, together with the top mount for the single rear suspension unit.

The most radical change was almost hidden by the sports fairing, although the telescopic forks looked fairly conventional. The aim was to split steering and suspension tasks between different components, as on a car's front axle; and the patented BMW Telelever system (see page 178) does indeed recall a car design. This, combined with the already established and patented BMW Paralever rear-wheel geometry (pioneered on the off-road GS 1000 models back in 1987), provides a quality of ride and suspension virtually unmatched by any other series production road-going motorcycle.

Four-Valve Single – The F650

The F650 Funduro, and its derivatives, has been one of BMW's success stories of the 1990s.

Launched in November 1993, it was also BMW's first major European joint venture in the motorcycle market, involving the German company, the Italian Aprilia motorcycle manufacturer, and the Austrian Bombardier Rotax engine-builder. Up to the end of 1997, some 45,000 examples had been sold worldwide.

BMW's idea was to introduce an entry-level model on to the market as quickly (and cheaply) as possible. Following initial discussions with potential system suppliers during the late 1980s, a vague idea slowly materialized into a fully fledged project. It was finalized by contract in Munich on 5 June 1993, and announced to the public via press release shortly afterwards.

The press release outlined that BMW would be taking responsibility for the new machine's styling, and for its technical concept, and that development would be undertaken by Aprilia at its modern plant in Noale. Power was to be provided by a four-valve Rotax engine displacing 652cc (100 x 83mm). Developed jointly by BMW and Rotax, the new liquid-cooled engine developed an output of 48bhp at 6,500rpm. Additionally, in accordance with the new two-tier driving licence regulations in Europe (also adopted in Britain from mid-1996), the F650 was also available restricted to 34bhp.

The F650 also broke new ground by being the first BMW motorcycle on which the rear wheel was not driven by shaft; instead, the 'Euro' single featured an 0-ring chain, in a logical decision for an engine with its crankshaft arranged crosswise to the direction of travel.

Other features of the F650 were its five-speed gearbox, dohc operated by chain balancer shaft, oil reservoir in the upper section of the tubular steel frame, twin 33-mm Mikuni carbs, twin spark plugs, stainless-steel exhaust system, 41-mm inverted front forks, single Showa rear shock absorbers, disc brakes front and rear, a 10,000-mile service internal, and a wide range of factory-approved accessories.

From 1925 through to 1966, BMW built no less than 230,000 single-cylinder motorcycles, ranging from 200 to 400cc. Therefore, although it was innovative in many areas, the F650 certainly did not break any new ground by being a vertical single, rather than a horizontally opposed twin.

The way it compensates for any conditions, from the slightest bump on the road through to exceedingly poor road surfaces, has to be experienced to be believed.

The R1100RS originally came with a 'three-quarter' fairing; later, as an option, BMW offered a section covering the area at the base of the cylinders. Fitted as standard, the 'three-quarter' type fairing has low air drag combined with relatively good protection from wind and weather, although not in the same class as the RT version. The drag coefficient of the standard-fitment fairing is (Cd x A) to 0.400 with the rider leaning forwards, and to 0.439 with the rider adopting an upright position.

All the fairing components are marked to indicate the specific type of synthetic material used, and can be completely recycled. The R1100RS is equipped with a 5.5-gallon (23-litre) fuel tank. A feature of all the new Boxers carried forward from the K1100 series is the combined ignition/handlebar lock in the upper fork bridge, allowing the front wheel to be secured both in left and right-hand lock after removal of the key. The latest improvement is the use of the two-sided key, which may be inserted into the lock on either side. The same key also fits the tank cap and set lock, while panniers may be ordered, with the locks allowing the rider to use one key all round.

One of the most outstanding innovations on the R1100RS is the ergonomics package fitted as standard. The machine can be modified individually to suit the individual rider, use and conditions. In all, there are three parts of the ergonomics package:

1. Adjustable fairing windshield.
The fairing windshield (screen) is adjustable through a range of 20 degrees by means of a rotating knob, and is streamlined to minimize drag resistance. The lowest position is intended above all for cruising on highways and country roads, while the topmost position offers optimum wind protection at high speeds.

2. Adjustable handlebar.
Incorporating forged precision teeth, the adjustment mechanism allows adjustment of the handlebar in seven stages by up to æin (20mm), plus three adjustment angles at increments of 6 degrees. The adjustment mechanism is easily accessible, by loosening one bolt.

3. Adjustable seat.
The adjustable seat is sub-divided into two sections. The rider's section may be adjusted in three stages by a total of 1.5in (40mm), allowing the rider to choose a seat height of 31in (780mm), 32in (800mm), or 32æin (820mm).

Instrumentation

The conventional instrumentation includes speedo and tacho, and also a series of the usual warning lights, such as direction

(Above) BMW's F650 engine, built by Rotax, assembled into the bike by Aprilia and sold as a BMW.

A joint venture between BMW, Aprilia and Rotax, the F650 Funduro single has been another four-valve success story for the German marque.

Battle of the Legends

Daytona International Speedway, Florida, where the Legends race series was staged

For several years, BMW of North America has supported racing at the legendary Daytona international speedway in Florida. at first by sponsoring the Daytona BMW Classic Cup Races. Also supported by AHRMA (American Historic Racing Motorcycle Association), the Classic Cup Races were open to all makes of machinery and attracted a vast number of competitors. The success of this series encouraged BMW to back an event for its own brand and, one day in early March 1992, ten riders – all famous names from the past – lined up on the Daytona tarmac ready to do battle. They rode identical R100R flat-twins, and all wore the same bright-red leathers!

According to Daytona Cycle Week's executive director Jeff Smith, the concept behind the BMW-only race was that the riders should get back on the track and have a good time, and most of all enjoy themselves.

The next Battle of the Legends took place on 1 March 1993. The impressive entry list read like a Who's Who of motorcycling, including eight-times world champion Phil Read from England; four-times world champion Walter Villa from Italy; two-times world champion Hugh Anderson; BMW's road-racing star of the early post-war period, Walter Zeller; former Kawasaki star, French-Canadian Yvon DuHamel; plus a host of famous Americans, including Gary Nixon, Don Vesco, Roger Reiman, Bart Markel, Dave Aldana and Jay Springsteen.

With the introduction of the new R1100RS by 1994, the Legends continued to grow in stature and spectator interest, and the machines continued to be entirely stock.

By 1995, the 'race' had become a well-attended three-day competition and a major highlight of Daytona's Motorcycle Week. No less than eleven former North American racing champions competed against each other in three heats. It was all highly organized, down to every detail of bike and rider. BMW of North America prepared the bikes with sponsorship now coming from Forbes FYI magazine. Winner after the three heats was 54-year-old Gary Nixon, the 1967 Daytona 200 winner, two-time AMA Grand National Champion and former Transatlantic Match Race series captain for the Americans. Sadly missed in 1995 was Walter Zeller, who had died a month before the event.

Keenly watching proceedings, as the old-timers fought it out on the track, were several personalities, including former car and motorcycle world champion John Surtees (still a great bike enthusiast), who also helped present the awards, together with publisher Steve Forbes.
The BMW Legends series continued until 1997.

indicators, idling speed, high-beam, fuel reserve (as soon as the level has dropped to approximately 1 gallon/4 litres), oil pressure, battery and ABS. BMW has also provided a rider information panel (housed in the offside interior fairing panel); this LCD (liquid crystal display) indicates the oil temperature, fuel level, time, and gear. The matching fairing panel on the near side houses three switches, for the hazard warning flashers, heated handlebar grips and ABS cancellation switch, standard since the 1994 model year.

Performance

Producing 90bhp at 7,250rpm, with maximum torque of 70ft/lb (95Nm) at 5,500rpm, the R1100RS has a capacity of 1085cc (90 x 70.5mm). Official BMW sources quote the R1100RS as having a maximum speed of 'over 125mph (200kph)', but this is clearly conservative, to say the least. *Motor Cycle News* electronically timed their test machine at 134mph (214.5kph) in their 26 January 1994 issue. It is also worth noting that the new R259 series engine can take up to 10,000 miles (16000km) to become fully bedded in. This is due in large part to the cylinder-coating process. A good quality non-synthetic oil should be used during those first important miles.

In the USA, Japan and Australia, as well as in several European countries, the R1100RS was voted 'Motorcycle of the Year'.

By autumn 1997, production of the R1100RS amounted to more than 22,000 examples.

THE R1100R AND R850R

The next model in the four-valve-per-cylinder line was the R1100GS (see Chapter 9), which was first shown at the Frankfurt Show in September 1993, and went on sale the following spring. BMW introduced the R1100R, the third model in the new Boxer generation and its smaller brother, the R850R, in autumn 1994; they were BMW's first all-new machines for years to have no form of fairing.

Engine, Suspension and Brakes

At the heart of both bikes was the essentially the same fuel-injected, shaft drive and air-/oil-cooled four-valve flat-twin engine that had already powered the RS sports tourer and the GS enduro. Both machines also used the pioneering Telelever front suspension system, Paralever rear suspension, and digital electronic ignition, BMW's adjustable riding position, and optional catalytic converter. ABS brakes were optional on the 850, and standard on the 1100.

The R1100R's power-plant, displacing 1085cc, was most closely related to that of the softer-tuned R1100GS. Like the GS, the

Technical Specifications 1998

		R1100RS	R1100RT
Engine			
Cubic capacity	cc	1085	
Bore/stroke	mm	99/70.5	
Max output	kW/bhp	66/90 at 7250 rpm	
Max torque	Nm	95 at 5500 rpm	
Design		Flat-twin	
No of cylinders		2	
Compression ratio/fuel grade		10.7/S	
Valve control		HC	
Valves per cylinder		4	
Intake/outlet dia	mm	36/31	
Fuel supply		Motronic MA 2.2.	
Electrical System			
Alternator	W	700	
Battery	V/Ah	12/19	
Headlight	W	H 4 55/60	
Starter	kW	1.1	
Transmission			
Gearbox			
Gear ratios	I	4.16/2.81	4.16/2.91
	II	2.91/2.81	2.91/2.91
	III	2.13/2.81	2.13/2.91
	IV	1.74/2.81	1.74/2.91
	V	1.45/2.81	1.45/2.91
Suspension			
Rear-wheel drive		BMW Paralever	
Clutch		Single-plate dry clutch rotating in opposite direction, dia 180mm	
Type of frame		Tubular space frame, engine serving as load-bearing component	
Spring travel front/rear	mm	120/135	120/135
Wheel castor	mm	111	122
Wheelbase	mm	1473	1485
Steering assembly angle	degrees	65.9	62.8
Brakes	Front	dual-disc brake, dia 305mm	dual-disc brake, dia 305mm
	Rear	Single-disc brake, dia 285mm	single-disc brake, dia 276mm

Wheels		Light-alloy	
	Front	3.50–17	
	Rear	4.50–18	
Tyres	Front	120/70 – Zr 17	
	Rear	160/60 – Zr 18	
Dimensions and weights			
Length, overall	mm	2175	2195
Width with mirrors	mm	920	898
Handlebar width	mm	738	898
Seat height	mm	780/800/820	780/800/820
Weight, unladen with full tank	kg		239 282
Max permissible weight	kg	450	490
Fuel tank	ltr	23	26
Performance			
Fuel consumption			
90km/h (56mph)	ltr	4.3	4.7
120 km/h (75mph)	ltr	5.2	5.6
Acceleration			
0–100 km/h (62mph)	sec	4.1	4.3
standing-start km	sec	23.7	24.3
Top speed	km/h	215 (134mph)	196 (122mph)

R's engine was designed not so much for maximum power but for grunty mid-range and low-down torque. The R produced 80bhp at a relatively laid-back 6,750rpm. Maximum torque was very slightly up on the RS, at an unchanged 5,250rpm. The R850R was a smaller-bore (87.5mm) version of the same engine (the stroke remaining changed), producing a maximum output of 70bhp at 7,000rpm, with maximum torque of 57ft/lb (77Nm) at 5,500rpm.

Both bikes featured the hi-rise stainless-steel exhaust system as specified for the R1100GS, but instead of the integral oil cooler beneath the headlight, both roadsters came equipped with a pair of small oil coolers fitted above each cylinder.

Styling

Styling was quirky. Functional, maybe, but certainly not pretty. There was a rounded-steel $4\frac{1}{2}$-gallon (21-litre) tank, together with a new two-piece seat designed to offer both rider and passenger maximum space and comfort. With the adjustable seat on the lowest setting, the two R models were the most accommodating of the new-generation Boxers for shorter riders. The seat height was variable from just 30in (760mm) to 32in (800mm). Both bikes were fitted with rubber-mounted forged aluminium 29-in (729-mm) handlebars and a hydraulic steering damper.

The speedo (there was no tacho on the

original launch model) and warning-lights console sat above the chrome-rimmed 6-in (160-mm) headlamp; a tacho and clock were optional extras. British-specification R850Rs featured wire wheels (of the type used on the R1100GS), but the three-spoke alloy wheels, standard on the 1100R, were available as an option.

When the motorcycles first went on sale in the UK, the R850R cost £6,795, the R1100R £7,795. Up to the autumn of 1997, production of these unfaired roadster models totalled more than 23,000 units.

CHANGES FOR 1997 AND 1998

In spring 1997, both versions were given a new face and a new cockpit. Since then, they have also featured a larger 6-in (170-mm) headlight, which was chrome-plated, including the shell which had formerly been painted silver. The headlight support and the all-new instrument support were made of aluminium; the chrome-plated instrument console housed not only the speedometer, but also the tachometer, now fitted as standard. Right at the top in the middle was a small analogue-face clock which, like the other two instruments, was surrounded by a polished stainless-steel ring.

Entering the 1998 model year, more changes have been made to the two road-sters. The rear-view mirrors and their supporting arms, as well as the handlebar weights, are now chrome-plated, while the brake and clutch levers, the passenger grab handle and oil-cooler covers are finished in silver paintwork. The footrest plate comes in a silver powder coating polished at the surface, and the rear frame section is also finished in silver powder. The direction indicator flasher housings and their support arms are in white aluminium paintwork.

COMPARING THE R1100R WITH THE R850R

So, what are these two roadsters like out on the street?

At first sight, the R850R looks like more or less the same motorcycle as the R1100R, offering a cheaper insurance premium and a slightly lower purchase price than the bigger version. In fact, it is the better of the two models and, as has so often been the case in the past (for example, the 1970s' R80 compared with the larger R100), it offers the better balance of performance and pleasure from the flat-twin configuration. Although its top speed is lower, at 118mph (189kph), compared with the bigger bike's theoretical 125mph (200kph), the rider is hard pressed to spot the difference. As *Motor Cycle News* found in its 14 December 1994 test, the R850R put out a genuine 75bhp, seven points up on the manufacturer's claim and only 5bhp less than the larger-engined model. At the test track, MCN proved that the 0–60mph time was only 0.2 seconds slower than that of the 1100 (4.1 seconds compared with 3.9 seconds).

The technical differences between the 850 and its larger brother are worth noting. BMW fitted a 3.36:1 secondary ratio on the 850's gearbox, compared to the R1100R's 3.0:1 set-up, giving the 850 slightly lower gearing. Of course, this means higher revs throughout the range and in top (fifth) gear, the 850 can be made to exceed the red line without too much effort. However, it also means that all the gear ratios are close together, improving acceleration. In fact, the differences in maxi-mum speed are immaterial because, without a fairing, any speed above 90mph (145kph) is simply too hard work.

To re-work the R as an 850, BMW reduced the bore (which led to lighter pistons), and made certain other modifications too. The lighter pistons mean that weight could be saved on the crankshaft and the out-of-balance forces are significantly reduced. Valve diameters are also reduced on the 850, with the inlet and exhaust 4mm smaller, at 32mm and 27mm respectively.

MCN ended its test by saying, 'The R850R undercuts its big brother by £1000 exactly – without any significant disadvantages. The handling agility of the 1100 is retained, the performance loss is barely noticeable in everyday riding, and the engine runs more sweetly. The bike doesn't look pretty, but it is distinctive, important when so many modern machines are getting so bland.

ANOTHER WINNER FOR BMW?

The R1100RT

The fourth and, perhaps, the final version of the 1100-series four-valve-per-cylinder boxer, the RT, made its world debut at the Frankfurt Show in September 1995. According to many people, this de luxe touring mount is the finest of the bunch, making the best use of the design's strong points.

Author and long-term BMW enthusiast Bruce Preston, testing the new R1100RT in the January 1996 issue of *Motorcycle Sport* had this to say: 'As always, I left my old R80RT at Bracknell [BMW's UK headquarters], so I had an immediate opportunity to compare the two. In truth there is no comparison, for the 13 years since my own bike was made have seen tremendous progress in so many aspects of motorcycling. As well as the aforementioned suspension system, the brakes have improved beyond recognition. Now they are Brembos using drilled twin discs front with

four-piston calipers, single disc rear, streets ahead of the twin front discs on my own machine. I made a mental note to take it easy when I collected my own bike; the last time I barely stopped at the first junction, such was the difference between the brakes of the new Boxer I had just returned and my own bike's! That's progress for you!'

Author's Impressions

The features of the R1100RT that impressed me most were the adjustable seat height (only for the rider); the ultra-powerful alternator capacity (three times more than old two-valve Boxers); the adjustable electric screen (not a first, as Suzuki debuted the concept on their GSX1100F sports tourer several year ago); the comprehensive fairing; the levers inside the fairing, which allow ducted hot air to be directed to the rider's torso; heated handlebar grips (probably BMW's most worthwhile and, at just over £100, most cost-effective option); the riding position; the large 5-gallon (26-litre) fuel tank, giving an effective range of over 250 miles (400km); the ease, for its size, of getting the bike on its centre stand; the side stand operation (possible without having to dismount); the mirrors, which double as hand protectors; and the general style and look of the machine. However, most impressive of all is its ability, as the October 1995 issue of *Ride* magazine said: 'For a tourer the RT can turn up the wick, but what really compresses journey times is the vast, police-like presence.'

On the minus side, the pillion section of the seat is not good enough – quite simply, the general view is that it is too hard for long trips; lack of self-cancelling indicators (strangely, as they are standard on the K-series); a dip beam which is too wide; a gear change which still requires a thoughtful

ABS II

BMW's second-generation ABS II was first introduced on the R1100RS, followed by the K1100 four-cylinder series. From the 1998 model year, virtually all the four-valve Boxer twins have ABS II as standard equipment (but do check a particular model and its market before purchase).

The highly efficient Brembo brake system is the same as on the K100 models, meaning that the front wheel features the same hydraulically operated double-disc brake with four-piston fixed calipers. Mounted in floating arrangement, the stainless-steel discs, with compensation for uneven wear and sintered metal brake linings to eliminate fading even in wet conditions, measure 305mm in diameter and 5mm across. The swept area is 100cm2, brake piston diameter 32 and 34mm, respectively.

The rear wheel features a single-disc brake with two-piston fixed calipers (38mm diameter). The disc measures 285mm in diameter and 5mm in width; its total swept area is 40cm2. BMW ABS anti-lock brakes are available as an option, and significantly increase safety when applying the brakes.

The various components – brake discs with gear sets, sensors and calipers, pressure modulator and control unit.

approach – it clunks if it is rushed; and a fuel gauge that tends to disappear far more rapidly once the half-empty reading has been reached. When the bike is fully laden and carrying a pillion, the centre stand digs in too early on left-handers, and even raising the rear end with the hydraulic pre-load adjuster doesn't entirely cure this trait.

One final point is that in place of 'RT' the name should really have the initials 'GT', for the motorcycle is indeed a 'Grand Tourer'.

In common with all the four-valve Boxers, the RT is not at its best at very low speeds, where a certain amount of jerkiness is experienced when going on or off the throttle. The motor also tends to shudder when pulling away in top gear below 3,000rpm. In every other part of its make-up, the RT's road behaviour is really superb.

When cruising between 45mph and 80mph (70-130kph), all is well, but above or below these figures (in top), a certain amount of roughness is detectable. Because of the handling – the Telelever front end separating braking and suspension – superb brakes and excellent riding position, it is possible to cruise safely just below 80mph (130kph) day and night, with the fierce headlight on main beam. The front-end dive while braking, which is often experienced on other machines, is not there on the RT.

BMW's ABS II is fitted as standard to several of the four-valve Boxer twins. There are sensor and gear sets on the front brake.

Four Anniversary Models Celebrate 75 Years of BMW Motorcycles

In 1998 BMW motorcycles celebrated their 75th Anniversary. To mark this event, four anniversary models were introduced; since the history of BMW motorcycles started back in 1923 with the flat-twin engined R32, it was appropriate that the anniversary models were all Boxers.

The special R1100R and R1100GS models arrived in dealer showrooms during March, shortly followed by the Anniversary R1100RS and R1100RT. The new bikes featured special colour schemes, incorporating the 75th Anniversary logo, as well as an enhanced standard equipment specification, including heated grips and pannier frames.

Prices remained the same as existing models, offering prospective owners of 75th Anniversary models even greater value for money. All owners received a commemorative certificate of origin, a high quality album of the history of BMW motorcycles, a leather key case and a 75th Anniversary lapel pin.

R1100R   Special paint   £8,430.00

     Night Black (730)
     Heated grips
     Pannier frames
     Alloy wheels (not spokes as shown)

R1100GS   Special paint   £9,335.00

     Marrakesh Red/Alpine White(737)
     Heated grips
     Pannier frames

R1100R 75th Anniversary, one of four special models produced by the company to celebrate the occasion (the others were the R1100RS, R1100RT and R1100GS). Models imported into the UK came with cast alloy wheels, not the spoked type shown in the photograph.

R1100RS   Special paint   £10,395.00

     Marrakesh Red/Arctic Silver (738)
     Heated grips
     Pannier frames

R1100RT   Special paint   £10,895.00

     Arctic Silver (705)
     Heated grips
     Radio preparation with speakers
     And second socket
     Seat and knee pads in Red or Black
     (please specify)

R1100RS 75th Anniversary model, launched March 1998. It has special paint in Marrakesh Red and Arctic silver ñ heated handlebar grips and pannier frames.

12 C for Cruiser

In June 1997, an event occurred that was unique in BMW's motorcycling history. The German company launched its very own cruiser, or easy-rider chopper. The launch, attended by the world's motorcycling press, took place in Tucson, Arizona, and the machine in question was the new R1200C.

The answer to the obvious question – why? – is simple.

During the late 1980s and the 1990s, various changes have taken place in the world motorcycle market, including the fact that sales of supersports bikes have dropped from 36 per cent to 21 per cent, while those in the cruiser sector have jumped from 18 per cent to 33 per cent. This trend is particularly clear in the two biggest markets, the USA and Germany; sales in the States have virtually doubled, from 58,000 to more than 100,000 units, while in Germany the number of cruisers sold has increased five-fold, from 8,000 to a staggering 40,000. It was clear that BMW had to respond to such a staggering increase in its own market, and the R1200C was the result of this realization.

EVOLUTION OF THE CRUISER

How did the custom cruiser evolve into what it is today?

Traditionally, many American bikes were

Tucson, Arizona was the venue for a unique event in BMW's motorcycling history – the launch of the R1200C, its very own cruiser.

R1200C

Engine

Type:	Four-stroke flat-twin
Valves:	Four per cylinder
Displacement:	1170cc
Bore and stroke:	101 x 73mm
Power output:	61bhp at 5,000rpm
Torque:	98Nm at 3,000rpm
Compression ratio:	10.0:1
Cooling:	Air/oil
Valve gear:	HC (high camshaft)
Fuel system:	Bosch Motronic MA 2.4
Catalytic converter:	Closed-loop, three-way, with metal monolith

Largest BMW flat-twin ever, the R1200C engine displaces 1170 (101 x 73mm), and produces 61bhp at a leisurely 5,000rpm.

Transmission

Clutch:	Single dry plate
Gearbox:	Five-speed
Overall ratio:	1st, 2.045; 2nd 1.600; 3rd 1.267; 4th 1.038; 5th 0.800
Final drive ratio:	1.2.54

Electrics

Engine management:	Bosch Motronic MA 2.4
Alternator:	700 watt
Battery:	12 volt, 19 amp hour

Frame and Running Gear

Frame;	Cat alloy front section
Front fork:	BMW Telelever with central suspension unit and anti-dive geometry
Front suspension travel:	144mm
Rear swinging arm:	Monolever
Drive:	Shaft
Rear suspension unit:	Mono, central
Rear suspension travel:	100mm
Brakes:	Front: dual 305mm floating discs, 4-piston fixed calipers
	Rear: single 285mm disc, with 2-piston floating caliper
Brake pads:	Sintered metallic (organic at rear)
Wheels:	Cross-spoke
Tyres:	Front: 100/90–18 tubeless
	Rear: 170/80–15 tubeless

Dimensions and Weight

Fuel tank capacity:	17 litres (3.2 gallons)
Seat height (at unladen weight):	740mm
Unladen weight, ready for road:	563lb (256kg)
Gross weight limit:	990lb (450kg)

Performance and FuelConsumption

Maximum speed:	105mph (168kph)
Fuel type:	Super (premium), unleaded, 95 octane (RON)

built and styled for long-distance touring and comfort; mudguards were deeply valanced, there were side-section 'balloon' tyres, and broad saddles. Handlebars were massive, and windshields, saddlebags and crash bars were very much part of the standard specification. The rider's feet rested not on pegs, as was the European practice, but on long, wide boards instead.

During the early post-war era it was discovered that, by junking all the unnecessary paraphernalia and substituting lighter components for the major bike, the Harley-Davidson or Indian rider could reduce his bike's overall weight by as much as 110lb (50kg). Small solo seats from a flat-track racer, a tiny peanut tank, straight-thru pipes, a total absence of front mudguarding, and narrower handlebars transformed the big 'hog' image into something more like imported European machinery. These early V-twins – their back bulk and unwanted equipment sliced – were nicknamed 'bobbed-jobs'. Later, the term 'chopping' was borrowed from the hot-rod fraternity.

Once established, the 'chopped' motorcycle quickly developed further and further from convention. The 'chopper' was still basically a 'bobbed-job'; the extensive use of chrome plate and garish paint designs was a legacy of the hot-rod days of the 1950s. Soon, high-rise 'ape hangers', back rests named 'sissy-bars', and extended front forks, hard tail and soft tail (denoting if the frame was rigid or sprung), and a host of other more minor alterations became part of the chopper's armoury.

Bike artist Dave Mann depicted the chopper as a long, lean warhorse, a motorcycle which looked aggressive even when stationary. Mann was largely responsible for creating the chopper on canvas, for others to create into reality out on the street.

Actually getting a 'Dave Mann look' was not always possible. Few owner-builders had the expertise (let alone the facilities) to extend a front end, or give a frame additional rake. A new cottage industry was born, producing everything for the custom freak, from King and Queen seats through to peanut tanks, and even complete bikes and, sometimes, trikes! By the mid-1970s, customizing had become a multi-million dollar business, with the chopper (now rapidly becoming known as the 'cruiser') an accepted feature of the bike world. The first manufacturers – the American Harley-Davidson and

Standard equipment

• Integrated ignition switch and steering lock (handlebars can be locked while turned to left or right)
• One-key system
• Handbrake lever with four-position adjustment
• Clutch lever with four-position adjustment
• Side (prop) stand with safety starter cut-out (engine can run in neutral when stand is extended, but stops if a gear is selected)
• Complete stainless-steel exhaust system with additional chrome-plated finish
• Exhaust emission control by closed-loop, three-way catalytic converter
• Two-section seat (pillion seat also acts as backrest for solo rider)
• Real leather set upholstery and handlebar grips
• Raised, single-piece steel tube handlebar
• Oil cooler integrated into front section of frame
• Telelever front suspension
• Monolever rear suspension
• Hazard warning flashers

Optional Extras

• ABS II (anti-lock braking system)
• Heated handlebar grips
• Low handlebar
• Seat and grips in Canyon brown with all paint finishes
• Seat and grips in black with ivory paint finish (no pinstriping)

The R1200C has lots of extra polished chrome and alloy; no tacho is deemed necessary for what is, after all, a cruising machine.

Japanese Kawasaki marques – now came on to the scene to sell factory-built customs. Soon, others were to follow, and in 1997 BMW joined in.

THE BMW CONCEPT

With the cruiser segment rapidly growing in size and significance, it was obvious that BMW should take a look at the cruiser too. It was also clear from the start of investigations that a BMW cruiser had to have two cylinders, and that these cylinders should not be arranged in the typical V-configuration to be found in nearly all other cruisers on the market.

After launching its four-valve R1100RS sports tourer in the spring of 1993, as the first model in the new Boxer generation, BMW completed the range by autumn 1995 with the enduro roadster and touring models so typical of the marque. All these models had been planned from the outset. A cruiser had not been planned, but one was now added into the four-valve concept. It was very much the idea of Dr Walter Hasselkus, who was appointed the new president of BMW's motorcycle division in autumn 1993, and is now seen as the 'god-

father' of the BMW R1200C. In 1994, the board of management of BMW AG at the Munich headquarters gave their approval, and the project was given the code-name R259C within the company. The man charged with bringing the concept through to production was David Robb, an ex-Audi and Chrysler car designer who had worked at BMW since 1984, and had transferred to the motorcycle design studio in 1993.

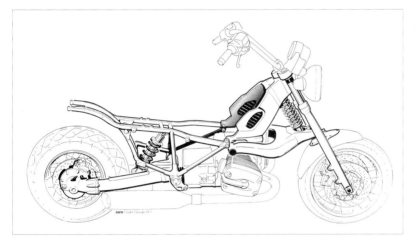

This view of the R1200C's chassis shows why the machine is so low.

BMW had been influenced by the rapid rise in sales of custom-type machine in its two major markets, the USA and Germany. On the home market, the number of cruisers sold has increased five-fold over a decade.

BMW Cruiser Rider Equipment and Lifestyle Products

BMW Cruiser	MAVERICK suit in jeans look, men's and women's
BMW Cruiser	CANYON two-piece leather suit, men's and women's
BMW Cruiser	ENDEAVOUR three-piece leather suit, women's
BMW Cruiser	LEATHERS leather waistcoat for men and women
BMW Cruiser	TWISTER windbreaker for men and women
BMW Cruiser	DUSTY light overcoat for men and women
BMW Cruiser	RAMBLER boots, full-length
BMW Cruiser	RANGER gloves, brown or black
BMW Cruiser	INDIAN SUMMER gloves, black
BMW Cruiser	shirt for men and women
BMW Cruiser	T-shirt, unisex
BMW Cruiser	T-shirt, women's
BMW Cruiser	sweater
BMW Cruiser	baggage roll
BMW Cruiser	rucksack
BMW Cruiser	lighter
BMW Cruiser	sunglasses
BMW Cruiser	cap
BMW Cruiser	pocket watch
BMW Cruiser	bandana
BMW Cruiser	leather belt
BMW Cruiser	braces
BMW Cruiser	lapel pin
BMW Cruiser	tie pin
BMW Cruiser	motorcycling goggles
BMW Cruiser	helmet

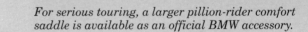

For serious touring, a larger pillion-rider comfort saddle is available as an official BMW accessory.

The Engine

BMW's engine specialists realized that, while the Boxer in its conventional form was perfectly adequate for its other roles, it was not suitable for the new cruiser. Their first and most important move in creating what they considered was the right kind of power base was to increase engine capacity; the engine of a real cruiser can never be too large. By increasing the bore from 99 to 101mm, and the stroke from 70.5 to 73mm, they were able to beef up the original power unit from 1085cc to 1170cc. In the process, they created the largest BMW motorcycle engine ever built.

The most obvious advantage of this modification was the effect on the torque curve, which one magazine described as 'like the back of a buffalo'. Another advantage was that, with such an abundance of torque, the engineering team was able to dispense with the need for a rev counter.

Accessories

- Pillion-rider comfort saddle
- Handrail for pillion passenger
- Cylinder guards
- Power socket with cover
- Saddlebags
- Saddlebag holders
- Inner bags

The standard pillion pad can double as a rider's backrest when needed.

Valve Diameter

The specification of the inlet valves on the R1200C is 34mm, the exhaust valves 29mm, as opposed to 36mm and 31mm, respectively, on the R1100RS.

New Camshaft Profile

The valve timing on the R1200C is 256 degrees, compared with 300 degrees on the R1100RS; the R1200C has a shorter valve stroke (inlet and exhaust, 8.23mm), compared with measurements of 9.85mm for the inlet, and 9.4mm for the exhaust, on the R1100RS.

Inlet System

The inlet manifold diameter measures 38mm, compared with 50mm on the R1100RS, ensuring optimum torque. A differing feature in this context is the configuration of the throttle butterfly manifolds (35mm in diameter, compared with 50mm on the R1100RS), which are connected to one anoth-

er and integrated in the inlet system to provide sufficient space for an automatic choke function. Accordingly, the R1200C, just like the four-cylinder K1200RS, is able to do without the usual choke lever on the handlebars.

THE BOSCH MOTRONIC ENGINE MANAGEMENT SYSTEM

New programming of the engine management system ensures a significant improvement of the special Motronic control concept (MA 2.4 as on the K1200RS) and, accordingly, a torque curve optimized for maximum torque at low engine speeds.

Performance

The power figures of 61bhp at only 5,000rpm may not appear very impressive on paper, but the way this power is delivered is what really matters out in the real world – on the street. In real-life cruising, the rider needs lots of power available whenever necessary, and supreme torque at low

The Cruiser Lifestyle

To many, the custom cruiser style of biking is a way of life, around which a cult has built up. The accent is on freedom. The film *Easy Rider* (1969), with its chopped Harley-Davidsons and breathtaking American landscapes, contemporary soundtrack and two of the most superbly customized machines ever seen on the big screen, caused a whole generation to convert, almost overnight, to a new sub-culture. The film fed fantasies depicting the customized cruiser life as one in which the sun always shone, the air was clean and the highways stretched on for as far as the eye could see, a straight arrow of asphalt unfolding into the distance.

The US, with its long, straight highways, is where the BMW cruiser is at its very best.

It is probably true that most of the followers of the custom cult either owned, have owned or still aspire to own a 'Hog' – Harley-speak for one of the much-revered V-twins built in Milwaukee, Wisconsin. As Harley-Davidson expert David K. Wright wrote: 'You don't just show up on a Harley. You arrive.' It's all a matter of presence. Owning a Harley, or any custom bike, is a statement. The rider wants to be noticed as an individual, and to live his or her life in an unconventional way.

Harleys do not remain standard for very long after they have left the factory. Each is personalized with either parts from HD's giant customising catalogue, or just as likely items from one of countless specialist after market goodies are added. Then there's the little matter of customising the owner and his passenger with jewellery, clothing and tattoos, or 'skin art'.

Harley-Davidson's clothing and accessories list makes almost as much money as its bike manufacturing arm. It includes items from designer sunglasses and expensive watches, to art trinkets, top-quality clothing, and much more. For some people, the machine, it seems, is almost incidental.

It is not hard to see the potential of this new market into which BMW has tapped by launching the R1200C. With BMW's name and prestige, the German marque is likely to be challenging established custom kings Harley-Davidson more quickly than many might have thought possible.

speeds. This is precisely why the R1200C engine develops its peak torque of 72ft/lb (98Nm) at just 3,000rpm. Throughout the entire range, from 2,500 to 4,500rpm, the rider consistently has in excess of 66ft/lb (90Nm) at his or her fingertips as soon as the throttle is fully opened.

Useful power and torque of the R1200C's engine extends from 1,500rpm all the way to 6,500rpm, if necessary. This means that, when riding in fifth (top) gear, the rider can accelerate smoothly from as low as 30mph (50kph) right through to the machine's maximum speed of more than 100mph (160kph). A laid-back style of riding can therefore be adopted – quite the opposite of the style used to ride a supersports machine.

To underline further the relaxed nature of the R1200C at low engine speeds, BMW's engine specialists added another technical feature. By significantly increasing the centrifugal mass on the crankdrive, they succeeded in giving the flat-twin a superior smoothness and refinement from just over 1,000rpm.

The R1200C has a twin tail pipe exhaust and a standard fitment three-way catalytic converter, which ensures that the new Boxer meets all noise and emissions regulations worldwide. A new five-speed gearbox (derived from the new six-speed K1200 unit) is harnessed via a hydraulic single-plate clutch.

Motorcycle Sport & Leisure achieved an average fuel consumption of 53mpg over 175 miles at the official launch in Tucson. The motorcycle has a galvanized steel 3.2-gallon (17-litre) tank with a gallon (4-litre) reserve.

Frame, Wheels and Brakes

Manufactured completely in stainless steel and finished in bright chrome, the entire exhaust is not only rustproof but offers a long service life. The exhaust pipes feature inner and outer walls. The insulating effect of this not only avoids discolouring (a problem on many older BMWs), but also keeps exhaust temperature upstream of the catalytic converter at a maximum, in the interest of a faster and better catalyst response.

A substantial cast-alloy frame runs from the steering head to the rear Telelever pivot, and is joined to a tubular steel rear sub-frame using the engine and gearbox as a stressed member. Rear suspension is taken care of by an extra-long Monolever unit, with a single-sleeve gas pressure damper and pre-load adjuster spring. Up front, BMW's Telelever system has a castor angle of 29.5 degrees, giving trail of just 86m, which is decidedly short in relation to the elongated wheelbase of 66in (1650mm), about 7in (177mm) more than the R1100R.

BMW has continued its excellent cross-spoked wire wheels, where the spokes connect to the outside of the rim and permit the use of tubeless tyres. The development team spent a considerable amount of time making sure it came up with the correct rubber; the front wheel (rim dimensions of 2.50 x 18) comes with a relatively slender 100/90–18 tyre, while the rear rim (4.00 x 15) runs a much broader 170/80–15 tyre.

Although dynamic riding characteristics are not so significant on a motorcycle of this type, BMW still considered it vital to provide powerful brakes. Thus the R1200C comes with a pair of drilled stainless-steel 305-mm discs on the front wheel measuring, as on the R1100GS. Brembo four-piston fixed calipers bite on to these, interacting with the single 285-mm rear disc, which features a two-piston floating caliper (also from the R1100GS). ABS is an optional extra.

Styling

Despite the compact appearance of BMW's cruiser, certain points and spaces have

Bond Success

Death-defying stunt scenes, and a stunning chase sequence are all part of BMW's R1200C's starring role in the 1997 James Bond film, *Tomorrow Never Dies*, which hit British screens in mid-December 1997. In an action-packed chase sequence, 007 (Pierce Brosnan) roars through packed city streets, with a helicopter in hot pursuit and his Kung Fu co-star (Michelle Yeoh) handcuffed to his wrist.

Stunt director Vic Armstrong has revealed that the scene took nine weeks to film at Pinewood Studios in St Albans, Hertfordshire. There, the crew re-created Ho Chi Minh City for the film. Armstrong went on to say that he was 'against having a bike chase, because good guys always escape on a bike. So, to make sure our film was different, we used the biggest and newest bike BMW could supply.' According to the film's producer, the stylish BMW was the perfect co-star for Brosnan, who did much of the stunt work himself.

For the potentially dangerous stunt work, Armstrong called in French jump legend Jean-Pierre Goy. Brosnan must have heaved a sigh of relief as Goy was blasted out of a tall building and shot over a helicopter!

Before work on the movie began, many observers thought that no cruiser would be up to the task, but the BMW proved entirely suitable. It surprised many, with its combination of easy-to-use power, safe handling and excellent brakes; certainly, no other custom cruiser would have coped as well.

In the feature film Tomorrow Never Dies, *James Bond (Pierce Brosnan) fights the baddies aboard a R1200C, with Chinese agent Wai Lin (co-star Michelle Yeoh).*

intentionally been left open to create a certain look when the R1200C is seen in silhouette from the side. Being able to see the Telelever spring components at the front, and the Monolever at the rear, gives a feeling of lightness, or of a machine reduced to the essential. The same goes for the materials used on the machine. These were selected not just for the specific purpose they have to fulfil, but also with regard for design and appearance. After all, a custom cruiser is about style above all else.

In common with Harley-Davidson, the BMW marque has a number of vital assets that it can use to encourage riders to buy into the laid-back lifestyle – its name, an engine layout which is automatically associated with the marque, aggressive lines and, most of all, 'street credibility'. BMW also has the advantage of a reputation for excellent finish and, clearly, so many plated and polished parts on a custom bike are vitally important in terms of customer satisfaction and pride of ownership.

The high cruiser handlebars on the R1200C are manufactured of 25-mm high-gloss chrome-plated tubing and contribute significantly to the rider's upright, but relaxed posture on this machine. The newly created cylinder head covers are also chrome-plated for additional style.

The only instrument above the chrome-plated round headlight on the R1200C is the speedometer, fitted on the near side and housing the oil-pressure and fuel-reserve warning lights. In keeping with the machine's particular style, the numbers on the speedo reflect the retro look of the 1950s. The remaining seven warning lights are in two rows, and fitted on to an aluminium plate to the right of the instrument. The dual-function ignition and handlebar lock is placed centrally.

The R1200C has a superbly comfortable leather-covered individual saddle – definitely a saddle, not a seat! However, even BMW admits that the much smaller (also leather-covered) pillion pad is best for short trips only, although an optional pillion 'comfort saddle' is available, at extra cost. When riding solo, the rider can move the pillion seat cushion to a vertical position, providing a backrest, which can be manually adjusted to three different angles.

There are air ducts on the inlet side of the fuel tank with high-gloss chrome-plated air-intake covers, and pearl-gloss chrome-plated scoops at the front. The front also houses the two oil coolers, clearly displaying this additional function by the opening for drawing in and expelling cooling air.

The Finish

All painted parts and components of the R1200C are treated to a very elaborate process. No less than two layers of clear topcoat are applied, in order to ensure a lasting gloss throughout the machine's lifespan. Those two layers are applied on top of the primer, filler and the actual surface colour. This is, of course, in addition to the special paint application method already well known to anyone who has visited BMW's Spandau plant, where workers display great skill and dexterity in applying colour-coordinated lines along the tank and the mudguards.

For the launch model year – 1998 – there are three colour choices for BMW's first custom model: night-black, with white lines and a black seat; canyon red metallic, with silver lining and a black saddle; and ivory, with lines along the tank and the mudguards, and a saddle in navy blue. As an option to this last colour scheme the seat may be specified in either black or canyon brown, in which case the blue lining is dropped.

All the chrome-plated components have been created to the highest standard, with three layers of copper, nickel and, finally, the chrome-plating itself. There is a combination of high-gloss and matt finishes, both representing different types of the same quality process. Polished aluminium can be found in several areas, including on the longitudinal Telelever arms according to BMW, this adds 'additional gloss and

Mobile Diagnosis Test Computer

BMW is the first motorcycle manufacturer in the world to introduce a Mobile Diagnosis Test Computer (MoDiTeC), on the four-cylinder K1200RS, and on the R1200C flat-twin. Connected to the motorcycle via a diagnostic plug, MoDiTeC is able consistently to check and monitor all electronic modules, and the bike's on-board electrical system.

After selecting the component or function he wishes to examine, the mechanic is guided by a display in locating possible defects, and receives all the technical information he needs in the process. Trouble-shooting is facilitated significantly by a comprehensive catalogue of possible symptoms. The mechanic enters the problem or deficiency perceived and the diagnostic system automatically guides him on, clearly presenting the steps to be taken.

The BMW MoDiTeC computer is not only a diagnostic and measuring unit, but also an electronic information system. It will help to shorten service and repair times and, accordingly, reduce the cost of ownership in respect of dealer servicing times and efficiency.

style to that typical cruiser look'.

As a finale to the R1200C's specification design and styling, it is worth recording that the handlebar grips are neither plastic nor even natural rubber, but top-quality weather-proof leather!

Out on the Road

The most surprising part of the BMW cruiser story is just how good the R1200C is out on the street – the best custom bike I have ever ridden, for a number of very good reasons.

For a start, the riding position, comfort and handling cannot be faulted. Low-speed handling is of the highest order, with feet-up U-turns being easily and safely accomplished. Out of town, narrow mountain roads, for example, are despatched effortlessly. Normally, a custom bike simply cannot compete with a conventional roadster, but this is one that can. I also like the 1200's distinctive growl, which is 'pleasant but unthreatening', according to *Motorcycle Sport and Leisure*, in their July 1997 issue.

The only 'faults' – if they can be called faults – are a lack of top-end power and ground clearance (although one would not want to use this bike like a sportster, anyway), and the seating arrangement for the owner who regularly carries a pillion passenger. And for those who do not like the cruiser styling, there are plenty of other BMWs to suit their tastes.

The new BMW is a fine cruiser, and an excellent road bike, which can probably appeal to a wider audience than any other custom bike. It suffers from none of the usual cruiser problems, such as weak brakes, soggy handling, or style at the expense of practicability, and it should be popular with bikers on both sides of the Atlantic in equal measure. And, of course, BMW has followed Harley-Davidson, by offering a host of matching lifestyle goodies, clothing and accessories.

BMW's target is to build 10,000 examples in the first twelve months of production; its an odds-on bet all of those will be sold without too much trouble. Only one question remains – why did it take BMW so long to join the cruiser club?

Index